INTO *Your* DREAMS

Decipher Your
Unique Dream Symbology
to Transform Your Waking Life

Janece O. Hudson, EdD

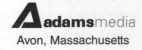

Avon, Massachusetts

DEDICATION
In loving memory of Elsie Sechrist
Friend, mentor, and second mother

Published by
Adams Media, a division of F+W Media, Inc.
57 Littlefield Street, Avon, MA 02322. U.S.A.
www.adamsmedia.com

ISBN 10: 1-4405-1267-1
ISBN 13: 978-1-4405-1267-4
eISBN 10: 1-4405-2503-X
eISBN 13: 978-1-4405-2503-2

Printed in the United States of America.

10   9   8   7   6   5   4   3   2   1

Library of Congress Cataloging-in-Publication Data
Hudson, Janece.
Into your dreams / Janece O. Hudson.
p. cm.
Includes index.
ISBN 978-1-4405-1267-4
1. Dream interpretation. I. Title.
BF1091.H83 2011
154.6'3—dc22
2011010230

This book is available at quantity discounts for bulk purchases.
For information, please call 1-800-289-0963.

Acknowledgments

I owe special thanks to many people, especially to those students, colleagues, clients, friends, and fellow dream workers who can't be named because they so graciously allowed me to use their dreams anonymously (with some details altered). My husband was extremely helpful as I was writing this book, and I appreciate his loving and generous spirit, as always. My editor, Katie Corcoran Lytle, was the epitome of patience and helpfulness and a joy to work with, as were all the folks at Adams Media. Wendy Simard deserves a medal. Huge thanks go to the following people (listed alphabetically by first name) for special acts of friendship, support, and/or information-sharing along my lengthy dream path: Anice Bullock, Anne Marie Palmer, Belle Johnson, Bess Harris, Carol Willis, Christie Craig, Deenie Cuenod, Dot Miller, Doug and Ida Stringfellow, Elizabeth Milstead, Gloria DesRoche, Jan Yonkin, Joyce Kaufmann, Linda Vandyck, Lynn Kurth, Lynn Turner, Mary Canada, Nadean Philips, Nancy Royal, Norma Jean Fredrickson, Pat Rosenblad, Pearl Lefevers, Sharon Werner, and Shirley Coleman. For those I've inadvertently omitted, forgive my brain blip; I salute you.

Contents

Introduction

Did you dream last night? If so, you contributed to more than a billion stories—dreams from the unconscious mind—that were created in bedrooms across the United States. All of them were unique, many of them vitally important for the people who dreamed them. However, lots of people don't recall or pay little attention to these nighttime stories. Have you been one of them? By ignoring your dreams, did you fail to heed a message to slow down and pay attention to your health? Did you miss the stock tip that could have made you rich or the creative idea that could have made your life a thousand times easier? Did you miss a key to greater happiness and fulfillment in your relationships?

Learning to tap that wondrous inner source of wisdom and to work with your dreams is one of the greatest gifts you can give yourself. The world's finest diagnostician, market analyst, creative thinker, sage, and counselor is as close as your pillow.

The advice is free, but deciphering it takes a bit of effort.

That's what this book is about—deciphering your unique dream symbology to transform your waking life.

THE PERSONAL NATURE OF DREAMS

Dreams fascinate almost everyone, going back as far as the second century A.D. when a Greek named Artemidorus penned *Oneirocritica*, his treatise on dream interpretation. Psychologists have constructed elaborate theories to explain the mysterious content of dreams; other analysts, more arcane and less scientific, propose their own sets of meanings to dream symbolism—many of which strain credibility or become unbelievably complex. All strive to make sense of the process in books filled with incomprehensible psychobabble or dictionaries of outlandish definitions for various dream elements.

But dreams are not one-size-fits-all. They are unique creations *by* you, *about* you, and based on *your* individual experiences. They are messages from your unconscious mind, and you are the best interpreter of your dreams. Of course, because we all share a culture, many of our symbols may be similar, but we bring our own meaning to them. For example, my feelings about an airplane may be very different from yours if I'm phobic about flying and you love air travel.

Interpreting dreams is not merely solving an interesting mind puzzle. After you figure out what your dreams mean, you have to *apply* the information to understand yourself and your behavior; make better choices; improve relationships; tend to your physical, mental, and spiritual health; and grow into the best person you can be. That's working with your dreams.

Into Your Dreams is an easy-to-read, common-sense approach to interpreting and working with your dreams, grounded in contemporary scientific research yet expansive enough to include viewpoints that run the gamut from behavioral psychologist B. F. Skinner to the psychic Edgar Cayce. Not everybody, even scientists and researchers, agrees about the nature of dreams and the unconscious. Some suggest that dreams are mere random bits of memory popping up with the firing of synapses in various parts of the brain and the content is of no particular significance. For others, the content is everything. Clearly, both the biology and physiology of dreaming *and* the content are important. Although the biological aspect is fascinating (and you'll get that occasionally), here we'll be dealing mostly with dream content.

I still remember a vivid dream from my childhood, so you can say that I've been working with dreams most of my life. More specifically, I've been formally pursuing the study of dreams and working with dreamers for nearly forty years. I've worked with dream groups, led seminars, taught college classes, and done scores of presentations on the subject. My graduate training was in counseling and educational psychology, my doctoral dissertation was on dreams, and I've published academic work in the field.

I still work with my own dreams regularly, and over the years I've come to like the notion of using dreams to understand our needs as defined by Abraham Maslow. Maslow was a popular humanistic psychologist whose paradigm of the hierarchy of needs is used frequently in the fields of psychology, business, education, and medicine. He suggested that needs range from the most basic physiological needs to transpersonal being needs (more on this in Chapter 1).

Using Maslow's notion of needs and an amalgam of other sources, you will discover that dreams are sometimes physical, sometimes mental or emotional, sometimes spiritual or transpersonal. Some dreams are funny, some mundane, some profound. They range from admonitions to eat more spinach to encouragements to reach for the stars. All are important.

USING THIS BOOK

Into Your Dreams is presented in two parts. The first part gives a brief summary about the history and nature of dreams and explains, with many examples, the various ways to recall, interpret, and work with your own dreams. You'll learn about the people, places, and things you encounter from your unconscious as well as common themes. Want to know what washing your hands means? Chapter 7 will look at some possibilities. How about dancing or crying or flying or running from a menacing stranger? And what about sex? Or dead people? It's all there in various chapters for you to consider and uncover your own interpretations. There are even exercises to help you along.

In the second part you'll find a listing of various symbols and some guidelines for possible meanings—but since dream symbols are highly individual, space is also provided for you to fill in the blanks for personal and/or expanded definitions. Think of this as a guide and not a dictionary. The list is divided into sections that parallel the chapters in Part 1.

If you've read this far, you must be one of those folks who's fascinated by dreams and eager to learn more. Let's begin.

PART 1

UNDERSTANDING YOUR DREAMS

CHAPTER 1

What Are Dreams?

People have always been fascinated by dreams, and throughout time dreams have been viewed in a variety of ways ranging from messages from God to random firings of synapses in the brain. In fact, every major religion in the world counts dreams as a part of its history and religious writings. In ancient times, before psychologists or psychiatrists, Chinese, Egyptians, Greeks, and others built temples for dream incubation to provide guidance for members of that society. While *incubation* sounds like something to do with hatching eggs, the idea was to pray, fast, and "hatch" a dream while sleeping in the temple. A priest or priestess would interpret your dream to solve your problem.

The theory and understanding of dreams has undergone many changes since this time, including during the Dark Ages when the study of dreams fell into disrepute. It wasn't until the late nineteenth century and the appearance of modern psychologists that dreams regained their importance as a valid area to be studied. Since that time, four major fields of psychology have emerged: psychoanalytic, behavioral, humanistic, and transpersonal. Each of these viewpoints and ways of looking at behavior (including dream behavior) has its proponents, as we'll see in the following pages.

SIGMUND FREUD (1856–1937)

History credits Sigmund Freud, considered the father of psychoanalysis as well as of modern psychology, with bringing dreams back into a legitimate area of study. In 1900, Freud's now famous *The Interpretation of Dreams* was first published. In it he wrote, "The interpretation of dreams is the royal road to a knowledge of the unconscious activities of the mind." Since the unconscious isn't directly accessible, examining the hidden meaning of dreams provides a method to study it.

Freud analyzed countless numbers of his own dreams as well as those of others, most of whom were his psychiatric patients with various neuroses, and concluded that dreams were expressed in symbols to disguise their real meaning. Freud saw most of those symbols as sexual in nature and stemming from repressed childhood impulses. Items such as rifles, sticks, snakes, canes, or knives represented phallic symbols, and containers such as caves, jars, rooms, or drawers represented the vagina. This insistence that most dreams were sexually motivated was (and remains) the most disputed of his theories. Many of Freud's colleagues rebelled at this overemphasis on sexual instinct but still used some of his ideas as a basis for their own theories concerning dream analysis. One such analyst was Carl Jung.

CARL G. JUNG (1875–1961)

Carl Jung, a Swiss psychiatrist and, for a number of years, one of Freud's close friends, is perhaps the most prominent name in dream analysis. Like Freud and other analysts, Jung worked primarily with his patients and their dreams to deal with the neuroses, complexes, and various conflicts arising from the unconscious. He also believed that dreams aided in the integration and individuation (the ultimate goal of self-realization or completeness) of the personality. Jung departed sharply from Freud when he introduced a new and extremely controversial viewpoint of the conscious and unconscious. He described the psyche, the personality as a whole, as follows:

1. **Consciousness** — The part of the mind known directly by the person. It likely appears before birth, and a child's conscious awareness develops over a lifetime through a variety of experiences and methods.

2. **Personal Unconscious** — The personal unconscious is the storehouse for every thought, feeling, and experience since birth. In the personal unconscious, groups of thoughts, memories, or experiences clump together to form a cluster or complex, what we might call a hang-up or a preoccupation. There are all sorts of complexes in the personal unconscious, and healthy growth dissolves them. Jung said they often arise in dreams.

3. **The Collective Unconscious** — Jung's discovery of the collective unconscious stirred great controversy as well as brought him fame as a great intellect and pioneer. He maintained that all people are born with a shared collective unconscious, a great reservoir of racial memory (feelings, thoughts, and fragments of experience passed down over generations) called *primordial images* that predisposed them to deal with the world in certain ways. The contents of the collective unconscious, these models and prototypes, are called *archetypes*.

Jung spent much of the last half of his life studying and writing about these innumerable archetypes that covered every typical situation in life. These latent prototypes can be seen by the similarities found in myths, art, and symbols in many diverse cultures. Among those many archetypes he described are persona, anima and animus, shadow, self, birth, death, rebirth (or reincarnation), the hero, the prophet, the child, God, power, the trickster, the demon, the wise old man, the earth mother, and a number of natural elements including the sun, moon, fire, and various plants and animals. Life experiences shape and add to these archetypes.

ROBERTO ASSAGIOLI (1888–1974)

Roberto Assagioli, Jung's colleague and the first Italian psychoanalyst, is best known for developing *psychosynthesis*, an integration first of the personality around the conscious self, then an integration centering on the higher self. Integration is a coming together, through growth, of the various parts of the personality. In simpler terms, it means getting it all together into a fully functioning and authentic person. This inclusion of a higher self as a part of the psyche is what makes him one of the early proponents of transpersonal psychology and adds a spiritual dimension to his understanding of behavior. In his practice, Assagioli used dream analysis as a technique for exploration of the unconscious, and he also encouraged patients to recount and analyze their own dreams. He emphasized that dream interpretation was only one technique for the understanding of the self and used many other projective methods including guided imagery (often likened to a waking dream), which you'll learn more about in Chapter 9.

While he didn't discount the idea of a collective unconscious—and indeed, spoke of it as something that surrounded the individual fields and could enter them by a sort of "psychological osmosis"—Assagioli's book, *Psychosynthesis: A Collection of Basic Writings,* delved deeper into the parts of the human psyche. Three of the major new ideas he presented were:

1. **The Higher Unconscious or Superconscious** — This area is the source of higher intuition, inspiration, genius, heroic

action, selfless love, spiritual ecstasy, and illumination. This theory discounted Freud's notion of a sublimated libido (sexual energy) being the generator of such behavior.

2. **Subpersonalities** — This concept speaks to the various selves within each person that need to be integrated into a fully functioning whole, while maintaining the advantageous traits of each. (We often see these various selves in dreams.) For example, here are some subpersonalities of Susan, an English teacher—she might be the teacher self, the belly dancer self, the daughter self, the pessimist self, and/or the little girl self depending on the situation.

3. **The Will** — Assagioli maintained that people are not wholly driven by instinctual urges, as Freud and others maintained. Instead, he argued that humans have the unique ability to make choices, to grow and relate, and to bring about changes in their own personalities. In other words, one couldn't continue to blame his parents or society or instinctual urges for their dysfunctional behavior.

ABRAHAM H. MASLOW (1908–1970)

Throughout most of his career, Brooklyn-born psychologist Abraham Maslow was a university professor and researcher into human nature. In particular, instead of studying animals in a laboratory or the worst in individuals, he purposely studied the most psychologically healthy examples of people he could find—thus the birth of *humanistic psychology*. Maslow is best known for his formulation of the hierarchy of needs that motivate human behavior. This theory, which went against the mainstream American psychological school of his day, was embraced by the public and still enjoys widespread use in business, health, and education fields. Among his many honors was his election to the presidency of the American Psychological Association, a group that had once been critical of his ideas.

Maslow's Hierarchy of Needs

In his book *Motivation and Personality*, Maslow maintained that a succession of needs motivated human behavior. (He also conceded that not *all* behavior was motivated.) This hierarchy is often illustrated by a pyramid with the most four most basic needs, sometimes called "deficiency motives" or "D-motives" at the base, and ascending to the highest level of "being needs" or "B-motives" at the apex.

His theory maintains that when a group of basic needs is met or mostly met, a restlessness arises for something more. This is similar to how we feel when we think if only we had something specific—a new car, friends, a particular job—we'd be happy, only to find that when we acquire those things, we want more.

While an individual works through these "needs" levels in a progressive manner, this doesn't mean that someone focused at a higher level can't also have needs associated with a more basic level. For example, if you're concerned about esteem needs, but you find yourself in a situation where an intruder ties you up and holds a pillow over your face, your most basic needs kick in. You're much more concerned about needs for air and for safety than whether your peers are going to elect you chairman of some committee, or if your neighbors are impressed by your new sports car.

This is the list of Maslow's needs, from the basic to the most advanced:

1. **The Physiological Needs** — the most basic of needs necessary to sustain life and health: oxygen, sleep, food, water, sex, elimination of body wastes.
2. **The Safety Needs** — security and stability; structure, order, law, and limits; freedom from fear, anxiety, and chaos.

3. **The Belongingness and Love Needs** — giving and receiving affection from a mate, children, friends, family, groups, and people in general. Anything that provides a feeling of inclusiveness.

4. **The Esteem Needs** — the desire to have a stable sense of self-respect or self-esteem in terms of competence, achievement, strength, and adequacy as well as have the esteem of others.

5. **The Self-Actualization Need** — the desire for self-fulfillment, to become everything you're capable of becoming, to find your sense of purpose.

While self-actualizers are unique in a variety of ways, Maslow noted certain characteristics in common and offered them as areas for further study. Among these are: a more accurate evaluation of reality; acceptance of self and others; spontaneity, creativity, and humor; ethics and values; and *peak experiences.*

Peak experiences are difficult to explain unless you've experienced one, but are likened to what has been called a mystical experience, though they're not necessarily tied to religion or particular religious beliefs. Still, it is a powerful feeling of great ecstasy, wonder, and awe. Not all self-actualized people experience such phenomena, but many report having them frequently.

Transpersonal Self-Actualization

In his later years, Maslow described something beyond self-actualization and spoke of those moving into that level as frequently having and valuing peak experiences. As a part of the newly emerging transpersonal psychology—sometimes called the fourth force—he described this state of transcendence in *The Farther Reaches of Human Nature* as "the very highest and most inclusive or holistic levels of human consciousness."

This is a glimpse of something beyond the ordinary self—a higher selfhood, if you will—into the spiritual realm of the mystic or the sage, and toward a more universal awareness.

Cognitive Needs

Maslow also identifies two additional needs that don't fit neatly into the hierarchy. This is likely because for some people these may be absent or weak; in others, they are observed to be more important than safety or belongingness:

1. The need for knowledge and understanding
2. The need for beauty, order, and symmetry (aesthetic needs)

Maslow and Dreams

Maslow didn't dwell much on dreams, although we do know that he considered dream interpretation an important part of therapy, and he believed that "unconscious needs commonly express themselves in dreams."

That small statement by Maslow is an important one and confirms the idea that dreams are about all sort of things and about every facet of our lives: physical, mental, and spiritual. They're about the mundane and the profound, about sex and relationships, about attitudes and aspirations, urging us onward to become better people. But how are we to know when dreams are about physiological concerns, or about mental or spiritual ones? As you work on interpreting a dream consider Maslow's hierarchy to see if particular needs may have sparked it.

EDGAR CAYCE (1877–1945)

Edgar Cayce is important to the study of dreams because he was one of the first to speak of not only the subconscious—but also of the super-conscious. He explored the emotional and spiritual side of dreams long before such holistic ideas were popular and had a most interesting source of material. Born in Hopkinsville, Kentucky, Edgar Cayce was neither a psychologist nor a psychiatrist. In fact, he had only an eighth- or ninth-grade education (not uncommon for the time, especially in rural areas). It may seem strange to place him among the previously listed august company, but he spoke frequently of the conscious mind: the unconscious, and subconscious, as well as the super-conscious. Too, he stressed the importance of will in the growth of an individual (similar to many ideas of Jung and Assagioli). A former studio photographer, Cayce was married with two sons and taught Sunday school most of his life. He was also America's most well-known and best-documented psychic.

After he accidentally discovered that he could put himself into a sort of sleep state and give "readings" on everything from diet issues to universal law and the meaning of life, Edgar Cayce drew the attention of people who ranged from the most ordinary folks to world-renowned entertainers, and even high-level politicians. People with desperate illnesses came to him for readings on diagnosis and treatment, usually after having exhausted the usual medical approaches, and when they followed his advice, they got better.

Stenographic copies of the more than 14,000 readings he gave are archived in Virginia Beach, Virginia, where he lived during the last several years of his life, and copies are available for study at the Association for Research and Enlightenment (A.R.E.) Library (and online for members of the organization). A great deal of study and research has been done with this clairvoyant material, and many of the treatments for various physical ailments, using a holistic approach, have proven that his advice was ahead of its time.

Levels of Consciousness

In one reading, Cayce spoke of the "correlation between the mental forces in its triune." [Edgar Cayce Reading 137-127] In other readings dating as far back as the early twenties, he described this triune as basically the conscious mind (manifested physically through one of the senses), the subconscious, and the spirit or superconscious.

(An aside here: The available material from Edgar Cayce's psychic discourses are anonymous and labeled with sets of numbers. The first number represents the individual or group for whom the reading was given. After a hyphen, the next number is the particular reading in cases where a person or group had multiple readings. For example, the above material was for a man, Mr. 137, who had many, many readings, and this is excerpted from his 127th.)

Throughout the many readings that mentioned one or more of the "triune of mental forces" and its variations, many of the ideas presented echoed those of Jung, Assagioli, and even Maslow.

Dreams and Readings

The readings touched on many subjects, some controversial to be sure, but Edgar Cayce stressed the importance of dreams: "In this age, at present, 1923, there is not sufficient credence given dreams; for the best development of the human family is to give the greater increase in knowledge of the subconscious, soul or spirit world." [3744-5]

Cayce gave more than 600 readings that included dream interpretations, with many readings addressing the meaning of dreams. Basically, he indicated that dreams are about many things and there are examples of physical, mental, and spiritual issues (similar to the ideas on dreams and needs that Maslow suggested.). He told one individual that many of his dreams "pertain to physical conditions . . . presented in emblematical form." [137-24] The Cayce readings offer one of the most comprehensive approaches to dream content and interpretation; for example, neither Jung nor Assagioli dealt with dreams and physiological needs and Freud was only concerned with dreams. Some of his interpretations spoke of diet, impending illness, attitudes, business, relationships, and profound spiritual experiences. They spoke both of the past and the future.

Mark Thurston, in his book *Dreams: Tonight's Answers for Tomorrow's Questions*, points out that the Cayce readings infer that dreams are real experiences, albeit in a different realm. B. F. Skinner, an American behavioral psychologist best known for his laboratory work on reinforcement principles with rats and pigeons, agreed with this general notion. He maintained that dream experiences should have the same positive or negative reinforcement capabilities as do real-life waking experiences.

Hugh Lynn Cayce (1907–1982), Edgar's eldest son, identified from the readings four broad types of dreams in *Dreams: The Language of the Unconscious*. The four classifications group dreams concerning:

1. Problems of the physical body (physiological dreams)
2. Self-understanding, unconscious problem solving, conflicts, and relationships (the largest by far of the groups)
3. Psychic information, precognition
4. Spiritual guidance

Many have found this broad description helpful in looking at the range of dreams they encounter. They illustrate the idea that the things that fill your days also fill your nights—a useful concept to keep in mind when you begin to analyze the meaning of your own dreams.

DREAMS AND THE MODERN LABORATORY

Beyond dream theories and analyses from great thinkers, one of the most momentous events for the study of dreams was the discovery, almost by accident, of something called Rapid Eye Movement (REM). REM occurs during certain periods of sleep and has an association with dreams. This information came out of the University of Chicago in the mid-fifties and brought an explosion of laboratory research on sleep stages, dreams, sleep disorders, and a variety of other sleep-related phenomena. Through laboratory research we know that everybody, with very rare exceptions, has periods of REM and experiences from four to seven dreams a night, depending on length of sleep and sleep cycles. By hooking up subjects to various electrodes to study brain waves and eye and muscle movement, scientists have learned that people dream in cycles with stages from light sleep through deeper levels, then reverse the process. When they've returned to the lightest stage again, the first REM stage briefly occurs, along with a dream. The cycle begins again, each one lasting for approximately an hour and a half, and the REM period lengthens with each cycle. Although the type of stories and images we usually associate with our dreams takes place during REM, scientists have discovered that some sort of mental process, more like thinking, occurs at other stages of sleep as well.

Does that mean that we're in light sleep when we dream? Yes. REM occurs when we're almost awake. Have you ever awakened and felt for a moment that you were paralyzed? You were. A mechanism at the base of the brain shuts down major motor movement so you don't jump up and run down the street when a monster chases you in a dream. This shutdown also prevents you from acting out in your sleep, such as yelling at the umpire or swatting your bed partner when you play a lively game of tennis in your dreams. How, then, do we explain sleepwalking and sleep-talking? These things ordinarily happen in the deepest, dead-to-the-world state of sleep, not during REM sleep.

While laboratory work has been valuable in teaching us about the physiology of sleep and dreams, these sorts of studies can't really add much to what dreams *mean*. Indeed, many such researchers believe dreams are simply an electrical brain phenomenon whose function is to keep the brain juiced up. According to them, dream material doesn't *mean* anything, at least nothing provable, and these folks aren't into vague, competing theory, conjecture, or anecdotal evidence. They value information that can be counted or measured or observed in some acceptable, objective way.

I've spent some time in a sleep lab studying, in particular, the dreams of anorexia nervosa patients. Although these young people claimed they weren't hungry, I could prove that they *dreamed* about food and other oral activities because I could *count* the number of times cheeseburgers, oranges, and meatloaf appeared in their dreams compared with a published database made up of people in their age range.

Laboratory research with dreams continues to provide valuable information about the physiology of dreaming and the dreaming process. We've seen some interesting studies on learning and problem solving as it relates to sleep and dreams, but if you want to know the meaning or the interpretation of your dreams, you're not likely to find that information in a research laboratory. At least, not yet.

SO WHAT ARE DREAMS?

After looking at several viewpoints, we're back to the question we started with: *What are dreams?* Understanding the different philosophies can give you a place from which to begin, but it honestly boils down to what makes sense to you, what works for you, and what you buy into about what makes people tick. This book assumes a premise that seems to work for many people—the idea that dreams have meaning. They're messages from the unconscious realms sent to help you enrich and transform your waking life.

While I wholeheartedly agree with the notion that dreams are about a variety of things, ranging from physiological warnings to spiritual guidance (akin to Jung's "big dreams" or Maslow's waking peak experiences), there's a basic problem with this idea. Because dreams are most often emblematic, how can you—without a Carl Jung or Edgar Cayce to interpret them—determine which kind of dream is which? For example, if you have a dream about heart problems, how can you tell if it's a literal physical warning or about your love life? If you see yourself eating from a cornucopia of luscious fruits, is that a reminder to eat more fruit or it is saying something about the fruits of the spirit?

To interpret a dream as something high-minded and transformative, when the dream is trying to convey a serious physical warning, isn't productive at all. Such mistakes often happen simply because it's difficult to determine which is which.

When Maslow's ideas are added into the mix, a missing piece of the puzzle is found. If dreams are about everything in our lives, dreams are also about the physical, mental, and spiritual needs that Maslow describes in his hierarchy. It's helpful to first consider your most basic needs, especially when it comes to disturbing or unpleasant dreams. If you don't find a source among the basic needs, then go up the hierarchy to see if the dream fits into a higher category. Sometimes it may not; most often it does. Don't worry if this sounds a bit confusing now; it will make more sense later.

I don't think that any school of thought has all the answers about exactly how the psyche works yet, nor do I believe that we have an exact system of dream interpretation. My own viewpoint of both dreams and the psyche is eclectic and evolving. This book contains an amalgam of theories and experiences. Some may call that eclecticism naïve or idealistic, but I agree with Maslow who said in *The Farther Reaches of Human Nature,* "I am Freudian and I am behavioristic and I am humanistic, and as a matter of fact I am developing . . . a psychology of transcendence as well."

Things to Remember and Exercises to Do

Remember:
- Everybody dreams every night.
- Dreams have meaning.
- Dreams may be about a range of needs.
- Deciphering your dreams can transform your life.

Exercises to Do:

1. Your first assignment is to make a basic needs chart. On a sheet of paper, draw a large equilateral triangle; draw four horizontal lines through it, equally spaced apart and parallel to the base so that it is divided into five sections. Beginning with the bottom section, label it "Physiological Needs" and name a few of those to help you remember. Go up the triangle/pyramid and label each section with the needs categories from Maslow's hierarchy, ending with "Self-Actualization." Label the area atop and outside the peak "Transpersonal Self-Actualization." To one side of the pyramid, list the cognitive needs "Need to Know and Understand" and "Aesthetic Needs." Making this drawing will help anchor these ideas in your mind. Tuck the paper into this book for future reference. You'll use it again.

2. You can get to know Carl Jung on YouTube if you have access to a computer. There you'll find several excellent interviews with Jung in his later years, including "Face to Face with Carl Jung" (parts 1–4). Watch one or more and note how you feel about Jung.

CHAPTER 2

Getting Started

Now that we've established that you dream and are committed to learning more about what your dreams mean, let's dive right into capturing all of the information that comes across when you sleep. If you aren't someone who generally recalls your dreams, consider this: A man in one of my seminars swore he hadn't remembered a dream in twenty years. By following the steps outlined in this chapter, he came back the next week with three dreams in his journal.

AND SPEAKING OF DREAM JOURNALS . . .

A woman named Eva said she'd been keeping a dream journal for many years and that she was continually surprised at how her dreams all eventually made sense even if at the time they didn't. She cites this example:

> *I dreamed I was at Disney on the ride "It's a Small World" with a woman with whom I wasn't really friends, but worked with as co-leader of a high school dance team.*

Eva wrote the dream in her journal but at the time thought it didn't make a bit of sense. Two years later she found herself in Florida and on that ride with that lady at Disney. It turned out the dance team won a championship and went to perform at the Citrus Bowl football game. Eva says, "It taught me to write down my dreams no matter how silly they seem. Also, if I had remembered it at the time, I would have had a lot more confidence in the outcome of that dance competition!"

Keeping a dream journal is really, really important. Over time, you'll begin to recognize patterns, and there will be occasions when you'll want to check back for dates or other details.

There are many types of dream journals, but the most important criteria in selecting one are that it appeals to you and makes recording and working with your dreams easy. If you want an attractively bound book of blank pages, go for it. Many people prefer a plain spiral notebook. They're cheap, easy to handle, and it's simple to write your dream on the right-hand page and your observations opposite it on the left page. Just *don't* use random slips of paper. They invariably get lost.

What about a computer, you ask? Sure. If you have a laptop or electronic notebook you can put on your bedside table and prefer using that method, that's okay. Using a desktop computer isn't optimal. This is because you're likely to stop by the bathroom or the coffeepot or make some other detour on the way to turn it on, and in that time your dream data fades. Immediate recording is preferable.

Some people use a tape or digital recorder. If you're faithful about transcribing your information or have someone you could trust who can do it for you, that's fine; otherwise, nix the use of a recorder. Most who've tried that method found they were often too busy to transcribe their dreams during the day, and trying to analyze dreams from a recording is far from ideal.

Learning to catch dreams for your journal is merely a matter of forming new habits. Try these steps before you go to sleep at night:

- Place your open journal and pencil or pen beside your bed.
- Suggest to yourself that you *will* remember your dreams.
- When you awaken and before you move, try to capture something from your dream—a feeling, a fragment, an entire dream. (Several authorities claim that the feelings evoked by a dream are as important as the content.)
- Write it down in as much detail as possible. Include emotions and body reactions.
- If you get nothing, roll over in bed and see if something comes. (Scientists have found that memory is jogged if you're in the same physical position as when the dream occurred.) Be careful that you don't drift off again!
- Date your entry and write a brief account of the previous day's activities (like a diary). Include thoughts, emotions, fights, awards, dilemmas, disappointments, decisions, etc.
- Name your dream at the top of the page. Choose something simple to describe it in one or two words. For example, in Eva's account above, a good name might be "Disney ride." The title will trigger the memory of it or help you locate it when searching your journal.
- Repeat the process each night for a week. You'll get results. I guarantee it!

Now that you have a dream to work with, read on to figure out how to begin interpreting it.

DECIPHERING TECHNIQUES

"Okay," you say, "I get the idea, but all that weird stuff I dream about doesn't make a lick of sense, so how can I use it for anything?"

You're not alone in your feelings. If dreams can be thought of as movies of the mind, lots of people feel as if they've stumbled into a theater playing a foreign film—with no subtitles. In many ways, that's exactly what they are. Dreams are played in another language, a language of images that's an amalgam of feeling and experience and unconscious scripts, and we have to learn to speak the language to be able to translate the meaning. That's what this book is all about.

You may wonder why you can't just use one of those dream dictionaries to find out what your dreams mean if you're serious about working with your dreams. Always remember this critical point: Dreams are very personal and highly individual, and *you* are the best interpreter of your own productions. While we can make some generalizations about themes, characters, and actions, everyone's experiences are different. If you dream about a St. Bernard, your experiences and associations with the big dogs may be miles apart from your friend Joe's. You may think of a St. Bernard as a rescuer (complete with the trusty brandy keg around its neck) and a benevolent symbol, while Joe, who was bitten by one as a child, may consider the shaggy, slobbering beasts as menacing creatures to be feared and avoided.

Don't trust books with lists of symbols and meanings stating such specifics as: dreaming of finding gold means you're going to be rich, or dreaming about black-eyed peas means that Aunt Harriet is coming to visit next Tuesday. It's not that simple.

Learning to interpret your dreams takes a little effort, but by using the tools provided in this book, you'll soon get the hang of it. Once you understand how to get the gist of the story and supply the subtitles, your dreams will begin to make perfect sense. Indeed, you'll discover that your wonderfully creative mind conjures up Academy Award–worthy productions.

Here are some techniques to help you tease out the meaning. You'll have to experiment with what works best for you, but most people have success employing some combination of them.

Immediate Insight

One of the easiest ways to interpret a dream can happen while you still have a foot in dreamland. The complete meaning may pop into your head as you're coming awake. The longer you work with dreams, the more frequently this may happen.

June F., who'd been diligently journaling and making an effort to interpret her dreams for several months, awoke from a long, convoluted dream and thought, "What in the world was that all about?"

Her answer came swiftly as a thought. *It's just as bad to have too little anger as too much. Use moderation in all things.* Wow! Instant insight. "Unfortunately," June said, "it was a while before this happened again, but I started getting immediate insight more frequently as I continued working with my dreams."

An important point about June's dream was that the interpretation and advice had relevance to her current life situation. June had been conditioned to rein in her childhood tendency to hotheadedness, to the point where she often completely repressed her anger. This dream started her thinking in a new way, and she said she feels healthier for it. Repressed anger often shows up not only in psychological problems but also in such physical ailments as digestive problems, damaged teeth, or more serious conditions.

In another example, Phyllis J. dreamed:

I call "home" and can't reach my parents so I go visit and learn they are dead, killed by my cousin Sylvia a while ago. My mother had welcomed her and was nice to her when she came to visit, but she attacked my parents with a knife, and the death scene is very bloody. (I'd seen the bloody scene somehow, and the setting was a version of my mother's grandmother's house.) I feel bereft and am upset that I wasn't notified, but my brother says he didn't want to upset me.

We can apply all sorts of techniques to determine the meaning of this dream, but Phyllis, a poet, woke up inspired to compose a poem about the relationship with her daughter, "to the effect of I am closer to my friends than to her, that all we share is blood." The dreamer said that her parents and Sylvia, a moody, distant cousin with her own problematic family relationships whom she rarely saw, were all deceased, and that she and her mother were never close. Phyllis wrote a poignant and lovely poem about the relationship of mothers and daughters. This is an excellent example of a dream sparking creative ideas or productions. Many musicians, authors, and artists have reported that dreams inspired certain works.

Common Themes

Everybody has dreamed about finding themselves naked in a crowd (exposed, vulnerable, or perhaps ashamed), flying, falling, failing an exam or being late to class (even long past school days), losing valuables, finding money or treasures, and being unable to move or run from danger. Every actor has dreamed of forgetting his lines. We've all dreamed about having problems with our vehicle (unable to brake, steer, or even find where we left it). We've sweated bullets being chased through countless scenes by every menacing entity ever imagined.

Many dream workers and researchers have noted that these and other similar themes often crop up in people's dreams. In her book *The Universal Dream Key*, Dr. Patricia Garfield, a noted dream expert and past president of the Association for the Study of Dreams, has proposed that particular dream themes are universal. After examining dream data from many different countries, she has compiled a list of the twelve most common themes and their variations, including the positive and negative aspect of the theme. (A variant of the falling or drowning theme would be its opposite: flying freely and jubilantly or swimming effortlessly.) We will explore many common themes throughout this book so you can begin to form connections when you seek the meaning in your own dreams.

The Dream in a Nutshell

Of course, not all of your dreams contain one of the most common themes. That would be too easy. But always ask yourself: What is the theme of this dream? What is the gist or central idea of the whole story? This sort of theme pertains to looking at the dream as a whole. Mark Thurston, in his book *Dreams: Tonight's Answers for Tomorrow's Questions,* calls a similar notion the storyline. I like to call it the central idea or the main concept—or the dream in a nutshell.

Let's take Frieda A.'s dream:

I am alone at home (not my current house but one from several years ago). It's night, and I'm in bed asleep when a noise rouses me. I awake to discover an intruder—a tall, dark man—and I know that he's come to loot the house. I don't feel personally threatened, and I don't care so much about his taking the TVs or silver, but I don't want to lose the information on my computer. Knowing that I need help, I run out the front door and try to yell for help, but my throat seems closed and no sound comes out. I keep trying to yell, "Help! Help!" until I'm finally able to get the words out. Now yelling loudly, I run to a neighbor's house, bang on the door, and ring the doorbell. By this time all my neighbors are gathering outside and coming to my rescue. I feel relieved.

Now, using general terms and only one or two sentences, tell what this dream is about. Describe the central idea of the dream as if this were a blurb for a TV show. Give it in a nutshell.

You might say: In a time of need, a woman has difficulty calling for help. When she does, people come to her aid.

Aha! Do you get what this "yelling for help" dream is telling Frieda? It's helpful to know that she's a very independent type, super-confident and efficient, who hates to ask anyone for assistance. (Perhaps she has some esteem needs?) Notice how hard it was for her to yell for help? Now that we have it in a nutshell, what's the moral of her dream story?

Yes, dreams have morals like in Aesop's fables. Very often the main intention of a dream is to reveal a truth to us. The moral to Frieda's dream might be that when a person needs help, she should ask for it, no matter how difficult it might be. This is the lesson to be learned, the behavior and attitude she needs to work on. As it happened, not long after the dream, she found herself overloaded and overwhelmed with work for a volunteer organization. Recalling her dream, she asked for help from several people in the organization. They all gladly pitched in to help.

Need Levels

At some point in your interpretation process—and that place often changes from dream to dream— you should try to determine whether your dream is associated with a need level of Maslow's hierarchy (if at all). Psychologically oriented people tend to think all dreams are about psychological issues, emotional growth, or unconscious conflicts. Spiritually oriented individuals are apt to focus on the notion that dreams are all about spiritual growth and high-minded ideals. However, putting your dreams into these predefined buckets renders you as short-sighted as those who claim dreams are merely random firings of synapses in the brain. Remember: Dreams are about *all* the things that affect your life; they cover *all* need levels from the basic physiological needs to the most sublime. Just because you're primarily concerned with self-esteem needs or with self-actualization during your ordinary waking life, that doesn't mean that other needs don't crop up and demand attention. They do crop up, often vehemently.

Look first to the most basic needs, then use common sense. Ask yourself these questions: Do I feel a little off physically? How about my diet? My exercise? Is there anything in the dream that could pertain to my physiological needs? What about my safety and security needs? During the recent severe recession, many people had dreams related to this because those needs were threatened. Catastrophic events sprout a rash of basic need dreams. Go up the pyramid, questioning at each level. (This is a good place to review those levels under Abraham Maslow in Chapter 1 and make that illustration if you didn't do it then.)

What need level do you think prompted Frieda's dream above? How did she feel in the beginning? Why did she leave and call for help? What would cause you to behave in the same way? Fear for her safety and security, most likely. She also was concerned with esteem needs (wanting others to see her as self-sufficient and able to handle any situation), but when a more basic need was threatened, that one became top priority. So she yelled for help.

A Picture Is Worth a Thousand Words

After you've first looked at the dream as a whole, you can—especially if you're still having trouble with the meaning—look at it in many additional ways to find what technique or combination of them works best for you. One way is to look at the pictures.

A woman dreamed that she had a bee buzzing around in her upswept hair; a man dreamed that a bear pushed him off the roof. Sound strange? If you know that the woman had a "bee in her bonnet" (was irritated) the day before and that the man is a stock investor in danger from a falling (bear) market, these dreams make sense.

Think of elements in a dream as concrete depictions of abstract concepts or figures of speech. Most dreams or parts of dreams are simply ideas expressed in symbolic language. Also, they may be something like a rebus, a picture puzzle (for example, a graphic image of a house with wings = house fly).

Metaphor

Most of us remember a bit about figures of speech from our English classes. There are hundreds of figures of speech, but one of the most common in dreams is the metaphor, defined in writing or speaking as saying that one thing is another, ordinarily dissimilar, thing. An example is a teacher saying that his classroom is a battleground. (Note that saying the classroom is *like* a battleground would make it a simile, another figure of speech.) We get an instant picture and feeling of contention. A complex idea is immediately portrayed with that simple statement. In a dream the teacher would be more likely to see only the battleground, and the events played out there could relate to his recent activities in school or a similar chaotic setting.

See if you can detect metaphor in this example. Bette M. had this tree dream:

> *I owned a large plot of ground in a lovely sylvan setting, and I wanted to make it more beautiful, so I started bringing in more trees to plant. I planted pines and oaks and flowering dogwood, magnolia, redbud, and plum. All were beautiful, so I kept planting more and more trees until the plot was crammed thick with them. One day I noticed that because the plot was so overcrowded, all my trees were turning sickly and dying. I was distressed.*

When Bette mulled over the dream, she recognized that, while her trees were all wonderful and good, by cramming the area so full, she had "too much of a good thing" and all the trees were suffering. Knowing this was in some way a metaphor for her current situation, she looked at her life for overcrowded situations. At that time she had a family, was a full-time graduate student, and was also a part-time teacher. She sat on two community boards, hosted a weekly study group, belonged to numerous organizations, and gave frequent talks to various gatherings. She realized immediately that the trees were her myriad activities, and she couldn't sustain the demands on her time and energy. (Maslow would say that her physiological needs were threatened. She needed more rest and less stress.) Just as the trees needed to be thinned, her activities needed to be thinned as well. She got some household help, resigned from one of the boards and most of the organizations, and said no more often to requests to help with fund-raising or various campaigns. There is an important lesson here: She *applied* the message from her dream to transform and balance her waking life. And when you begin to interpret your own dreams, I believe you'll come to find the more you use the information, the more you receive.

Hyperbole

Hyperbole is another figure of speech that we frequently see in dreams. Hyperbole is simply a grossly exaggerated statement made for emphasis. For example: He was tall as a pine tree, or bigger than the side of a house. (Of course not, but you get the idea.) They had a ton of money. (Again, not likely, but you have a clear picture of the situation.)

In the following dream, see if you can spot the hyperbole.

Jean dreamed she was beating her teenaged daughter with a gigantic tongue. Just picture the scene. Think rebus. Think hyperbole. Her dream referred to a tongue-lashing she'd given her daughter the day before. How big was it? Huge. Jean conceded that she had overreacted to the teen's messy room. What did she do with the new information? She apologized to her daughter for her outburst and calmly discussed the rules for cleaning.

Onomatopoeia

Onomatopoeia is a fun word, especially when it's said with an Italian accent. The sound of it can remind us that onomatopoeias are words that imitate the sound of the object or action referred to. *Buzz*, *hiss*, *zip*, *murmur*, and *chug* are examples. These show up in dreams occasionally, probably as a function of the brain in the REM state not being as efficient in coordinating information and needing to convey meaning by sounds instead of pictures. An excellent example is the "sniff" incubation dream in Chapter 9.

Personification

Personification is a figure of speech in which an abstraction or an object is given human characteristics. Uncle Sam is a personification, as is Father Time or the Grim Reaper. This device is frequently seen in dreams and will be addressed in greater detail in Chapter 3 when we discuss the people in your dreams.

Roleplaying

Roleplaying, a technique made popular in the sixties and seventies by Gestalt therapist Fritz Perls and expanded by Dr. Ann Faraday and others, is still a helpful tool in examining dreams. It usually begins by relating the dream in first person, present tense. This takes some practice because the tendency is to relate a dream in past tense. Make the extra effort, and you'll find that using the present tense puts you back into the dream experience and brings on its sensations and emotions instead of distancing you from it. Closing your eyes can help you use the present tense when you relate a dream.

Continue by taking the part of each person or element in the dream. If you dream of Uncle Mel, step into his shoes for a few moments and tell us about yourself. Since many of our dreams' elements are projections of ourselves, it's difficult for some folks to get the hang of this technique at first. (Projections will be discussed more in the following chapter, but basically it's assigning certain characteristics of our own personality or behavior to someone or something else.)

"I am Uncle Mel," you begin. "He's a tall and dark . . . "

Oops, you've slipped from *being* Uncle Mel to *telling about* him. It's a common slip. Sometimes people feel a little silly using this technique; other times you don't want to *own* the characteristics of Uncle Mel, especially if he's someone you don't particularly admire. Uncle Mel has probably shown up as a character in your dream to represent some quality or behavior in yourself.

"I am Mel," you say, starting again. "I'm opinionated and quarrelsome. People avoid me."

Are you like Mel, opinionated and quarrelsome?

"I hope not," you say. "I'm usually pretty easygoing."

What about yesterday?

"Ahhh," you say, remembering an exchange with a coworker. You thought his ideas on a team project were totally screwy, and you cut him off sharply in a meeting. (Sounds like self-esteem needs might be prompting this dream.) "I acted like Uncle Mel," you say, feeling sheepish.

Projections don't always come in the form of a person. A dog, a diamond, a house, an onion, or a baseball bat can have the same purpose. Here's a great roleplaying exercise to use with groups to help them understand how objects can represent bigger meanings. First, gather a large number of random items into a big paper bag or box. Any items will do: a rock, a vegetable, a flashlight, a string of pearls, a roll of toilet paper, a book, a doll, a shoe, a box of bandages, a ruler . . . literally anything. Use lots of various things.

Spread the objects out on a table for all to see and examine. Each person selects an object that catches her eye for some reason and examines it closely. In turn everyone roleplays the object chosen. Don't just stick with outward descriptions; imagine yourself in an avant-garde acting class and *become* the object. If someone is particularly uncomfortable speaking, he may write instead, but speaking aloud is best. It's easy to slip into saying, "I am a rock. It's hard . . . "

"I am a cucumber. I'm cool. I am cut into little pieces and mixed up. Some people don't like me. I am . . . " As you can see, this makes for a revealing exercise on many levels.

Beginnings, Middles, and Ends

Another important way to analyze content is to examine the structure of a dream for clues to meaning. The setting or the beginning often reveals the subject of a dream; the middle is the meat; the end provides a direction. In the dream of the bear pushing the man off a building roof, the beginning showed the man walking into an office building. We might anticipate that the subject of the dream might be related to business. In Chapter 5 we'll discuss this topic in more detail.

Analyzing Each Element

To illustrate another technique, consider Irene's dream:

I am walking down a road and come upon two turtles fighting. I stop to watch and discover that one of them is my pet turtle. I walk on and find that my pet turtle has one of my fingers in his mouth and is hanging on as I walk. This is uncomfortable, and I complain about it.

Suddenly I find that, instead of the turtle, a bag of lotion is around my finger. It feels much better.

I continue my walk and come upon my pet turtle again. This time it's on its back, feet kicking in the air. Concerned, I start to turn it over, and a voice says, "No, leave it alone. That's a very important lesson to learn."

Clear as mud, right?

It will be—as soon as you analyze each element. Using a variety of methods to translate each symbol of the dream is probably the most common way people interpret dreams.

The *dreamer* (not a dream dictionary, or her mother-in-law, or even a dream analyst) supplies the answer to: What do you associate with a turtle, fingers, lotion?

These were Irene's associations with each element:

- **Road** — the way you travel
- **Turtle** — something with a hard, protective shell
- **Fighting** — conflict
- **Pet** — favorite
- **Fingers** — for feeling; for doing everything really
- **Lotion** — softens
- **Turtle on back** — vulnerable
- **Voice** — higher self, inner counselor

Remembering that most dreams are about yourself, it becomes clear that the dreamer in this instance has an inner struggle or conflict (the beginning). Irene's preference (pet) is to keep a protective shell around herself, but this behavior is growing uncomfortable and preventing her from feeling and doing other things. Softness is better. The ending, and the *moral* to the story, suggests that she needs to learn to allow herself to be vulnerable to invite closer relationships with others. (Love and belongingness need.)

Sounds great, but does the interpretation fit?

Yes. Not only did Irene confirm the interpretation verbally, but she also reported feeling a "ding"—an important body reaction (like the proverbial light bulb) that almost always occurs when the translation is on target. It's that "Eureka!" moment that many people feel when they've hit the meaning of a dream. Something resonates inside them and it's experienced as a physical sensation—so much so, others can almost see the light bulb that's gone off over your head.

Things to Remember and Exercises to Do

Remember:
- The feeling the dream causes is important.
- Sometimes you can figure out a dream's meaning while drowsy.
- Look at the dream in a nutshell.
- The moral of the story is important.
- Identify the need, according to Maslow's hierarchy, motivating your dream.
- Look for figures of speech and common themes.
- Try acting out roles of people, places, and things.
- Try analyzing each element by associations.
- The "ding" is the thing.

Exercises to Do:

1. Carefully select a dream journal (make a special trip to the store if you can) and a pencil or pen to put beside your bed, and follow the directions for catching your dreams. The sooner you begin recalling and recording your dreams, the sooner you'll begin to have new insights into yourself and your behavior. Go!

2. Have a friend or family member gather ten or more random items in a bag. Select two or three of those items that appeal most to you or catch your attention. Hold each of them, one at a time, and pretend to be that item. Then follow the roleplaying directions in this chapter. Some items may cause positive,

neutral, or negative feelings. That's not unusual. You may do this either alone or with a partner. (It's okay for another person to select the same items you select.) If possible, use a recorder so that you can listen to your comments later, or merely write down your responses. Next, select one or two items that you dislike or repel you. Roleplay with those objects in the same manner. Examine your answers for insights into yourself. Any surprises?

CHAPTER 3

The People in Your Dreams

Most of the time the people you dream about are familiar: They're family, friends, people you work with, characters you read about or see on TV, or folks from your past such as your third grade teacher or an old love. Sometimes the people you dream about can be surprising or even startling. Why would you dream about your boss riding a camel to the Sphinx or your deceased Aunt Estelle standing naked on Broadway? These various people show up to teach you different things about yourself or your life situation. Although occasionally these folks appear as themselves, most of the time they're symbolic of something else altogether.

Most often the people in your dream represent:

- Some aspect of your personality or behavior *projected* onto other people, or
- Some general quality or situation *personified* by the actor

We'll get into more detail about these ideas throughout this chapter, but the first cardinal rule in dream interpretation is that the people in your dream most often represent parts of yourself. The second rule is, don't make any drastic decisions or rash moves until you've taken the time to properly analyze what the players in your dream represent and you're very clear in your understanding of the information. If you act before analyzing, you risk dire consequences. An extreme and tragic example of this occurred when a man dreamed his wife was having an adulterous affair with another man. He woke up infuriated by his dream of her infidelity, grabbed his pistol, and shot her dead.

Had this man known the cardinal rules of interpretation, he'd have discovered his wife was innocent of any wrongdoing. The newspaper account didn't give any more information, but you might wonder about the man's own fidelity—either literally or figuratively. Although you may occasionally see someone playing themselves in your dreams, most often they are representing a quality or trait in you. The man in the newspaper article didn't take time to analyze before he acted.

SYMBOLIC VERSUS REAL

If people in dreams are sometimes real and sometimes not, how can you tell which is which? If it's not clear, using common sense can go a long way towards guiding you, so take your time and think it through.

Ask yourself if the dream is logically about someone else. Take the tongue-lashing example from the previous chapter: Jean dreamed that she was beating her teenaged daughter with a gigantic tongue. How do we know the daughter who appeared in her dream was her actual daughter and not representative of an aspect of Jean herself?

While it's true that most of the time people in your dreams are parts of yourself, consider another important principle: *Dreams are about current events in your life*. Since Jean's dream dealt with a current issue with her daughter, it's reasonable to assume that the daughter was actually the daughter in this case and not a projection.

PROJECTION

Exactly what is projection, anyhow? Freud and others explain projection as a defense mechanism for the ego or conscious self. Simply put, defense mechanisms are attitudes or excuses that keep us feeling okay about ourselves. We attribute our own traits and behaviors to others, either as a form of denial or simply by viewing the world through lenses colored by our own personality and experience. The child says of his imaginary playmate, "Mike broke the lamp." The grumpy man growls, "Everybody I've met today is in a lousy mood." It's easier to blame someone else than admit our failings. That's projection.

Some psychological tests use the concept of projection to reveal something about the personality of an individual. The Rorschach test, commonly known as the inkblot test, is an example of this. It consists of a group of standardized cards which were originally made by literally dropping ink onto a piece of paper, then folding it in half to make a mirror image. Most are black on a white background, although some cards use colored ink on a white background. People joke about it, but the fact is, when interpreted by a trained psychologist, it's a remarkable tool for diagnosing a number of psychological issues. People really can see specific images in the cards. Your descriptions tell a lot about you because you *project* yourself onto the images on the cards. Could you do the same thing with cloud-watching? Sure. And you can with dreams, too.

When you project (and everybody does it), it's much easier to be objective if you see situations acted out by others; that way, you can distance yourself from the emotions of your personal issues. If you remember that those actors on your inner stages are parts of you, dreams, like inkblot tests, will show you what dream expert Elsie Sechrist, author of *Dreams: Your Magic Mirror*, calls "magic mirrors"— the reflection of your inner self.

For an excellent illustration of projection, read Connie's dream:

I saw my neighbor Betsy walking along a garden pathway toward me. The garden was lovely, ethereal, abloom with a variety of colorful flowers and lush plants, and Betsy was just as lovely. Head high, she was dressed in a shimmering white gown, and her face glowed with an

inner radiance as she approached me, nodded, and smiled. Knowing,
even in the dream, that Betsy represented a part of myself, I was feeling
a bit smug with the positive portrayal—until she turned around.

The whole back of her gown was missing and her bare bottom was
showing. I woke up laughing.

Using a technique that often helps to determine what various dream
people represent, I had Connie list Betsy's qualities—a column for positive ones and a column for negative ones. Betsy had many positive attributes, but also she tended to act a bit holier-than-thou at times. Know
the type? I had a strong hunch that Connie's dream wasn't talking about
Betsy's positive traits. Quickly and easily Connie realized that her dream
was mirroring her own pompous attitude with her cousin the day before
when she'd shown her "rear end." (Remember that dreams are about current events.) Connie ended up apologizing to the cousin and vowed to
stop acting self-righteous and taking herself so seriously.

Projection isn't the only way your subconscious gets its message
across. It also uses a figure of speech called personification to clue you
in to something you need to know.

PERSONIFICATION

Personification is attributing personal or human characteristics to
abstract ideas, qualities, or situations. In other words, a person is
used to represent an idea. If, for example, the man who killed his wife
thought of her as a personification of loyalty, then his dream might
have been calling his own loyalty into question.

In another instance, a young mother was distraught when she dreamed
that her own mother had died. When asked what she associated with her
mother, she said, "My mother is the soul of patience." (Don't we often
say things like "patience personified" or "evil personified"?) After being

questioned further about her own patience the day before, the woman admitted that she had "lost it" with her own children, and they'd thought her a real witch. Her inner counselor was showing her, through personification, how distressing her own behavior was. Her own "patient-mother" virtue had "died," and her self-esteem had suffered.

While we're on the topic of "evil personified," what can we learn from Beverly S.'s dream that she contended with the devil?

The devil was in the form of a handsome man, and I couldn't seem to make the other people around me aware of how dangerous he was. I tore at his face, which was made of paper, and tried to set fire to him, but the flames went out and his face regenerated itself. Though I didn't fear for my life, I knew he wanted to possess me, and I fought valiantly against his powers. Only one rather ineffective woman tried to help me at all; I was virtually alone in my efforts to defeat him. I woke up with a sense that I was still struggling.

Beverly knew the cardinal rules of dream interpretation, and she understood about projection and personification, but try as she might, she couldn't come up with any inner "struggle with evil" (the obvious dream theme) that made any sense. Later in the day, still puzzling over her dream, her throat began to get scratchy. By evening she felt worse. The following day, she had a full-blown case of the flu. She didn't understand her dream until a friend called to ask how she was feeling.

"Like the very devil," she croaked.

Then it hit her. She had personified the flu virus as a devil. She had struggled to marshal her defenses against the disease threatening to possess or "take over" her body, but for some reason her immune system (personified by the other people around) hadn't responded as it should have.

Again, always look to the most basic needs first when interpreting a dream, especially a disturbing or puzzling one. Threats to physiological needs are often conveyed by nightmares.

In a similar dream, Ralph W. reported:

> *I stood in a field by my house and watched hordes of very tiny Chinese soldiers, in full battle dress and complete with miniature guns, parachuting from the sky. As they landed they began attacking me in droves. I had only a stick to fight them off.*

That dream, too, was a puzzler until he developed a bad cold a couple of days later. Aha! He had been attacked by "tiny foreign bodies"—cold germs. His and Beverly's physiological need dreams were *prodromal*.

PRODROMAL DREAMS

Prodromal dreams are dreams that warn of upcoming ill health— think of them as an alarm system that goes off before a disease or illness appears. They are frequently reported.

You may be thinking, *You mean we know when we're going to get sick?* Yes. We aren't disconnected from the other parts of ourselves. We are mind, body, and spirit—and that body is made up of a vast number of components and systems that operate to keep us healthy and functioning. While those systems normally work automatically, research has shown that we can consciously affect their workings. For example, through the use of special biofeedback techniques, subjects can learn to raise the temperature of their hands to ward off migraines, and others can concentrate to successfully lower blood pressure. This is possible due to communication between the mind and the body at a subconscious level. As an example of using biofeedback to raise the temperature of the hands, a subject's fingers would be connected to a temperature gauge that would beep when the fingers got warmer. The subject would imagine the hands getting warmer, perhaps by visualizing the hands dipped in warm water or under a heating pad. Beeps would provide positive feedback to let the person know that the efforts were working. With practice, it's fairly easy to learn to raise the temperature of the hands, thus rerouting blood from the brain to the hands and forestalling a headache.

If you can accept the idea of mind-body connection and communication, prodromal dreams make sense. The mind is aware that trouble is brewing in the body.

Literature is full of people who have actually saved their own lives by paying attention to prodromal dreams, and I know of many such cases that have been warned of cancer, heart disease, and other grave illnesses. (See the ambulance dream in Chapter 6.) There's an adage that says nothing of any consequence happens in your life that hasn't been previewed in a dream. By getting into the habit of recording and interpreting your dreams, you could possibly save your own life.

SUB-PERSONALITIES

As mentioned in Chapter 1, Italian psychiatrist Roberto Assagioli suggested that we are all normally made up of different sub-personalities, various selves that are expressed in the different roles we play in everyday life—as teacher, parent, child, employee or employer, student, and many others—each distinct enough to identify.

In waking life you might be a pragmatic engineer with a wife and two kids. But there are other parts of you that make up the whole—perhaps the poet who secretly pens sonnets, the adventurer who aches to climb Mt. Everest, the little boy who is afraid of spiders, the grandmother who bakes cinnamon rolls on Sunday morning, the general who is a strict disciplinarian.

Is it unhealthy to think of ourselves as separate parts with separate identities? Only if they're not integrated. We're not talking multiple personality disorders like in *The Three Faces of Eve* here. The abnormal side of this notion is depicted by people like the woman in the aforementioned book and movie whose sub-personalities aren't integrated because of some psychological trauma, and they become distinct, incomplete, and unhealthy personalities. We're all made up of many parts to our personality, which, when combined, make us who we are. Many of these various sub-parts show up as people in our dreams.

The trick in dealing with different role-players is to be able to identify the characters that are a part of you and claim those parts. Below are some general guidelines and examples illustrating several of the various types of individuals who appear in your dreams.

Familiar People

Often the people who appear in your dreams are people you know—family members, friends, coworkers, neighbors, people you see every day. First ask yourself, as I asked the young mother, what do I associate with this person? Patience? Warmth? Cruelty? Sense of humor? Procrastination? Honor? Or, if you don't know this person, describe him or her. Substitute whatever major quality you associate with that person and see if the dream message makes sense. Or, as in the dream about Betsy in the garden, make lists of positive and negative traits. Even if the person is a football hero from high school, someone you haven't thought of in years, or if the character is deceased, the same principle applies.

Consider the dream Marilyn, a mother with two adult children, had:

I'm on a bus with my son, and we're trying to get off an island. My daughter appears and says, "Take the first right turn." I ignore her advice, thinking that the other way looks shorter and better. Instead, we have to drive for a long time, twisting and turning through jungles, and we end up back where we started.

The central idea of the dream is which path to take—and indeed, Marilyn had been trying to make a decision about an employee. She knew that sooner or later she was going to have to dismiss the incompetent employee, but being a tenderhearted sort, she hated to take the initiative and wanted to give the person one more chance, hoping that conditions would improve and she could avoid a confrontation.

When asked to describe her daughter, Marilyn said, "She's an attorney and a very decisive, no-nonsense sort of person." Her son? "He's more like me."

Of course, after analyzing the dream we see it's counseling a quick exit—immediate dismissal of the employee—or else the situation will go on and on and nothing will be accomplished.

Carole B. frequently dreamed that her close friend Margaret was in trouble. She couldn't figure out what her dreams meant, but on the off-chance that her friend really was in distress (it happens occasionally), she checked on her. As it turns out, Margaret was fine, but Carole continued to have dreams with the same theme. Finally, she realized that Margaret was a person who had a problem saying no. When Carole examined her own situation, she discovered that she had overextended herself to the point of exhaustion—all because she couldn't say no.

Dark or Menacing Strangers

We'll look more at menacing characters in the next chapter, but in general, these people are parts of the dreamer, too. Dream analyst Carl Jung called these menacing strangers the archetypal shadow, which represents the primitive side of our personality as well as material repressed as shameful or unpleasant, the part of ourselves we wish to deny. However, it also provides positive spontaneous traits such as creativity, strong emotions, deep insights, and wisdom from its instinctual nature. A shadow shows up as an unsavory character, usually the same sex as the dreamer, and represents aspects of the self that have been denied and remain unconscious because of their threatening or unpleasant nature. According to Jung, we have to recognize these qualities within ourselves, accept them, and integrate them into our personality to be healthy and whole, a notion similar to that of Assagioli. We often find that these denied aspects aren't as bad as we imagined and actually add dimension to our personality. Some contemporary Jungian analysts suggest that the shadow may not be limited to same-sex characters but may include other symbols as well.

A typical shadow dream by Naomi:

Late at night, I am walking down a street alone when I hear the sound of footsteps behind me. I glance over my shoulder and see only a shadowy form. I'm afraid that I may be attacked and begin to run.

If Naomi frequently goes walking alone at night, the dream may be a literal caution to her, but if not, we would look at the content symbolically. This dream illustrates a threat to her safety and security needs. Who among us is comfortable turning and facing such a threat? Actually, facing the shadowy character is exactly what she needs to do.

I have successfully used the following method for working with dreams, especially with children who need to confront a frightening figure of their dream. In this technique, the person is directed to:

- Imagine he is back in the dream setting, and keep his eyes closed.
- Retell his dream in present tense.
- Turn and confront the figure instead of fleeing.
- Demand, in his imagination or aloud, that it tell him who it is or what it wants. If that prospect seems too frightening, he can

conjure up a powerful helper—two or more, if necessary. (Give me an armed superhero, and I'll confront any shadowy stranger.)

- Have a dialogue with the figure: Ask what it wants from him, then listen. Something should pop into his mind.

You may be surprised at what you discover when you dig deep. The woman used this method and discovered her stalker was only a scruffy kitten, wanting to be cuddled—and this from a woman who prided herself on her independence and lack of sentimentality.

At other times, dark and/or shadowy figures might represent something that hasn't "come to light" yet; that is, something in the future. For example, LaJuan dreamed that a dark man was sneaking into her bank late at night and stealing large amounts of cash. She dreamed this two or three times, each time awakening concerned about her money. She tried working with it symbolically, but nothing seemed to fit. A few weeks later her bank was taken over by a federal agency and closed; the CEO had embezzled millions. Although her funds were ultimately safe, she had to wait several days to gain access to her account, and this caused hardship.

GENERAL CATEGORIES OF PEOPLE

Frequently, characters in dreams are defined by their category or occupation, whether strangers or people we know casually. We make general associations with those in various roles; an airline pilot would represent one idea, a newborn baby another. In every case we should consider a play on words as well as role or occupational characteristics. Though not exhaustive, the following are some common sorts of people dreamers encounter, along with some possible meanings to consider. Always remember, *your* associations are individual and, because of your unique life experiences, may be different from the examples given here.

Babies and Children

Both babies and children may represent innocence, playfulness, naïveté, or immaturity. They may also be symbolic of "the child within," an aspect often injured or repressed in the past and not allowed to be expressed freely. While children may be unruly or undisciplined, they are also honest, creative, and adventuresome.

JoAnna V. dreamed:

I saw a dark-haired little girl about four years old sitting on a bench in a deserted station of some sort. Her fingers were tucked between her knees, and her head drooped as if she were very sad and lonely. I felt that perhaps she was lost or had been deserted.

Using this dreamette, as Dr. Ann Faraday calls short dream scenes, we dramatized the dream with JoAnna taking the roles of various parts of her dream. When she began to speak as the child and describe her loneliness and sadness, tears trickled down JoAnna's cheeks. For the past several years, all her time had been focused on her very demanding work and on caring for her aging parents. She knew immediately that the dream was dramatizing her need to express her carefree, playful inner child. She vowed to give herself a few hours every week to do something fun and frivolous—to go skating in the park, camping with friends, or to take up ceramics again.

Babies frequently represent new ideas, new undertakings, or new beginnings. Sometimes the age of the baby is related to the age of the project. Rhonda dreamed that she gave birth to a baby, and was distressed to discover that the baby had an IQ of 12. (A point of information: A baby with an IQ of 12 would be completely nonfunctional.)

The day before, Rhonda and her friend had discussed the idea of going into business together. They had gone so far as to consider names for their venture and property to house it. Needless to say, Rhonda rethought the whole notion and decided that it was, as her dream had suggested, a really "idiotic" idea.

Policemen, Sheriffs, and Other Law Enforcement Personnel

Everybody dreams of cops at one time or another. Does that mean you're going to get into trouble? Maybe, but it's more likely that the cop is a part of you—an archetype, a subpersonality, or a personification of a principle. Law enforcement officials are just that. They remind us, indeed, *require* us, to obey the law, whether the law is a matter of personal ethics, enacted by government or another body, or the edict of a higher power. These officers may represent conscience, moral codes, or universal law, as in Ellen V.'s dream:

I am driving down the access road beside a major freeway, speeding along at fifty miles an hour—well over the speed limit. A policeman pulls me over. "You know, you can get on the freeway and go faster without breaking the law," he says. He writes me a ticket that carries a fifty-dollar fine.

At a friend's urging, Ellen had made an appointment with a psychic for a reading. Ellen, who was accustomed to receiving her own guidance through avenues such as reasonable thought, meditation, and dream work (the "free" way), considered breaking the appointment after her dream, but didn't want to disappoint her friend, who had extolled the abilities of the clairvoyant.

As it turned out, she learned nothing of any value from the psychic (the side road). The clairvoyant's charge? Fifty dollars.

A reminder: Not all lawmen are benevolent or righteous. Some, depending on their deportment in the dream, may personify what psychologist Fritz Perls called the "top dog" character, the internal voice of authority. Ann Faraday suggests that the top dog is a perfectionist, a dogmatist, or a bully. He is often a sanctimonious preacher spreading guilt with his "shoulds" and "oughts," and a hypocrite to boot—a true Pharisee. This is a sort often stereotyped in movies as the big-bellied, cigar-chomping southern sheriff who jails or beats minorities with no provocation, or the "Smoky" character who chases Burt Reynolds and his buddies down highways and back roads.

Messengers

Messengers of one sort or another are frequent characters in dreams. They run the gamut from FedEx couriers to skywriters, and are always trying to tell us something—either warning us away from trouble or imparting important information. Some common messengers that may show up in your dreams are postal or package delivery people, telephone callers, and e-mailers. Animals or birds may also act as messengers, but we'll talk about that more in a later chapter.

Teachers

Obviously teachers imply lessons to be learned, but there are good teachers and bad teachers (and some that serve as "top dog"), so individual characteristics will color the meaning here. The subject being taught is also important. Whereas an English teacher evokes images of words, language, writing, and reading material, a history teacher is concerned with the past, and a math teacher may deal with something to be "figured out" or making things "add up."

Ministers, Rabbis, Priests, Nuns, and Other Religious Leaders

Religious leaders in dreams often signal dreams with a spiritual content, but not always.

A Protestant woman dreamed that a priest was serving Communion using pitchers and pitchers of milk lined up on the rail. As he poured glass after glass for communicants, he said to someone beside him, "I thought this would be enough, but it's not. Bring some more milk."

It turned out the woman was seriously low on calcium and needed strong supplements. She used this symbolism because, for her, the Communion elements become part of the body and nourish it just as calcium, a major nutrient in milk, becomes part of the body and nourishes it. Her physiological needs prompted the dream.

Doctors and Nurses

Those in healing professions who show up in dream roles often signal health concerns to the dreamer, but they may also suggest concerns with psychological or spiritual health as well. Doctors may symbolize the "diagnosis" of a problem, or a nurse might remind us to use TLC (tender loving care) in a particular situation.

John, who had been suffering with a pain in his shoulder, reported this simple dream:

> *A doctor appeared before me and said, "Eat okra." I told him that nobody else in my family liked okra. He merely smiled and said, "Eat okra."*

Thinking this might be a physiologically motivated dream and with nothing to lose, John prevailed upon his wife to cook okra for him. After eating a large helping one night, he ate the leftovers the next day, and his shoulder pain had disappeared by the following morning. Coincidence? Perhaps, but John believes that some property of the okra speeded the healing process. There was no harm in giving it a try.

Dentists and Oral Hygienists

Dentists and oral hygienists deal with the teeth, those things in your mouth. Dreaming of either type of person could mean a literal need to attend to your teeth. On the other hand, teeth and the whole oral constellation may symbolize words or language—those other things from the mouth (more on teeth later).

Glenn, who frequently used profanity that offended his family and coworkers, dreamed that an oral hygienist was cleaning his rotting teeth with a floor mop and a water hose. (In reality, his teeth were healthy.) Little interpretation is required to understand that Glenn needed to clean up his language or wash out his mouth. Since people were avoiding him or visibly wincing at his salty talk, and this was beginning to bother him, his needs for belongingness and the esteem of others motivated his dream.

Counselors and Therapists

Counselors and various types of therapists are people who help you deal with issues of living, or perhaps problems of the past. These may be real people, your own inner counselor, or even a spiritual counselor.

Maria G. and her husband had been having serious marital problems. They were in counseling, but it wasn't working. Their fighting continued, and she felt totally hopeless about the future of her marriage. She remembered thinking one night that they would have to settle for simply co-existing and never having a true relationship again.

She dreamed:

> My husband and I were meeting with our counselor, explaining how nothing was working. The counselor told us it was time for a specialized counselor, one who handled tough situations like ours.
>
> She made the introduction. It was a man. I didn't see his face, but I remember he walked me to my car. He was holding my elbow—not a romantic gesture, but one of concern. It gave me a great sense of comfort and hope.

"I awoke the next morning feeling hopeful," Maria said. "I wanted to seek out a new counselor that could help us. But before that, I went to a new Bible study starting that day. Something was said in the presentation to the effect that sometimes God will allow us to get so low that we have no other choice but to look up and seek him. Those words pierced me. I remember so well, driving home with my baby in the back seat, talking to God, and basically saying, 'Uncle.'"

Things slowly started improving in Maria's marriage. She started to hold her sharp tongue, they continued counseling, and things improved considerably. Later at Bible study they discussed different names often given to Jesus. One of these was "Counselor." It hit her that he was the "specialized counselor" who had brought her comfort and helped her fix things.

Other Categories

You may dream of many, many categories of people including soldiers and warriors, musicians, artists, presidents, kings, queens, and hobos. The key thing to remember is to first look at the obvious, then look beyond literal meanings to symbolic meanings. With a bit of practice and experience, you'll find the process simple and automatic.

CLOSE-UP ON BODY PARTS

Sometimes important elements in our dreams are those that focus on certain body parts rather than on a whole person. These specific features have special meanings as well. As in all symbolism, body parts must be interpreted from your individual experience, but here are some examples that will illustrate how the procedure works and give you a starting point. A few of the most common parts are given below.

Teeth

Teeth show up frequently in dreams. As mentioned earlier, if your real teeth are healthy, look to symbolic meanings.

A common myth is that dreaming of losing teeth means that a death will occur. While I occasionally hear of a person who seems to use this symbol to signal an upcoming death, more frequently such a dream has to do with words (as do dreams of tongues or mouths).

Once Hugh Lynn Cayce, Edgar Cayce's elder son, laughed as he told the story of a woman who always talked a mile a minute, chattering, chattering, chattering, and not letting anyone get a word in edgewise. She dreamed that bunches and bunches of teeth were falling out of her mouth and scattering everywhere while she tried desperately to rake them into a big pile to save. She asked Hugh Lynn what that meant, but continued to talk so much that he didn't have an opportunity to explain.

Hair

Another common symbol, the hair on our heads is a perfect analogy for ideas, thoughts, or thinking. Matted or disheveled tresses may signify tangled, confused thinking, while shining locks are positive mental aspects.

A woman dreamed that she was cutting off masses of long hair into a shorter style that was easier to care for. (In reality, her hair was of medium length.) Her dream was advising her to cut off so much thinking and start *doing*.

Hair was an important consideration for Samson (strength), Rapunzel (access), and for a Broadway cast who frolicked nude while singing about it. We're all familiar with "letting down your hair" or the scene in a movie when the dowdy secretary takes off her glasses and shakes out her bun to reveal sexy tresses. Everybody knows about the stereotypical dumb blondes and fiery redheads, the gray/white hair of wise folks. Often those stereotypes appear as dream symbols.

Heads

Heads house our brains and most of our sense organs. When we say things like "use your head," we're saying *think*, use logic.

There are many figures of speech referring to the head, including "out of his head" and having a "big head." In addition, we have corporate heads, heads of state, the head of the line, and the headless horseman.

A man once asked Edgar Cayce about the meaning of a dream about a headless sailor. The reply was like a moral to the story. "Do not lose the head too much in duty . . . to accomplish the greater lessons . . . in things more spiritual." [137-360]

One of my favorite head dreams came from the journal of Sara J., an older college student, who dreamed:

Heads were being used for bowling balls; however, the bowlers when finishing their turns at bowling were not putting the heads back on the right people, or they were not putting them back at all.

Unfortunately, the dream was never interpreted, and she failed to note current events in her life, but we can see the obvious figures of speech there. "Heads will roll" and "getting heads on right/straight" as well as the idea of not using heads properly or losing heads are all referenced here. Do you wonder about what was going on in her life at the time to cause such a vivid message? Hopefully she got it through her own head, subliminally.

Hands and Fingers

Hands and fingers are commonly highlighted in dreams and are complex symbols with many possibilities. They may represent feelings (as in the turtle dream in Chapter 2), service, work, help ("give a hand"), praise (as in applause), creativity (the hands of artists, musicians, writers), communication, or any of a number of productive ways we use our hands. They can also signal disdain, idleness, or getting into mischief.

Feet

Since feet are used to stand, they're often used to illustrate "understanding" or perhaps bases (on "firm footing," or "feet made of clay"). They're also our main method of locomotion, so feet may represent our path in life or our direction. Bare feet are especially vulnerable to the environment, so they may represent sensitivity or being a tenderfoot (a novice). Toes are extensions of the feet and help with balance. They can also have to do with sensitivity or with testing ("sticking a toe in the water").

Tamara had the following "split-toe dream":

My husband and I were entering a house, maybe one we used to have. My brother was there, or maybe it was my son—some young guy. He turned up dead, and we realized he'd been bitten by a boa on his split left big toe, which was fatal. Since I also had a split left big toe, we were searching for the boa (which really looked like a cobra) so it wouldn't kill me too. The whole time we searched, I was upset that we were ignoring the dead guy and not taking him to a hospital or something, even though I knew he was dead.

When asked what had been going on in her life at the time, Tamara said that one of her sons had invited the extended family to come spend Thanksgiving with his family in his new home in another state. Parents, two sisters, and one brother-in-law all traveled there. The occasion was a disaster. There were venomous family squabbles and high drama. The son's (and the mother's) idea of a lovely family affair was devastated.

She felt the dream was about this situation. The split big toe was baffling, but the big toe sometimes relates to balance and sensitivity. The left side sometimes refers to the unconscious, hidden, or weak side. Certainly the disastrous occasion was about sensitivity, division, and venom.

Luckily, Tamara woke up at four in the morning after the first dream with an interpretation. It was a "Eureka!" moment, she said. The dead young man wasn't a real person, but the vision of a peaceful, happy family gathering. The split toe, she realized, was shaped like a valentine heart and the acrimony had struck at the heart of the occasion and killed it. She should be careful not to let the ruinous visit pierce her sensitive heart and "kill" her, too. Can you see how her interpretation fits the very strange split toe dream? Knowing what was going on in her life was critical to discovering the meaning.

Eyes

Of course, eyes are considered windows to the soul. Dreaming of having a third eye is common and signals a spiritual awakening, an ability to "see" beyond the mundane.

A woman was thrilled to discover in her dream that she had an extra eye in the back of her head. The eye, rather than looking grotesque, was beautiful. She determined that she was learning to see the past clearly and deal with the pain there; the message was a progress report from her inner counselor who said, "Well done." Losing your sight might suggest "losing sight" of some objective, purpose, or ideal or being blind to certain realities.

Internal Organs

We often see internal organs referred to as "having guts" or not having them, or as something "eating our guts out." This gruesome dream is a good example. Leanne K. dreamed:

> I was captured by some jungle people and thrown in a cell with a very low ceiling. Then I was brought out and presented to the king or head guy. They sliced me open from neck to bowels, and he reached inside, took out some organs, and ate them. Then he said, "Sew her up. I'll

snack on her later." They crudely stitched me up and threw me back in the cell. I looked down at myself and said, "I'm really screwed."

At the time Leanne said she had a terrible boss, the whole work situation was horrible—with a jungle mentality—and she felt as if she were being eaten alive. Her dream indicated that things weren't going to get any better, and her most basic unconscious needs had prompted this attention-getting illustration. Being a smart lady, she left the place and found a much less stressful job.

The Endocrine Glands

The Edgar Cayce readings spoke of seven endocrine glands that corresponded with spiritual centers. These areas are very similar to chakras, or energy vortices, associated with the kundalini (or vital force) raised along the spine during some eastern meditations and yoga. These centers are often linked with other various groups of seven, including the seven churches in the Bible, parts of the Lord's Prayer, and with the seven colors of the rainbow, beginning with the red of the gonads and moving upward to the violet of the pituitary, or master gland. The first four are considered the lower, earth centers, and the top three are considered the higher centers. (Sounds a bit like Maslow's need hierarchy, doesn't it?) Here are some associated meanings for the endocrine glands as specified in the Edgar Cayce readings (slightly different from the chakra system of the Eastern philosophies):

1. **The gonads (testes or ovaries)** — red, sexual energy, desire, creation, daily bread
2. **Cells of leydig** — orange, soul in the earth, balance, temptation
3. **Adrenals or solar plexus** — yellow, energy, power, debts or trespasses

4. **Thymus or heart center** — green, love, healing, passion, keeping from evil
5. **Thyroid** — blue, choices, will
6. **Pineal** — indigo, third eye, Christ consciousness, enlightenment
7. **Pituitary** — violet, highest master center, Father in Heaven

You might notice the colors associated with the various centers. In Chapter 5, we'll discuss colors in greater depth.

Things to Remember and Exercises to Do

Remember:
- Dreams are mostly about *you*.
- Dreams are usually about current events in your life.
- Don't make any drastic moves until you're sure of your dream interpretation.
- Nothing of any consequence happens in your life that hasn't been previewed in a dream.

Exercises to Do:

1. Since people you know often appear in your dreams, make a list of your closest relatives and friends and write out your first impressions of them—positive and negative. Imagine you're describing them to a stranger and think of specific characteristics of each. Roleplaying may help. (You might also consider giving each a pseudonym in case someone peeks at your notes.) Keep this list and review it occasionally, adding to it or changing it as needed.

2. Read the following dream and imagine that it's yours. Decide what this dream would mean to you using the "Analyzing Each Element" method from Chapter 2 (and writing down the symbols). Particularly note the people and/or body parts. You'll encounter this example in a later chapter. When you do, ask yourself if your dream meaning was very different from the real dreamer's. If so, why do you think it was different?

My husband and I had just returned home from a plane trip and were unpacking. The doorbell rang. It was my long time friend. Seeing her reminded me that this was the night for our bridge game at my house. When I invited her in, she told me that she hadn't eaten and was very hungry. I took her to the kitchen, hoping I had something to fix for her. I found and prepared a nice piece of salmon for her (in reality, she doesn't care for salmon) and some leftover green beans from the fridge. I was looking for another vegetable for her and decided against either corn or potatoes, which she had suggested. I went outside to a group of magical people who grew vegetables from their chests (I could see stalks peeking out of the shirt of one, and others had one particular kind of veggie coming out of their V-neck T-shirts). They also had magical hands to harvest and prepare these vegetables. I selected some small yellow tomatoes, cooked them, and added them to the plate. My friend said it looked delicious, ate every bite, and said the tomatoes were amazing.

CHAPTER 4

Flora, Fauna, and Other Creatures

In the physical world, "flora" and "fauna" are the terms used to describe the plant and animal life indigenous to a particular geographic area. For example, rattlesnakes are common in Texas, but not in Australia. You're not likely to see a kangaroo or a koala in Texas unless it's in a zoo, nor are you likely to see a eucalyptus tree among the tall pines of East Texas. In the real world, certain plants and animals are native to certain areas. However flora and fauna indigenous to our *dream* worlds include *everything*—even some that may not exist on Earth. The daisies and dogs of your dreams may seem ordinary, or they may talk and be polka-dotted. Most often they will be symbolic of something else altogether, just as people in your dreams are. When trying to discern meaning, the key is to determine your associations with these elements using the same techniques.

"Other creatures" is a catch-all category that's widely divergent. It includes everything that is likely to show up in your nighttime adventures, from angels to zombies. They're not exactly normal people, plants, or animals, but they play similar roles, and dreams with these players should be interpreted like any other dream.

FLORA

Flowers seem to appear more often in women's dreams than men's, perhaps because women in general are more likely to be more concerned about flowers. Of course there are exceptions, including a well-known surgeon who is an expert on roses, as well as men who are florists or horticulturists. But the fact is, many men—and lots of women—wouldn't know the difference between a delphinium and a daisy, thyme and marjoram, or between aspidistra and papyrus plant. It's unlikely that plants you don't recognize would have some hidden esoteric meaning in your dreams.

Still, flora shows up from time to time and must mean something. Plants can be metaphors just as people are. There is a difference between a sturdy oak tree and a gracefully swaying weeping willow. Let's figure out what those differences might mean.

Say It with Flowers

Back in romantic Victorian times, suitors often sent bouquets of particular flowers to impart messages to the young ladies they were wooing. The specific type of blossom, along with its color, sent a message. Even the number of flowers meant something. A quick online search reveals several lists of flowers and their meanings. Unfortunately, not everyone agrees on all the meanings—which is just as well for our purposes. These lists are useless to anyone except Victorian ladies and gents. (And florists.)

As always, the issue is: What do particular flowers mean to *you*? Judging by the number sold on Valentine's Day, I think we might all agree that a majority of people associate red roses with "I love you" or "Be mine."

Jackie S. says that carnations remind her of death and the smell of funerals, but Sandra C. is reminded of youth and her senior prom. Bob T. says that magnolia blossoms make him think of his grandmother, who had a huge tree in her yard, and his grandmother represents comfort and unconditional love to him. When shown a photo of a calla lily, Will says he remembers from his days of reading comic books that corpses were often shown holding such a flower, so they make him think of death.

Some people walk into a florist shop and are drawn to exotic or unusual arrangements or flowers; others are drawn to the more traditional bouquets. Which do you prefer? Sifting through those types of memories and experiences will give clues as to what certain blooms mean to you, as in Marilyn P.'s dream:

> *I heard a bee buzzing around in my upswept hairdo and was alarmed. I knew if I swatted it I was likely to get stung. After thinking for a moment, I took a white rose and gently enticed it from my hair.*

We already know that the bee in her hair was a variation of the figure of speech "a bee in her bonnet" (irritation). The question is how to handle the disturbing situation. An aggressive, head-on approach (swatting) wouldn't work. What did the white rose mean to Marilyn? She said she was reminded of sweetness and purity, a delicate connotation. Using gentle enticement and higher principles was the way to handle her problem, a variation on the adage "you can catch more flies with honey than with vinegar."

Because of traditions, advertising, TV, movies, poetry, songs, books, and stories from our childhood, we all probably have more flower and plant associations tucked away than we would think. Carl Jung suggested that the lotus blossom, because of its circular pattern of unfolding, was an archetype of the unfolding or individuation of the self, a process that leads to the ultimate goal of self-realization or completeness—a state that's rarely reached in life. The lotus is a sacred symbol in many cultures and religions and is a frequent motif in early

Egyptian art. But do you personally know the difference between a lotus blossom and a squash blossom? Have you ever seen a lotus blossom or even a picture of one? (In case you don't know, the lotus is somewhat similar to a water lily.)

The distinct smells of different flowers are often cataloged in our internal storage system. Strangely, the English language has a vast number of words that specifically describe things we see, but there are fewer that name specific scents. Only a small number of words specifically describe odors, and those mostly describe a general class of smells (reeking, acrid, fragrant), not precise ones. We have to resort to something smelling *like* a rose, cinnamon, smoke, garbage, sweat, cookies, lavender, etc.

A vast number of memories and associations are stored by scent. A woman reported that her mother once had a serious reaction to pain medications after surgery and was behaving erratically. Nothing, not even heavy doses of antipsychotic drugs, could calm her, and she had to be restrained for her own safety. The mother didn't seem to recognize her daughter or the sound of her voice, but finally, and abruptly, the mother settled down. Later she said, "I remember all of the experience. It was like a crazy bad dream, and I was frightened. I didn't recognize you or anybody. I thought you were Bess and wanted to hurt me, but when I finally smelled your perfume, I knew it was you, and I was safe."

The idea here is that you probably have more associations with flowers than you think, but they may be tucked away in your unconscious. Consider the following list:

- Easter lilies
- Red roses
- Pulling petals off daisies or other flowers
- Lilacs or honeysuckle

- A funeral
- A first corsage (given or received)
- Poinsettias
- A flower garden

Do some of these flower connections bring a constellation of memories and associations to mind, including smells? This will be useful for helping you decipher their meanings when they appear in your dreams.

Trees and Other Plants

Lady Bird Johnson, the former first lady who loved plants and sought to beautify her surroundings with them, campaigned to beautify the nation and was the force behind many of the plantings along the country's highways. Those bushes and shrubs, as well as herbs, grasses, vines, and other plants, follow the same principles as flowers. Who hasn't heard of a prickly cactus, a four-leaf clover, or waving fields of grain, and then made immediate associations with crotchetiness, luck, or plenty?

Trees seem to have developed characters of their own, many of an almost universal nature. In *Man and His Symbols*, Carl Jung states that trees are one of the symbols that often appear in dreams, and have a wide variety of meanings—everything from a phallic symbol to a representation of physical or psychological growth, or even death (as in on the cross) or evolution.

You may have never seen a spreading chestnut tree in your life, but you may conjure up thoughts of chestnut trees having strength because you associate them with the village smithy in Longfellow's poem "The Village Blacksmith." East Texas, Louisiana, and Georgia pines are tall and stately, but they're softer than the soaring, stoic pines of Colorado or Northern California. The latter seem unyielding, stately, austere. Could you imagine wind *playing* among the branches of a stolid mountain pine? It wouldn't dare. Wind might blow, whistle, or whip through those giants, not dance or play. But southern pines aren't so unyielding; their needles are longer and their branches sway as wind plays through them. See? Even trees have different personalities or traits.

Most people think of a mighty oak and its strength, or the olive tree and the peace represented by its branch. Rows of flowering cherry trees might remind us of Japan's gift to the United States, which beautifies Washington, D.C. We see palm trees and think of tropical settings and water, or date palms bring to mind an oasis and camels in the desert. Christmas trees stir memories of gifts and family; maple trees might make us think of Vermont and tapping for syrup. Apple trees might bring to mind the forbidden tree in the garden of Eden, biting into a sweet, crisp fruit, or a song about apple trees or apple blossoms.

Yet some of our memories and associations of particular trees are quite different from one another. A young mother loved the weeping willow in the family's backyard, enjoyed seeing and hearing the sway of its graceful branches. The children loved to run through the branches, sweeping them aside and pretending they were in a jungle. Her husband hated that same tree. For him it was a nuisance, a monster with tentacles that wrestled with him and banged his head every time he mowed under it.

The following sayings—the Tree of Life, a family tree, and "not being able to see the forest for the trees"—all mention trees, but aren't referring to real ones growing in the ground. In the same way, you'll see real trees in your dreams representing those and other ideas.

Trees go through the life cycle of the year's seasons, and the deciduous ones especially signal the passing of time when their leaves and colors change depending on whether it's fall, winter, spring, or summer. The seasonal states of dream trees often give important clues to the message presented.

One winter Ellen K. dreamed:

I saw a magnificent tree covered with large fragrant blossoms like none I'd ever seen. Two nests were in the tree's branches, and I watched birds building up the nests, lining them with colorful ribbons and feathers until they were quite beautiful.

She awoke with feelings of awe and anticipation. She knew that birds are sometimes associated with messages (think of the owls in the Harry Potter books), and that blossoming trees and preparing nests come in spring. Ellen decided her dream meant to be prepared for something very positive coming in the spring. And in the spring she actually received two wonderful work-related awards (parallels to the two nests of her dream). She "feathered her nest," monetarily in one case and figuratively, with prestige, in the second.

Consider the following figures of speech:

- Barking up the wrong tree
- Up a tree
- A bad tree doesn't yield good fruit
- An apple doesn't fall far from the tree
- A hanging tree

What do you associate with them? How would you picture them?

FAUNA

Animals in dreams are simply actors and actresses with fur, feathers, and scales. It is important here, as it is with human characters, to rely on *your* associations rather than on some other source. Certainly we can get clues from such sources, but look for the unique definition of these projections of the dreamer.

Interestingly, research has shown that children dream of animals more often than adults do, with the percentage of animal dreams decreasing as age increases. Still, animals crop up frequently in adult dreams.

Family Pets

The usual furry creature is a family pet, a dog or a cat. Anyone who has pets in the household knows that while we might generally associate loyalty with dogs and independence with cats, every dog, every cat, and every bird has its own distinct personality and characteristics. Consider the presence of familiar animals in your dreams the same way you consider humans in your dreams. Is Max so friendly that he's useless as a guard dog? Is Skittles so shy that she hides under the bed when the doorbell rings? Is Tweety the canary always cheerful and singing? Is Dexter the gerbil playful? You get the idea.

Birds

Birds are harbingers of spring, remind us that the early one gets the worm, sometime serve as messengers, and, like any other symbols, deliver a message unique to our interpretation. Birds are among the most beautiful and colorful of all the fauna, so they tend to be positive symbols—except for maybe turkey vultures (buzzards) and, in some cases, pigeons and a few others that are a nuisance for cars, sidewalks, and statues.

In the United States we think of the bald eagle and immediately associate it with freedom, courage, and strength. If I asked which bird represents peace to you, the common response would be "a dove." Most of us associate owls with wisdom. In ancient Greece, Athena was the goddess of wisdom, among other things, and is often pictured with an owl. Rice University in Houston, known for its scholarly student body, even chose the owl as its mascot.

We've heard about the bluebird of happiness and may vaguely remember all the little bluebirds cheerily helping Cinderella ready her dress for the ball, or recall a refrain about singing like the birdies sing. Just as we have an association with vultures circling, we know what a buzzard sitting on a fencepost means—the anticipation of something negative, or someone exploiting weakness.

Let's take a look at two bird dreams, a duck dream and a swan dream. These two dreams are very different, but have some similarities as well.

Sam P.'s duck dream at first seemed silly to him, but since he believes all dreams are meaningful, he wrote it down and worked with it. As it turned out, it wasn't silly at all:

> One night I dreamed about a duck wearing a life preserver. That's all I remember.
>
> It was a Sunday, and when I looked at the Sunday comic section in the newspaper, I found two different cartoons featuring a duck wearing a life preserver. I thought it was quite funny to have the redundancy, or synchronicity.

"Synchronicity" is a term Jung coined which is a *significant coincidence* of a causal physical and psychological phenomena. In this case, the psychological phenomenon was the dream, the comics the physical. Neither caused the other, but the timing was significantly coincidental to Sam.

After he gave the dream more thought, Sam realized it was quite meaningful. He'd been pondering an issue in his life that seemed potentially threatening and fearful. He noted that a duck wearing a life preserver was absurd because a duck couldn't drown if it tried. The dream was showing him that he had no more reason to be afraid in his life than a duck needs to fear the water. He was being overly cautious because of a threat to his safety and security needs.

Rose P. had the following swan dream:

> I dreamed that I was in a shipwreck and was being tossed around between rocks on a very stormy sea. I had about decided I was going to drown when suddenly I came to an inlet. On the other side was a beautiful, perfectly calm sea, like a sea of glass. A huge swan came up beside me. He had a seat in his back. I knew I should climb into that seat and did so. Then the swan carried me to shore. As I sat on his back I had a strong sense that he was very wise and very good, and that I was safe. I felt very calm, serene, and trusting.

This dream is filled with symbolism and emotion, and Rose felt that it was an important one, right up Carl Jung's alley with archetypes and transformation symbols galore. Let's break down the depiction to its various components and Rose's association with each part.

- **Shipwreck** — disastrous upset
- **Stormy sea** — emotional battering and turmoil
- **Rocks** — problems
- **Drowning** — overwhelmed and helpless, dying
- **Inlet** — a way out
- **Calm sea** — emotional tranquility
- **Swan** — peace and grace, tranquility, the soul, a God-like figure
- **Seat on back** — the way out
- **Shore** — safety, feet on the ground and away from the turmoil

She felt calm when she awoke. What would you ask Rose first?

"Is there some sort of serious emotional upset going on in your life?" I asked Rose.

"Yes," she replied. Her husband's drinking problem had escalated, and she had a rebellious teenager causing chaos. It's no wonder she felt overwhelmed, battered, and drowning in emotional upset. But there was a way out of her turmoil—the swan.

The swan is a complex symbol. Carl Jung suggested that a swan was a symbol of transformation. Even Hans Christian Andersen would agree. Remember the ugly duckling story? Ancient Greek myth suggests that Zeus changed himself into a swan to ravish Leda, a woman he had his eye on. But why is a swan a transformative figure, and what is the subtext of that story? Could it be an allegorical connection of the mortal and the divine? Perhaps. There is a striking similarity among Jung, Andersen, the Greek myth, and Rose's associations with a swan. The dream itself did its work in calming her emotions: She was left with the reminder that the swan is within her, a part of her. The swan, the soul, the higher self, the divine within will lead her in her life journey with grace and serenity.

In the end, Sam's and Rose's dreams chose very different ways to convey the same message: Don't be afraid.

Other Mammals

When you encounter generic, unfamiliar animals in your dreams, treat them the same way you do other symbols. How is a guide dog different from a junkyard dog? What do you associate with a German shepherd? A poodle? A pit bull?

Dana dreamed:

I was in a travel trailer nestled on the edge of the woods—not sure where, but it was green; the time was dusk. I was with some other people, but I'm not sure who they were. This lady (warrior type), tall, thin but muscular with something over her shoulder, brought me a very large black dog and told me to look into his eyes, and he would show me the way. Then she just turned and left. It was as if she and I had seen each other's inner souls. An instant trust was there. After that there was no one else around us; the other people were gone. I didn't see how they left or where they went. When the dog and I went out, he took me into the woods, and that's when I woke up.

Dana said, "After I awoke, I felt as if I needed to find that dog. I remember not feeling afraid, just at peace." She also reported going through some serious family problems at the time.

As we discussed the dream, it became clear that the warrior woman was her strong higher self bringing her peace and giving her strength (the dog) to guide and protect her through the unknown (the woods) as she moved on (the travel trailer).

What about other strange animals? Have you ever dreamed about . . . a monkey? A skunk? A hippo? A groundhog? How about a lion?

Who can forget the Cowardly Lion in *The Wizard of Oz*? (That movie is filled with symbolism. The whole thing can be interpreted as you would any dream.) Most of us are familiar with the MGM trademark of the roaring lion or certainly *The Lion King*. A majority of us would probably associate a lion with being the king of the jungle, courageous, powerful, and aggressive. Some associate the lion with the solar plexus or adrenal glands that secrete adrenaline when we need to be courageous and aggressive (the fight-or-flight response). Lions are also mentioned frequently in the Bible and other religious writings, and in myths.

Here is John's lion dream:

I was standing aside watching the action unfold. I could see a dark-skinned young man, who I knew was me, dressed in a simple loincloth. He/I was in a clearing amid several dome-shaped huts that seemed to be a primitive setting in Africa. In the clearing was a large, sandy, circular path in the grass, and there was some sort of initiation or testing going on that involved a lion. The object was to walk around the circle until he met the lion. At that point he would stop, face the lion without fear, and speak a magical incantation. If done properly, the lion would be tamed and walk beside him under his control. If he showed fear or didn't say the proper words, the lion would attack and devour him.

This is a good example of an important principle of dream interpretation: *Dreams may be allegories or analogies on more than one level and have different interpretations, all of which may be correct.* We can look at this as a dream of transformation, of individuation à la Jung, in which the primitive self is harnessing the power of the lion on the way to wholeness (the circle). That's a good interpretation. We can take a more pragmatic approach and ask John if he is learning (or needs to learn) how to harness and control his aggressiveness and/or his power by choosing the right words in combative situations. For John, both interpretations rang true.

Further, if we think of the lion as representing the adrenal glands and remember that adrenaline is released in times of stress, as well as the damage that can be done to the body and mind under prolonged and/or extreme stress, we discover another possible meaning. Is John's dream pointing out the need to "tame the lion" before it "eats him alive"? He agreed with that interpretation as well. His doctor had warned him about health changes. In this case you see needs addressed at several levels, from the most basic physiological needs, to esteem needs, to being needs.

What about Snakes?

In our waking world, snakes are normally seen as scary or creepy. But how do you determine in your dreamworld whether a snake is good or bad? Is the dream snake representing the age-old temptation from Eden, the healing power of the doctor's caduceus, or the kundalini of Eastern philosophies? Is it a snake in the grass, a sexual or phallic symbol as Freud might insist; a transformative motif as Jung might offer; or a magnification of a snakelike infection in the body? In dreams, snakes show up fairly often and in many guises.

An audience member at one of my speaking engagements once described a dream of terrible small snakes of an undetermined species teeming in a small container of murky water. She woke up feeling concerned. Trying to picture the scene as she related details, I asked, "Do you have kidney or bladder problems?" (It never hurts to start with the most basic concerns first: the physical needs.)

Yes, she acknowledged, she did. She had to have dialysis treatment shortly after the dream. This is another example of the prodromal dream discussed in Chapter 3.

A young mother reported another snake dream:

I opened the doors to a closet, and there on one of the shelves was a cute green frog. I picked it up and held it. As I did so, it turned into a snake. I wasn't afraid of it. I raised it over my head and stood with one foot in front of the other in a position that resembled an Egyptian hieroglyph. Then I said, "Oh, and this has the power to divide itself in two." And the serpent divided into two. "And then it has to power to become one again." And it became one again!

The dreamer felt that this was a spiritual dream. She had recently begun meditating as well as studying all sort of metaphysical ideas along with her traditional Christian Bible. For her, the closet symbolized her inner self, and the cute frog reminded her of the fairy tale frog waiting to be transformed into a prince. The raised serpent is a common symbol for the raised kundalini, the spiritual life force flowing upward in meditation that is healing and transforming. The raised serpent is often seen on the headdresses of Egyptian pharaohs, and both a raised serpent and entwined serpents had Biblical meaning to the woman as well. To her, this was a powerful, affirming dream of spiritual truth and growth.

More on Animals

Animals of a more general nature, from guppies to elephants, may metaphorically represent qualities, attitudes, or situations. Or they may be a play on words. Think of the following terms and phrases: rat race, catty, horsing around, eagle-eyed, playing chicken, overbearing, eating like a pig, and a zoo full of other common figures of speech. The fish is often associated with Christianity, a bull with a brokerage firm, and a gecko with a popular insurance company. In football, teams are called Rams, Eagles, Bears, or Tigers. American Indians used various animals as totems because of their specific qualities; they often took names from animals, sometimes seen in dreams or visions, like Spotted Horse, Sitting Bull, Running Bear, or Little Fawn.

Are you allergic to any animals? As a child were you bitten by a monkey, stepped on by a horse, divebombed by a blue jay, or stung by a jellyfish? Did you pray every night for a puppy, have a little yellow kitten, get a turtle for your birthday, or feed bugs to a lizard you caught on the front porch? Past experiences with animals shape our dream symbols. Think about some of your associations.

If you couldn't be a person and had to be an animal, which one would you be? Why?

What's Bugging You?

Spiders and other creepy crawlers with more than six legs aren't technically bugs, but for our purposes, let's lump them together. They range from lowly dust mites and chiggers to Egypt's sacred scarab beetle. Who doesn't love butterflies, dragonflies, and lightning bugs? We admire the industry and cooperative nature of ants and honeybees, but abhor the mean mounds of fire ants moving across the country, as well as the vicious Africanized bee colonies following their path northward.

Take these two examples as different ways dreamers apply their own meaning to a creature. Spiders, except for the nasty little brown recluse, might not bother Sue, although she's not likely to have a tarantula or a black widow as a pet. On the other hand, Elton is absolutely phobic about the eight-legged critters. Therefore, Sue's and Elton's dreams of spiders would mean vastly different things. Sue might think of the webs they spin, and they might represent webs of deceit, things that lure her in and get her stuck, or too much time spent on the Internet and the World Wide Web. Elton, on the other hand, might react by sweating and trying to escape his nightmare.

As prevalent as bugs are in our world, we're bound to see them in our dreams. Estimates suggest that insects outnumber us by about a billion and a half to one, and they, along with other creepy crawlers, are a vital part of our ecosystem. Besides the critical pollination chores of many of these creatures, they also aerate soil, act as scavengers to consume or transform decaying matter, and serve as food for predators higher on the food chain. Have you ever eaten chocolate-covered grasshoppers, or captured lightning bugs in a jar? Think about some of your unique associations with bugs. How do you feel about roaches? You might be surprised at how often they show up as symbols.

Byron R. dreamed:

I'm in a white room, lying on a bed covered with white sheets, and I'm dying. I look up at the ceiling, and there is a huge roach there. Suddenly, I leap out of bed, get a swatter, and start trying to kill the roach.

Was Byron ill? No. He was perfectly healthy. But his work situation wasn't. There were rumors of a major shakeup and lots of gloom and anxiety on the job. His anxiety was growing as well. It was interfering with his sleep. (How often have we said, "I'm dying here"?) But what about a cockroach? Byron said he thought of a cockroach as a thing carrying disease. We played with that idea for a while. Disease. Disease. Dis-ease. He was uneasy (the dis-ease) about the shakeup. What should he do? Kill that "roach." The stress or uneasiness of the situation was causing a problem at the most basic physiological level, and his safety and security needs were threatened as well. He needed to get rid of the anxiety and develop a more positive attitude. Sometimes dreams remind us that all we can change is our attitude.

OTHER CREATURES AND SCARY STUFF

Besides flora, fauna, and regular people, other creatures show up in our dreams from time to time—everything from aliens to monsters, and from angels to other unworldly or ethereal beings. Some may be people, but they're not regular folks; they may be savages out to kill us, or menacing strangers chasing us or trying to do us harm. Some are benevolent, even holy; others scare the pants off us.

Nightmares are the bad dreams most of us have from time to time, and they mostly occur in REM sleep. They're heart-pounders about monsters and ghouls and other awful things chasing us or trying to do us in. I'm also often asked about something called night terrors (*pavor nocturnus*) in children. Night terrors are events in which kids start screaming, flailing, maybe trying to climb the wall as if to escape some unknown horror, and in the process, scare their parents to death. The kids are difficult to awaken, but when finally awake they're usually perfectly calm and don't even remember a bad dream, while their parents are basket cases. *Pavor nocturnus*, which usually occurs in the deepest stages of sleep (non-REM), is a sleep disorder, perhaps a result of heredity (did Daddy suffer with this when he was a child?) or a developmental or brain wiring issue. The good news is that children almost always grow out of it. A pediatrician can tell you more and may prescribe medication or other remedies for night terrors.

Monsters

By now, you're probably starting to detect a theme when it comes to making associations in your dreamworld. Just as with animals, monsters can represent different things to different people. For example, take a man who had recently become intrigued with genealogy. He began to spend every extra moment reading books about it (sometimes three or four at a time) and searching through old records, maps, and histories. He neglected his family and friends as he dug through the lives of his long-dead ancestors. One night he dreamed there was a monster in the library, and he desperately needed to escape. The man needed no interpretation of his dream. His monster was excess. His family and other facets of his life were threatened by this imbalance and overindulgence in his new interest. He cut down on his study to get his life in better balance.

Another dreamer, Susan L., recalls a nightmare:

I was at a lively party with a large number of people. Everybody was talking and enjoying themselves in a long room with two doors, one on each end of the room that led to a hallway. No one knew of the horror that lurked just outside the doors except me. A frightening, grotesque monster growled and paced in the hallway, anxious to get at the people and commit mayhem. Knowing that the only thing keeping him at bay was my vigilance, I stood and glanced back and forth between the two doors, mentally barring his entry.

The dreamer was mulling over the "monster in the hallway" in the drowsy state when the meaning suddenly popped into her mind: "Let not fear enter in." The woman was undergoing major life transitions, and the dream reminded her, even reassured her, not to let the "monster" (her fear) in the hallway (changes, transition from one room to another) disrupt the joy in her life.

Very often monsters represent our fears of one sort or another, and nowhere are our "need" dreams more obvious than in those that scare us. Whether it's doing battle with hordes of tiny Chinese soldiers (foreign bodies) parachuting into a field or running from a tiger threatening to rip us to shreds, nightmares often signal issues with the physiological, or safety and security, or other basic needs.

Survivors frequently have nightmares in disaster-stricken areas (from explosions, hurricanes, shooting rampages, wars, etc.) where needs that were previously taken for granted are suddenly challenged. This may be because dreaming can discharge pent-up anxiety or can help establish a form of mastery by repeating exposure to the fear. This is similar to the almost compulsive retelling of an automobile accident, a near miss, surgery, or other traumatic event.

Menacing Strangers

In Sandy D.'s "knock at the door" dream, it wasn't a monster who threatened her but the often-seen "menacing stranger":

I answered a knock at the door and opened it to find a man standing with his back to me. He had on dark blue slacks with a matching shirt and sported a military style haircut. I remember thinking he must be a police officer.

He was standing inside a screened porch (which my current house does not have). I kept my hand on the handle of the storm door as I asked, "May I help you?"

He turned around. His shirt was unbuttoned and opened all the way down in the front, revealing a white T-shirt. His expression was a mixture of anger and confusion. He stepped forward without saying a word and thrust a small, wrinkled slip of paper toward me.

I hesitantly opened the screen door just wide enough to take the paper. When I did, he pulled it open and shoved me back into the room. I saw

his hand pull a knife from his pocket. I yelled over my shoulder to my
husband who was in the bedroom, "Run. Get out of here, Jim, run!"

The intruder knocked me down and held the knife over my throat
while pressing my shoulder against the floor. I saw it come down and
somehow knew he was cutting my throat, but then I woke up.

Scary? You bet. Here it's important to know the current events in Sandy's life. Because of the economic downturn, her husband lost his job and they were going to have to relocate. She loved her house, her friends, and her community, and she was resentful about losing everything. Turning to the dream and remembering that this menacing stranger was a projection of herself who brought a message (the crumpled paper), she could begin to decipher its meaning.

Screened porches represented pleasant times to her, but she allowed this guy (anger and confusion) to intrude. Her attitude was threatening her husband's self-esteem (he already felt diminished by the circumstances), and she was "cutting her own throat" by dwelling on the negatives in the situation. All her basic needs felt threatened, but as a person working toward self-actualization, she realized that an attitude adjustment would make the changes easier. She vowed to look forward to the future as a new adventure.

Dead People

As discussed in an earlier chapter, people, living or dead, usually represent parts of yourself. Sometimes, however, dreams of deceased friends and relatives come to comfort us in our grief. A still-distraught mother whose son had died three years before dreamed that he came to her and begged her to burn his clothes—a plea to cease her mourning.

A man dreamed he was digging up a gravesite in a cemetery. An ancient and decomposing corpse rose up from the dirt and grabbed him by the leg. The obvious lesson here is that some things are best left buried, i.e., don't dig up old stuff (in his case, dead and buried old family squabbles) and cause problems for yourself.

Kathie P., in her mid-twenties, was very close to her grandmother. The grandmother's death hit her hard, shook her up, and made her really think about the whole issue of life, death, and dying for the first time. She also regretted not spending more time with her grandmother toward the end of her life.

Kathie recounts a dream that she said was the most powerful dream she'd ever had:

I was hanging out at my grandmother's house with friends and family, and Grandma was still alive. I had to go, so I left her house. On the street outside, someone had been shot—like a drive-by—and this lovely woman of about forty was bleeding out. I quickly helped her into my car to drive her to the hospital. I was panicked the whole time, knowing that I needed to save this woman in the passenger seat, and I didn't know how to help except get to the hospital as quickly as I could.

But when we got there, I realized she was dead. And she turned to me (yes, the dead woman turned to me—it was like one of those movies where I could see the dead, still person but at the same time I could see her turning to me and speaking) and said, very gently, "See? Death is so soft, you didn't even realize I'd died."

Kathie said she woke up startled, but with an intense sense of peace. She said, "I realized that the woman was a stand-in for my grandmother. She'd switched bodies with the woman who was shot so I wouldn't freak out at seeing Grandma shot and miss the point. What she was saying was that I shouldn't stress out about death. I may not understand it or see it coming, but it's not crushing, or fireworks. It's slipping quietly away, and the dead woman was at peace with her death. She didn't blame me or even wish that I'd saved her."

In Chapter 8, we'll delve deeper into what it means to see dead people in your dreams.

OTHER UNEARTHLY BEINGS

If monsters and other menacing creatures are at one end of the spectrum, angels, beings of light, and religious figures are at the other. These higher order beings may represent the very best aspects of ourselves or appear to impart a truth or give comfort. They may have come from the superconscious mind as proposed by Assagioli or Cayce, be archetypal as Jung would suggest, or deal with transpersonal self-actualization needs as defined by Maslow.

What if you dream about a space ship landing in your backyard, and an alien being steps out? What is an alien to you? Perhaps it's simply a personification of an idea, behavior, or experience that is "alien" to you and outside of your usual realm.

What do you associate with angels? In the Bible, angels are most often portrayed as messengers from God. At other times angels act as heavenly guides. We also refer to someone who is exceptionally sweet or good as an angel. Mother Teresa and others like her were angels of mercy. In your dreams, an angel might simply be a figure of speech and not a visitation from above—but then again, perhaps it is. It depends on the personal lens through which you view the angel.

What do you associate with Jesus, Yahweh, Buddha, Mohammed, Krishna, Viracocha, or other religious and spiritual figures? Are they visitations during sleep and dreams, or are they personifications of love? Truth? Wisdom? Sacrifice? Perfection? Guidance? We'll also take a closer look at this in Chapter 8.

Things to Remember and Exercises to Do

Remember:

- Any creature—even those with fur, feathers, sap, or scales—is usually a projection of you and your situation.
- Flora, fauna, monsters, and angels are often figures of speech.
- Dreams are analogies that may be interpreted on more than one level, all of which are correct.
- Sometimes all you can change is your attitude.

Exercises to Do:

1. If possible, take a walk in a wooded area or park near your home. You might take a camera and a small notebook along. Notice the differences in the trees. Feel the bark, examine a leaf, study the root system. Do you know the names of those you see? If not, find out. Which is your favorite? Why? How do you feel in the environment? Observe the other plants around. Anything special you notice about them? Absorb your surroundings. Make notes about the things you see in nature. If you live in a treeless area or a walk in the woods isn't possible for some other reason, use a book or the Internet to study some different kinds of trees and plants. Have you seen any of these trees and plants in your dreams?

2. Make a list of current or past family pets and the qualities you associate with them. Which was your favorite? Why?

CHAPTER 5

Settings, Clothing, and Objects

When we think of movies, plays, or television shows, our attention is first drawn to the characters and the story. Big deals are made at the Oscar presentations for the stars, the directors, and the best stories, but we rarely pay much attention (or recognize the names) of set directors, costume designers, and special effects people. Yet these responsibilities are vitally important to the color and flavor of the movies. Our dream productions are no different.

SETTINGS

Dreaming of walking along Broadway in New York amid the bright lights and nighttime bustle of the city paints a very different picture than walking down Broadway in Galveston, Texas, and heading toward the Gulf of Mexico on a lazy summer afternoon. Settings immediately set the mood and provide important clues to the meaning of your dreams.

Houses

In the movie *Gone with the Wind,* Tara, the gracious southern home, represented Scarlett O'Hara's identity and her state of awareness; she was bound to Tara as if it were a living, breathing entity. Tara *was* Scarlett. So, too, are the houses in our dreams; often they are direct representations of us. Using that analogy, we can go a step further and understand that attics are places where lots of things are stored (our minds, conscious or forgotten). The basement may be a deeper part of our awareness or the subconscious. The front yard is the part presented to the world (like Jung's *persona*), while the back is the part "hidden" behind a fence.

Just as the beautiful Tara mirrored Scarlett in her carefree days, so did the ruined Tara mirror Scarlett's later despair. Similar information can be revealed about our own states of consciousness when we dream about houses. Take Kay's dream, for example:

I was traveling to my vacation home (in reality I have no vacation home). When I arrived there were two women there, intruders. Unhappy about them being there, I told them to leave.

Since vacation homes are places we go to relax and get away from it all, that's what Kay's dream was advising—taking a breather from irritations and intrusions.

Laurel dreamed frequently of a very large house she lived in that was not really her house in waking life. Downstairs were many, many large rooms: living spaces, an ideal kitchen, an indoor basketball court and swimming pool, bedrooms, bathrooms, and meeting rooms. As she explored the house in various dreams, she discovered a large number of bedroom suites upstairs as well as meeting rooms and snack rooms, all nicely furnished. Each time she dreamed of the house, she discovered something new, including more rooms tucked away, a large garden outside, an outdoor pool and beautiful wooded area with secret cabins and places to explore.

At first she thought the dream house was much too big for her family, and she needed to scale down. Later on in her dreams, she began inviting people to stay, saying, "I have plenty of room." In her waking life, Laurel began to realize that she, like Scarlett, *was* the house; her inner self was telling her she needed to share her knowledge by writing, mentoring, and teaching.

What do different kinds of houses mean to you? What would you associate with a haunted house? A shack? A mud hut? A castle? Your grandmother's house? The place where you grew up? A doghouse? A Victorian house? A beach cottage? Our experiences shape our associations. When some people think of a castle, they picture the Disney logo and think of magic and happiness. Another person might think of the German castle she visited on her honeymoon, while someone else would recall the gloomy, ruined castle he explored in Scotland. In our dreams, these houses tell us something about ourselves and/ or about our situation, our state of mind, or even our physical health.

Specific rooms in the house give us more information and clues to dream meanings. Kitchens may have to do with diet, bathrooms with elimination (literal or figurative), hallways with transitions or connections, bedrooms with rest, sex, or privacy. And what's in your garage? The house's "plumbing" may pertain to some corresponding body structures, either urinary or sexual; electrical systems are good analogies for neurological ones.

Schools

Being late for class or a test (even long after graduation), not being able to find our classroom, or other frustrations involving school are settings and common themes for many people. These anxiety dreams may mirror our frustrations or fears about not being able to measure up or being unprepared in some way for current life situations.

What was your experience in school? This will color your interpretation of school symbols. Many of us associate schools and the buildings housing them with lessons, learning, and being tested, so they may appear in our dreams to signal just that. After all, isn't life a series of learning experiences, tests, and evaluations?

Jennifer, who had just turned thirty, dreamed:

I was on a college campus. It was sunny out, and I had somewhere I needed to be. I stopped by a building that looked like it was under construction: There was scaffolding, construction dust, etc. I stepped inside and immediately got the feeling that something bad was going to happen. At first I was the only one in there, but then I was with my sister. I knew other people (dangerous people) were in the building as well. I never saw them, but the feeling that they were there was with me for the rest of the dream.

At this point, I've become my sister in my dream. I (as my sister) walked through a bunch of rooms that were decorated with things like old suits of armor, old paintings, etc. The rooms were progressively higher in the building as I walked. As I walked I realized that I was going to be executed and started to look for a last meal. For some reason there were plates with food on them throughout the rooms. I passed over a chicken dish, then found one of those Half-Moon cookies that I grabbed instead. I made it up the attic/belfry and realized I was going to be hanged. One whole wall was covered in dead rats that had been previously hanged. Their faces all pointed outwards at me. I started to walk up the stairs to the noose (which I didn't actually see) and then I stopped being my sister and became myself again. I watched my sister walk up the stairs and out of view.

Then I started my own ascent up the stairs and my sister met me halfway up, eating the Half-Moon cookie. She told me what happened, and as she was telling it I could see it happen. She was in the noose, and, as she was pushed off the stairs, my brother caught her and held her until she freed her neck. Then he put her down and she came to meet me. Then we started to walk down the stairs again and I woke up.

Let's break this one down.

- **College campus** — learning situation
- **Building under construction** — growing, undergoing changes

- **Bad feelings, scary unseen people** — anxiety about the unknown, dread
- **Sister** — currently undergoing changes in her life
- **Rooms with old things** — vestiges of the past
- **Armor, etc.** — old protective attitudes
- **Execution by hanging** — cutting off air
- **Half-Moon cookie** — comfort food, yin/yang kind of thing representing either harmony or conflict
- **Rats** — negative associations, disease carriers, gnawing
- **Going higher, attic** — consciousness raising, places that hold the past
- **Brother** — loving, but a take-charge kind of guy, overly protective

Remembering that all these symbols are parts of herself (including the rat "hang-ups"), what is this execution dream conveying to her? If we use the central idea method, we might say: A woman faces something she dreads, and when she does, there's a positive outcome. That's the lesson here.

Jennifer said that she had been having recent problems with her brother and others thinking they knew what's best for her, even when their advice was contrary to her own ideas. It had been so distressing that she had been having anxiety attacks where she felt as if her throat closed up and she couldn't breathe.

She felt the dream was telling her that she needed to stop walking in other people's shoes (her sister's) and caring so much about other people's advice, and just do what she needed to do in her own time and in her own way. It could also represent her desire to move from the need of esteem from others to a more self-actualized state of being.

Hotels and Motels

Hotels, motels, inns, and other sorts of temporary housing may, depending on the type and condition, have to do with temporary states of consciousness, a need for relaxation, or a complex situation involving many people or facets of yourself. If you're a businessman who is required to travel and dislikes living out of a suitcase and being away from his family, hotels might have a different meaning than for a man who owns a hotel, or for the woman who loves staying at a hotel and being pampered with room service and housekeeping.

Trisha dreamed a long and convoluted dream about being with a friend at a conference hotel. They were to share a room, but things turned chaotic. Other people were sharing the space as well, and the room was a mess—dirty, inadequate bathroom facilities, inconvenient in many ways. It directly joined an indoor swimming pool, and there was little privacy. Everybody was pitching in, trying to clean up the room and get dressed for various events. It turned into a fun party.

Luckily, when Trisha awoke, the moral of the dream popped into her head: *Make the best of a temporary situation.* (The conference hotel equates to a temporary situation.) She held onto that thought for the next couple of days when all sorts of unexpected intrusions interfered with her plans. Her dream warning helped her keep her sanity and a good attitude. When life handed her lemons, she made lemonade.

Cafeterias, Restaurants, Grocery Stores, and Other Eateries

Any place that has to do with food, including kitchens, naturally reminds us first of our diet (physiological needs). Often these symbols show up in dreams to emphasize our eating habits. Look first at these symbols to see if particular foods are featured. Are they good choices or poor choices? If all you're eating is desserts, as one man dreamed, this is probably calling attention to an overabundance of sugar in your diet. It might alternatively suggest that he'd been "ingesting too much fluff" rather than something of substance and might refer to anything from entertainment or reading choices to business concerns.

If you find yourself wandering through the produce section of a grocery store or a similar location in your dream, and all the fruits and vegetables look mouthwatering, check out your diet to see if you need more of these healthy things and less fast food. Seeing cases and cases of wonderful seafood at an eatery or store may be a simple reminder to up your intake of these foods in lieu of heavier proteins. Consider Nora's "magical vegetables" dream—the dream you were asked to analyze as an exercise in Chapter 3:

> *My husband and I had just returned home from a plane trip and were unpacking. The doorbell rang. It was my long time friend. Seeing her reminded me that this was the night for our bridge game at my house. When I invited her in, she told me that she hadn't eaten and was very hungry. I took her to the kitchen, hoping I had something to fix for her. I found and prepared a nice piece of salmon for her (in reality, she doesn't care for salmon) and some leftover green beans from the fridge. I was looking for another vegetable for her and decided against either corn or potatoes, which she had suggested. I went outside to a group of magical people who grew vegetables from their chests (I could see stalks peeking out of the shirt of one, and others had one particular kind of veggie coming out of their V-neck T-shirts). They also had fluttering hands to harvest and prepare these vegetables. I selected some small yellow tomatoes, cooked them, and added them to the plate. My friend said it looked delicious, ate every bite, and said the tomatoes were amazing.*

To find the meaning of her rather odd dream, Nora decided to analyze each symbol.

- **Husband** — helpful (loves salmon)
- **Plane trip** — higher plane, high ideas and ideals
- **Ursula** — longtime friend, has health issues and severe back problems

- **Bridge** — strategy, playing cards right
- **Food** — what's needed, real food? Metaphorical food?
- **Salmon** — healthy fish, food, high in omega-3 fatty acids, good for heart, cholesterol
- **Green beans** — low calorie, low carb, high in nutrition
- **Corn and potatoes** — starchy, high carb
- **Yellow tomatoes** — low calorie, low carb, high in potassium, good for immune system
- **Chest** — heart, healing (thymus), heart healthy?
- **Fluttering hands** — gesture like falling rain, butterfly or bird wings, fluttering heart
- **Compliment on food** — well done, suitable

Nora decided this had all the markings of a dream about her diet, especially since she'd been having health problems (immune system, high cholesterol, aching joints, weight concerns). Her friend represented these health issues they had in common. It was a helpful message (husband) from a higher plane (airplane trip) about a strategy (bridge) for healthy eating with examples of the types of food she needed. Fresh vegetables that were low in calories, low in carbs, and heart healthy would be magical (veggie people) and healing (thymus) for her (make her heart flutter in a good way). She would like the result.

While dreams that focus on various areas of food preparation are often related to your diet, eateries may be symbolic of other things as well. Sherri T. had this "cafeteria shoes" dream:

I was standing in line at a cafeteria. I looked down at my shoes and saw that they didn't match. They were the same color, navy, but one shoe had a cutout design on the vamp and the other was plain. I was concerned about this and knew I had to go home and change so that my shoes matched. It didn't seem to matter which pair of shoes I chose, only that they matched.

Sherri associated cafeterias with choices (sometimes difficult choices). She felt shoes served both as a protection for the feet and as a fashion accessory. She also considered the expression "putting yourself in someone else's shoes" which meant position or life direction.

Because the setting was a cafeteria (about choices), the first question to ask was if she'd been concerned about a choice or choices in her life. Yes, she had. She'd been having some health problems, and her doctor had suggested surgery (cutout design shoe as the way to go) as the best and easiest solution. She could avoid surgery, at least for a while, by going another arduous route of treatment (not cutout shoe). Highly anxious and frozen by indecision about which to choose, she was doing nothing about her problem (waiting in line).

Her dream seemed to advise making a decision to go one way or the other. It didn't matter which way she chose, only that she choose and get her treatment underway—a very basic need. She chose surgery and had a positive outcome.

Churches, Synagogues, and Other Religious Buildings

Most of the time, dreams set in religious buildings or circumstances have to do with our spiritual life in some way. Patty, a soldier stationed in Iraq, had this dream:

I went home to the church I grew up in, but the building was gone, and the people had scattered. I was very distraught to see a blank space where the church had stood. Suddenly I saw a black panther behind me, poised to leap at me, and I was very frightened.

When I asked Patty much later if anything was going on in her spiritual life at that time, she replied that she'd been studying some other religions and questioning her former beliefs. The panther represented her fear, both for her safety in a hostile country and the spiritual void left in her life. As it turned out, she reaffirmed her life-long faith, and when she came home, she happily went back to her church (which was still standing).

Bodies of Water

Bodies of water are considered universal symbols for emotional states (although this is not a steadfast rule). Does a peaceful pool evoke the same mood as a raging river? No; these scenes portray very different things. Just as roiling water may indicate emotional upheaval, gentle seas may represent smooth sailing. (Note the waters in the swan dream in the bird section of Chapter 4.) An ocean may represent vastness to one person, seasickness to another, terror to a person afraid of water, and a spiritual journey to still another. Like paths or roads, rivers may symbolize a life journey or the way a person is currently headed.

Brita, an older woman, had the following river and roots dream:

I'm swimming in a wide, treacherous river, struggling to make headway. Up ahead, my friend (a person she admires as "having it all together") is swimming easily and beckoning me to come on. I shout to her that I can't, that I'm tangled up in a bunch of roots.

Brita's present-tense retelling of her dream gave it a sense of immediacy, and with a bit of questioning, it became obvious that she was having a difficult time emotionally (the river). She was trying to get it all together (catch up with her friend), but she was impeded by "roots" (issues in her past, dealing with family and background).

Several of this woman's dreams indicated that she was trying to come to grips with events from her past. In one, she was taking a shower and trying to wash "dirt" from her "back." Themes repeated in dreams are like exclamation points saying, "Pay attention!" These issues need to be given special consideration, perhaps by seeking professional help or at least the ear of a friend.

What images, memories, or figures of speech come to mind when you think of the following:

- The Atlantic or Pacific oceans?
- A Colorado stream? The Mississippi River?
- A body of water near your childhood home? One near your current home?
- A swimming pool?
- A spring? A pond? A lake?
- A waterfall?

Were you surprised at the material evoked by each of the bodies of water listed? Are other bodies of water significant to you personally? You might make a note of your responses and tuck them into the book for future reference.

Outdoors

Dreams frequently feature a journey into a dark forest with hidden dangers lurking behind every tree, while others boast spring gardens in full bloom or fields ripe with wind-rippled wheat. Often the dark forests in dreams suggest fears or uncharted territory, while spring gardens evoke thoughts of reawakening or promise. The wheat field might hint of fulfillment, a celebration of the time of reaping.

Close your eyes and picture a beach scene, then picture a mountain scene. How did each scene make you feel? What moods were evoked? Which did you prefer? Why?

OPENING SCENES AND WEATHER

"It was a dark and stormy night . . . "

We may groan at this clichéd opening for a story, but it sets an undeniable mood, especially when a car is driving up a winding road, flanked by tall, wind-whipped trees, toward a gloomy gothic mansion on the hill. We know instantly this isn't going to be a rollicking comedy, but the venue of nightmares or something mysterious.

Weather in general is often an important aspect of our dreams. Ask yourself the following questions: How is a gentle rain different from a storm? How do I feel about lightning? The boom of thunder? Does a sunny, mild day lighten my mood? Do I enjoy the soaring heat of a summer day? The chill of winter? Snow? Sleet?

As mentioned previously, the opening scene of a dream is often critical in understanding the dream's content. Dreams, like movies or books, have beginnings, middles, and ends. The opening scene sets the mood and gives the first clue as to what the dream is about. An office building may signal a dream about work or business matters; a school, lessons to be learned; a church, spiritual issues; a den, family matters. Being in a jungle, or slogging through a desert, or wandering through an intricate maze conjure up very different expectations. Or do they? Remember, your specific circumstances impact the meaning. Normally, the middle part of your dream represents working out or working through an issue, and the ending indicates the appropriate direction or resolution.

Clothing

In storytelling, clothing can convey attitude. Mike Myers adopts a wacky mindset when he dons his Austin Powers outfit; Glenda Jackson or Helen Mirren become regal in their Queen Elizabeth raiment; and who can forget the mild-mannered reporter who steps into a phone booth and emerges in tights and a red cape? Indeed, the clothes a person wears becomes part of his or her persona in various situations and frequently defines the role of the character. Clothing may also represent attitudes in your dreams. Assagioli talks about these various selves as sub-personalities that need to be recognized and integrated.

The white uniforms of doctors and nurses, the distinctive collar of clergy, the apron of a cook, the uniform of a sheriff or a soldier all define roles and give clues to the meaning of a dream.

Shoes, or the lack thereof, often show up in dreams. They may symbolize such ideas as understanding, foundation, direction (such as the path we walk), or other similar notions. Hats of various kinds may simply be part of the costume—like an Indian headdress, a Scottish tam, or an army helmet—or it may call attention to the head and its activities, like thoughts and ideation, egoism (swelled head), and identity or role (e.g., "he wore several different hats").

Lack of Clothing

What about those dreams of being as naked as a jaybird? Being unclothed or improperly dressed in public is a common and universal dream theme frequently mentioned in dream research as noted by Patricia Garfield, Ann Faraday, Elsie Sechrist, and others. These dreams can have a wide array of interpretations, depending, as usual, on current events in the dreamer's life. It may be saying that you should be ashamed of yourself about your recent behavior. At the other extreme, such a dream may be encouraging you to stop hiding behind a facade, attitude, or a role (represented by your clothes) and simply be yourself. Naked dreams might also illustrate fears or anxiety about having the world see you as you really are.

OBJECTS

Who's in charge of the props? The dreamer, of course. And props, the inanimate objects that show up in dreams, are selected for a reason, particularly those spotlighted in some way. They add richness to the meaning of dreams and may supply the central element to understanding the message. Scissors, hammers, bouquets, suitcases, footballs, lamps, letters, jewelry, books, clocks, and kitchen sinks—all these objects have meaning and give clues, in context, to the communication from the unconscious. Without the statue in the *Maltese Falcon* or the stone of *Romancing the Stone*, there would be no story. Each of these props was critical.

Weapons

Certainly weapons—handguns, shotguns, rifles, knifes, spears, and various large artillery—can be sexual and aggressive symbols, as Freud suggested. They may also be objects for self-protection or for "killing off" various enemies such as bad habits, fears, anxiety, or even germs.

But weapons, like any dream prop, may also simply carry a message from the unconscious to the conscious. An anecdote that shows up in dream literature tells of Elias Howe's struggle with his new prototype for a sewing machine. He was having trouble with the needle and thread concept when he dreamed of a group of primitive natives carrying spears that had holes near the end of the tips. The following morning he awoke with a "Eureka!" moment and realized that the hole for the thread belonged near the tip of the needle instead of higher on the shaft. A variation of the story claims he saw a jousting knight with a hole at the end of his spear.

Weapons used against us may represent various forms of attack or self-attack (as in the attack of the tiny Chinese soldiers with guns, or germs, mentioned in Chapter 3), verbal attacks, or animosity and rebuffs of assorted kinds. We've all heard such expressions as "like a knife to my heart," "cut me to the quick/core," "stabbed in the back," "blew a hole in my idea," "shot down my suggestion," "chopped me off at the knees," "blasted me," and "put a gun to my head." These all have associations that are figurative in nature, and you need to unravel the real meaning when they show up in your dreams.

Household Items

Kitchen items such as pots, pans, dishes, and utensils frequently signal dreams of diet, ingestion (of food, information, or experience), or even service of various sorts. We also speak of plotting or planning as "cooking up" something.

Clocks, watches, and other timepieces emphasize time, reminding us that time may be running out or the time has come for something to happen.

Tools such as hammers, saws, and lumber can speak of building, expanding, and growing, while axes and hatchets are ordinarily associated with cutting down, cutting off, and getting rid of—either a good thing or a bad thing, depending on context.

Office and Communication Items

A file cabinet reminds us of organization or of things filed away for future reference; a desk is where work gets done. A computer can conjure up all kinds of analogies, including the brain or the mind, where information is stored. It provides business, professional, and social connections and communications, and brings messages and knowledge from all sorts of unseen sources. Telephones and cell phones of all kinds signal messages and communication.

All of these things seem so obvious, but you'd be surprised at how often someone asks, "What does it mean when you dream of a phone call?" It means, "Here's a message for you. Here's some new information. Here's a connection. Pay attention!"

Valuables

Included among valuables are all sorts of treasure, gold, silver, jewels, money, wallets, and purses. They can be lost, found, or stolen. Rarely are these symbols representative of real riches; most often they are metaphors for the things you treasure or value, such as talent, love, your good name, spiritual riches, knowledge, and accomplishments. Losing valuables may be saying that in some way you've lost (or are in danger of losing) something important, perhaps a friendship, self-esteem, truths, or happiness.

Finding treasure is just the opposite: You've gained something valuable in your life, perhaps a new awareness, accomplishment, or an inner reward for some service you've performed. How would you feel if you found a real bag of gold or diamonds, or dug up a treasure chest in your backyard? I suspect the sensation would be similar to the feeling you experience when you have a flying dream—exhilaration. Sometimes such dreams are a pat on the back; sometimes they come to lift our spirits and compensate for a lousy day.

When things are stolen, this may indicate that you're allowing someone or something to take away your joy, confidence, serenity, or other positive attribute—and that someone may be you.

If, in reality, you've ever misplaced your wallet or purse, you were probably less concerned about your cash (unless it was a very large amount) than about credit cards and identification. Canceling credit cards and having new ones issued along with getting a new driver's license, insurance cards, and others pieces of identification that represent *you* can be a real pain. The wallet or purse may represent your sense of identity, your self, your individuality. What do you usually carry in your wallet or purse?

COLORS

Does everybody dream in color? Probably. Many people just aren't aware of the colors that show up. Women are generally more aware of colors than men (except artists, designers, and others who work with color). This came up in a seminar once, and a man said, "I don't dream in color." He had related a dream a few minutes before, so I asked him what color shirt he had worn in the dream. "Blue," he said, then laughed. He hadn't even noticed.

Occasionally people dream in black and white for emphasis, and waking color-blindness may affect color awareness in dreams, but usually dream apples are red, the sky is blue, and grass is green.

Do colors have special meaning in dreams? Sometimes. Many of us share an association with specific colors, but others don't pay much attention to color or have very individual feelings about particular colors. Spend a minute thinking about what color means to you by answering the following questions.

- What's your favorite color?
- What color do you associate with danger, passion, or anger?
- What color represents jealously, envy, or greed to you?
- What color do you dislike?
- What color represents the unknown to you? Death?
- What color or colors represent happiness to you?
- What color is serenity, peace, or purity to you?
- What does pink make you think of?
- What color represents autumn to you?

We probably have some answers in common, others are different. It's been said that colors correspond to notes of the musical scale or to the spiritual centers of the body (see the section on endocrine glands in the body in Chapter 3). Whole studies have been made of colors and their meanings, but it's beyond the scope of this book. If you're interested in exploring this idea further, you can look up some of Bob Hoss's work online for more information on his work with color in dreams. (Try *www.dreamgate.com/dream/hoss/* to start with.)

NUMBERS

Numbers frequently occur in dreams and may have a variety of meanings. In the literature dealing with dreams, they range from Freud's contention that the number 3 represented the male genitals, to Jung's report of a complex system of a man's adding together various birthdays of himself, his family, and his mistress to arrive at the number 2477, which was significant in a dream relating to his conflict between family and mistress.

It seems much more reasonable to look first at the obvious meaning of a number. A case in point is a dream I came across several years ago about a man who dreamed he was driving his family down a street and past a house with a huge sign in the front yard with the number 409 written in large script on it. He sped away. How did he feel? Uncomfortable, embarrassed, he said. Did the house have any special meaning to him? Yes, the woman with whom he was having an affair lived there. Was 409 the house number? No. To the man, 409 was a cleaning product. The dream's advice: Don't expose your family to this. Clean up your act.

Edgar Cayce also interpreted many dreams involving numbers and emphasized the importance of those symbols, some literal, some figurative. There are many meanings for numbers, often of universal significance, to which we may look for clues in deciphering our own dream numbers. Here are a few:

- **One** — numero uno, the beginning, wholeness, God, one and only
- **Three** — the Holy Trinity, a triangle, three dimensions
- **Four** — the four elements (air, water, earth, fire), a square, four corners of the earth
- **Seven** — this number appears frequently in our culture, from "lucky seven" to the seven days of the week, seven spiritual centers of the body, seven deadly sins, seven knots in Mohammed's rope, seven seas, and more
- **Forty** — an extension of four which occurs frequently in Biblical accounts and represents a period of testing or preparation including the wandering of Moses and the Israelites, Noah's flood, Jesus' fasting in the desert, and others

One morning Julia C. awoke with a number in her head—276. She tried looking at the meaning of each number, then adding the numbers together (2 + 7 + 6 = 15, then 1 + 5 = 6) but nothing registered. She dressed and went on to a scheduled morning meeting. Her husband called her there and said the hospital in her hometown had been trying to contact her. Julia's mother had been in a serious automobile accident. She made the two-hour drive in considerably less time, immediately ran to the front desk, and asked for her mother's room number. And—you guessed it—her room was 276.

The number was literal, and the dream was precognitive (we'll talk more about precognitive dreams in Chapter 8). Here again, as in the case of the meaning of flowers, be cautious not to get too carried away by the meanings of various numbers, unless you're a numerologist. Pay attention when specific numbers show up in your dream, but don't go too far afield and miss the obvious.

Things to Remember and Exercises to Do

Remember:
- Settings describe the dreamer and current life situations.
- The opening scene is a clue to what a dream is about.
- Repeated themes are important!
- Clothing and costumes give clues to attitude and role.
- Objects, colors, and numbers have special meaning.

Exercises to Do:

1. Assemble photographs of houses where you formerly lived and currently live. If you don't have photographs, that's okay. You can use memories to fill in the gaps. Find a quiet, comfortable place and bring along a writing pad. Think back to

the first house you remember as a child. Select the photograph if available, study it, then close your eyes and mentally wander through the house and picture yourself then. What are your memories there? How did you feel?

Go through your various houses in the same manner, allowing memories to emerge and making notes. If at any time you begin to feel uncomfortable doing this, put the exercise aside or skip the exploration of that house and move to another until you've come to the current house you occupy.

Which house was your favorite? Why? Which house did you like least? Why? Where were you the happiest? The saddest? Did you feel like a different person in each place? How were these houses like you?

2. Using magazines, parts of boxes, or odd bits of paper available, cut and gather solid colored pieces of paper about one to one and a half inches square, one for each color of the rainbow: red, orange, yellow, green, blue, indigo, and violet. Add black and white to those seven, plus any other colors you want. (Paint sample charts are great for this.) If you have a file folder handy, use it to tape or glue the various squares inside, leaving some room to write under each color. Plain sheets of paper will do in lieu of the folder. Have a pencil or a pen handy. Stop reading the exercise here and return an hour or more later.

When you return to your color exercise, open the folder, look at the first square and write down the first adjective you think of, then move on. Work very quickly; use first impressions. When you're done, circle your two favorites and two least favorites. Keep your folder handy as a reference for possible meanings of the colors in your dreams.

CHAPTER 6

Transportation, Signposts, and Maps

Transportation, signposts, and maps are all things that help us get around, navigate the world, give us direction, or show us the way. These objects, activities, and systems frequently appear in our dreams. Here we'll look at symbolism ranging from the ordinary, like cars, stop signs, and road maps, to the unconventional, like levitation and astrological terms.

TRANSPORTATION

In your dreams you might find a range of transportation, from horses to space ships and flying like a superhero to taking planes, trains, and automobiles. Let's look at the most common modes first.

Automobiles

Certainly cars, like everything else, can have individual meaning, but very frequently cars represent the actual vehicle you get around in—your physical body. Over and over I hear dreams in which a car is wrecked, hits a barrier or a wall, loses its brakes or steering, or gets stopped for speeding. Most of these dreams are telling the dreamers to slow down and/or take better care of their body and their basic physiological needs. Often, the parts of the auto correspond to your various body parts, e.g., the engine might be your heart; the headlights or the windshield, your eyes; the gas tank, your stomach. Seeing your car with all the tires flat needs little interpretation—you're "flat-tired."

Jeri dreamed:

I was in a white van driving around town. I kept driving and driving and driving. My brakes weren't working right, and it was difficult to slow down or stop. Finally, as if in slow motion, I ran into a brick wall and the van stopped.

The white van represented work to Jeri. She'd been working and driving herself, without making herself slow down or stop, until she had driven herself into exhaustion, hit a wall, and was forced to stop and rest. At least there wasn't extensive damage (illness) to the van (her body). This dream spoke to an obvious physiological need.

Remember that the dream could also come as a warning, and it may *literally* be guiding you to take care in your driving.

For cases in which vehicles represent something other than the body or a warning about driving habits, the automobiles are still some facet of us and refer to the manner or direction we're traveling in life.

Joe dreamed:

I was in my car at an intersection, and I wanted to go straight ahead on an uphill street that was under construction. A traffic cop kept motioning for me to turn instead of going up the hill. Being determined, I shook my head and went straight ahead. I kept sliding back down the hill and was finally forced to turn around and go in the direction the policeman indicated.

Hills and mountains often equate to problems to overcome, and road construction is something blocking the way. Joe realized immediately this was about a problematic work project and his tendency to handle things in a "damn the torpedoes, full speed ahead" manner. His inner guidance (the traffic cop) was telling him to circumvent the problem by going at it another way.

Dream cars come in all different shapes, colors, and sizes—each with distinct associations. A black car represents something different than a yellow one; a Mini Cooper something different than a Hummer. What do you think about when you see:

- A sleek black sports car? A red one?
- A jeep?
- A rattle-trap?
- A chauffeured limousine?
- A station wagon or a SUV?
- A taxi?
- Your "if price were no object" preferred car to own?

Trucks

From pickup trucks to semis, these vehicles carry or haul stuff around. Sometimes it's garbage or heavy stuff from the past that needs to be dumped. They're often associated with work and/or something big. I'm sure you're familiar with the expressions, "I feel like I've been run over by a truck," or "big as a truck," or "a truckload of grief/problems/misery."

Angie, a working mother with two small children, often dreamed that she was driving an eighteen-wheeler, struggling to keep it on the road and worrying about being able to manage it. That one hardly needs any thought. Clearly Angie is feeling anxious about the "big load" she's hauling with all the demands on her time, concentration, and energy.

Frank, a meat and potatoes man, dreamed of a pickup hauling fruits and vegetables to market. His dream is a no-brainer, too. To work properly, his body needs those fruits and veggies in his diet. Both these dreams are addressing basic physiological needs: stress relief and proper diet.

Trains

We often speak of "losing our train of thought," "training a dog," or even the "little engine that could." But the trains in dreams may represent the path we're traveling or the way we're headed. Trains have some things in common with buses (see below), but one aspect is very different—the tracks. If we get off-track or derailed, we're not on our prescribed path and aren't going anywhere. Our forward motion is stopped. Abbie dreamed:

I was on a train, and we came to a place where an antiques shop was set up on and around the track. The train came together with the antique furniture and a car driven by an elderly lady. It didn't crash but came to a gradual stop—like its momentum had been stopped by the car and all the stuff in the way. I jumped out and started to move things away from the track. But the train workers didn't want me to do it; they wanted to do it themselves. So I began to browse around, looking at the antiques. The next I knew, the train had left without me.

A couple of nights later, she dreamed this:

I was on a bus heading north. I wasn't sure of the exact route of the bus, but I felt it was going in the general direction that I needed to go. I thought it would be good to see a map, but there was no map on the bus. I decided to get off at the next stop to get a map, then get back on. I didn't find a map right away in the store where the bus stopped; I got distracted and the next I knew the bus had left without me.

In both cases, Abbie felt distressed to have been left behind and didn't know how she would get to where she was going.

Abbie, a longtime member of a group that does dream work, realized that both dreams were telling her the same thing, one on a train, one on a bus. She interpreted her dream as warning her not to get distracted from her journey and where she was trying to go, or "miss the bus." She first thought about what was going on in her life. What was she missing? She and her husband had been "moving in the direction" of downsizing, but she'd decided to put off such a consideration for a year so she could help her recently widowed mother adjust to her life. One of the things she'd wanted to do for her mother was to clean out old stuff that she didn't need any longer. Her dreams were telling her that she couldn't get distracted from her own journey by focusing on her mother's journey. Abbie felt that she needed to clear her own life of stuff from the past and move ahead into the future and allow her mother to do the same, as shown in her dream by the train workers who didn't want Abbie messing with the antiques.

Buses

You've probably heard the expressions "thrown under the bus," "hit by a bus," or "big as a bus." I'll bet you've also used other bus metaphors.

Did you ride a school bus growing up? What was your experience? Can you almost smell the bologna sandwiches, or hear the laughter as you rode to a football game? How about a tour bus, a city bus, a chartered bus, or a Greyhound? They all conjure up very different types of memories and experiences. One thing they do have in common is that a bus carries a group of people with a common goal or destiny. Those various people may depict a family, parts of the self (like Assagioli's sub-personalities), or simply a group of known or unknown individuals with shared interests. As noted in the pair of dreams above, buses and trains have many similarities.

A bus, like other conveyances, may depict your body as well. A bus dream may well be about excess poundage, acting as a reminder to lay off the ice cream and Alfredo sauce and take up jogging.

Ambulances and Fire Trucks

We see flashing lights and hear sirens, and immediately think, "Emergency!" The same thought should arise when an ambulance, fire truck, or other such vehicle pops up in dreams.

Sharon M. dreamed:

I was on a gurney in the back of an ambulance. They were rushing me to the hospital, but the driver kept running into roadblocks, and we'd have to go in another direction. I knew it was critical that we get there quickly, and I told him to run the blockades.

She awoke with her hand on her breast and felt a lump beneath her fingers. As someone who worked with her dreams regularly, Sharon knew it was important to see her doctor immediately. She knew that her dream could be symbolic and the lump might prove to be a mere cyst, but she had a feeling it was more. After examining the lump, her physician assured her that it was probably nothing and suggested they watch her breast for a few weeks. Sharon refused to follow his suggestion and insisted on an immediate biopsy. As it turned out, the biopsy showed a malignancy, and she had life-saving surgery at once.

Bicycles

In Lance Armstrong circles where bicycles are more common than spurs, bicycles mean exercise, competition, training, and endurance. For others, balance is a big part of riding, so bicycles equal balance. Stationary bikes that don't go anywhere definitely imply exercise, or putting out a lot of effort and making no progress. For some, riding means relaxation, and still others ride bikes as their only means of transportation. Your particular experience will influence the meaning of bikes in your dream. Bikes with training wheels or tricycles are a younger, more immature, inexperienced version of the bicycle symbol.

Sue Ann dreamed that a thief stole her bicycle, although she didn't own one and hadn't ridden in years. Other elements in her dream and in her current life suggested that a particularly vehement attitude about a political issue was robbing her of her balance and centeredness. She was stealing from herself.

Motorcycles

One person may think of motorcycles as loud, wild, and dangerous, while someone else may consider them the epitome of freedom, fun, and power. An important issue here is who's on the motorcycle—a Hell's Angel, a daredevil, a teenager, you, or a cop? A newspaper comic strip called *Rose Is Rose* often shows Rose, a normal, polite, young mom, turn into her alter-ego when she desperately wants to act against type. Her alter-ego (or subpersonality) is a leather-clad, wild-haired motorcycle mama who speaks her piece, or hops on her "hawg" and roars off along the open road. You may have a similar experience in a dream, an invitation to express another facet of yourself, to loosen up or broaden your horizons.

A mother dreamed that her daughter, away at college, was wearing garish makeup and riding on the back of a motorcycle behind a scruffy-looking guy. When the daughter's grades came out and the two had a serious talk, the mother understood the dream. No real motorcycle or rider was involved, but the daughter had followed the path of many students away from home for the first time; she'd gone wild. Parents may often sense these things because they've dreamed about them, but they may or may not have remembered.

Does this show some sort of psychic connection to her child? Yes. Such reports and experiences are fairly common among people who watch their dreams.

Watercraft

Large seagoing ships and boats may represent a spiritual journey because of travel into the vastness of the ocean, while submarines are the parts of us that delve into the subconscious or look beneath the surface. The ocean voyage, too, may be seen as a journey into the vast unconscious as described by various theorists. Pleasure craft may speak of a need for relaxation. If the craft is on a body of turbulent water, often a time of emotional upheaval is indicated. The swan dream in Chapter 4 is an example of this.

Aircraft

As you might expect by now, the type of aircraft and the situation dictate the meaning of a dream. Is it a commercial airline, a fighter plane, a rescue helicopter, or a glider? Flying in an airplane is a fast and convenient mode of travel these days, and we have many figures of speech associated with planes and other aircraft. Planes don't have the constraints of buses, ships, or trains. They're on a "higher plane" that may be referring to lofty ideals and high-mindedness.

Angela, a neighbor, once invited me over for brunch. I had a cup of coffee and she had a gin and tonic, and we chatted while she finished baking a casserole. Knowing of my interest in dreams, she told me of a disturbing recurring dream she'd been having. I was still sipping my coffee; she fixed herself another gin and tonic and related her dream.

I'm on an airplane, and it's in trouble. I know it's going to crash, and I'm panicked. It starts into a nosedive and everybody, including me, is screaming. We're going to die, and I wake up, just before we crash, in a cold sweat.

"What does that mean?" Angela asked.

I was pretty sure what her dream might be telling her, but it was her dream to figure out, so I said, "Planes usually represent a part of ourselves. Is there some way you've currently fallen or nose-dived from your ideals or put yourself in physical danger?"

She looked at me sharply and said vehemently, "I know you think this is about my drinking, but it's not!"

Even though I now realized her dreams were the reason for my brunch invitation, I could only shrug and back away. "I didn't say anything about your drinking. It's your dream, and only you can interpret it."

She was working hard at denial, but she knew exactly what her recurring dream was shouting at her: Wake up! You're killing yourself! (This dream was concerned with both her physiological needs and safety needs.)

A couple of things to note about dreams with planes:

1. Plane crash dreams aren't usually about real crashes, but never say never. Use common sense when making your interpretation.
2. There is no truth to the myth that if you crash, you'll die. Many people have crashed, fallen, hit bottom, and died in their dreams—even repeatedly. They're still here.

Horses

"The British are coming!" shouted the messenger as he galloped from place to place. Long before Paul Revere or the Pony Express, horses were associated with messages or messengers. We still use horsepower as a unit of measurement of power, most familiarly in relation to our car engines. Horse and buggy days remind us of old-fashioned things. There are wild horses, show horses, race horses, and work horses, as well as people who horse around. We may think of the four horsemen of the Apocalypse, who may represent various things including the four lower chakras or endocrine centers. A knight in shining armor (or other hero) rides a white horse, while the villain is astride one as black as his hat.

Look, Ma, I'm Flying!

If you've ever had a flying dream (sans aircraft) you know the feeling of true exhilaration, true freedom. To be able to sail above the treetops and zip to faraway places gives you a high like no other. But what do these flying dreams mean? They can have many meanings; however, such experiences often happen after a particularly trying time when we need our spirits to be lifted. Jung talked about *compensatory* dreams, those dreams that occur to keep us in balance and headed down the road to individuation. If we need something to pull us out of feeling dispirited, we fly. If we're getting a little too big for our britches, as my grandmother used to say, we have dreams that take us down a notch to keep us balanced.

Flying, levitating, or teleporting dreams may have other motivations as well. Perhaps they come to remind us not to get too bogged down in the heaviness of life or figurative gravity, and to rise above negative situations. They encourage us to look beyond the limitations imposed on us, to a belief that anything is possible. Like Maslow's peak experiences (which they are, in a way), these may be a promise of transpersonal self-actualization, of transcending the lower self and reaching for the true self, the higher self, which Jung, Assagioli, Cayce, and Maslow agree is the ultimate goal.

SIGNPOSTS AND MAPS

Dreams are like good sheep dogs that keep the various parts of ourselves together and traveling in the right direction. There are many signposts and maps pointing the way and marking the trail. These may appear in our dreams as literal signs, or they may simply be cues or emblematic things to remind us who we are and where we're going.

Road Signs

Often, literal traffic signs, billboards, and signals appear in our dreams to give particular instructions. Little interpretation is needed if we see a red stop sign, a straight ahead or a no U-turn sign, a yellow caution light, or the 409 billboard dream mentioned in Chapter 5.

One of my favorite sign dreams is one supplied by a friend several years ago:

> *I was walking down a paved road in what seemed like a nice rural area with trees and meadows. As I walked, I began to notice arrow-shaped signs staked along the left side of the road. All the signs were pointing straight ahead, and each was printed with the directions "To Hell."*
>
> *The road quickly became rough, rocky, and downward sloping. The signs were posted closer and closer together and continued to point the way as the descent became darker and steeper. I grew frightened and stopped, refusing to go any farther, turned, and hurried back the way I'd come.*

We were in a group when the friend related the dream, and someone piped up, "What was the road paved with? Good intentions?"

We all laughed, and my friend flashed a startled I've-been-caught expression, signaling that she got it. She was notorious for not following through with her grandiose plans and ideas, and her "road to hell" was "paved with good intentions." She swore she was going to change her ways. Did she? For a while. Change is hard, and sometimes we can only manage a little bit at a time.

Which Way Is Up?

Signs direct us to elevators, escalators, and stairs. Are we going up—to higher parts of the mind, rising in our awareness or to the occasion, going up in the world, seeking higher goals, or seeing a rise in the stock market or blood pressure? Are we going down—delving into the unconscious, losing ground in some way, or coming down to earth? Which floor are you traveling to? The numbered buttons in an elevator may have some particular meaning as well. Your current life situation, your thoughts and actions of the day before will give important clues as to the meaning.

No Left Turns

Left and right can also have many meanings. Right may mean the correct way, or it may mean something like the future, while the left indicates the past. Occasionally the right is masculine, the left feminine. We speak of the political left as liberal, the right as conservative. Being "out in left field" indicates an extreme position, completely outside the norm in thought or action, or someone who's not "with it."

Which hand do you use? Your handedness may influence your perception.

Compass Readings

Think of all the directional references we use in our everyday language. In migration, we equate north with cold and south with warmer climates. East makes you think of the mysterious Orient, where the sun rises, and the Atlantic states, while west makes you think of parts of Europe and the United States, the West Coast, "moving west" to new beginnings for settlers, the wild west, and the setting sun. In some cultures, notably ancient Egypt, east is associated with birth or rebirth, and west represents dying or death. East can be right, west left, north up, and south down. If a business or an idea is failing, we say things are headed south.

Having a compass gives us a sense of direction, and keeps us from getting lost. Knowing where north is on either a compass or a map orients us so we can find our way. Remember Abbie's bus dream in which the bus was headed north? Why do you think it was headed in that direction? There are several possible reasons for this coming up in her dream, but plausible explanation was that an area she and her husband were considering for relocation was north of their existing home.

Water Faucets

Faucets in the sink, shower, or tub indicate which is hot (marked H or red, a warm color) and which is cold (marked C or blue, a cool color). How often have you said someone was "in hot water"? Note that even if faucets aren't marked we know that hot is left, cold is right.

Shapes and Figures as Signposts

Jung spent many years researching mandalas—circular symbols of perfection, wholeness, and completion found in various cultures and religions. Circles may represent oneness or coming full circle. There is the circle of life and the circle of a ring or a crown. We know the importance of being square in the positive sense (being truthful and honest) and in the negative (being nerdy or boring). The triangle and pyramid symbols abound in our culture, both ancient and modern. You have only to read the books of Dan Brown to see how often our Masonic forefathers placed powerful symbols on our currency and in our capital's architecture, or how churches use various symbols to speak subliminally to our unconscious minds. Other such symbolic shapes include the cross, the menorah, the ankh, the symbol of infinity, and the spiral of the labyrinth. These are part of the language of the collective unconscious or generations of lore, of myth, or of memories.

The Four Elements

The elements of earth, water, fire, and air often appear in various ways, especially as related to an ancient understanding of the basic elements in the formation of all matter. A fifth element was sometimes added, a sort of heavenly substance. These basic elements are often associated with the four lower chakras. This notion of elements evolved into medieval alchemy. (Jung spent a great deal of time studying alchemy, insisting the practice wasn't about turning base material into gold, but a philosophical search for transformation of the self.) The notion of elements is seen in astrology, where each astrological sign is assigned to one of the group of elements. Many folks maintain that astrological symbols have importance in the dream realm, and we'll look at that a bit later.

The elements in and of themselves also have meaning in dreams:

1. **Earth** — Involves things that are solid, but also concepts like "earthy"
2. **Water** — Involves things that are liquid, but also the unconscious or the emotions
3. **Fire** — Involves things that destroy, but also anger, hatred, temper
4. **Air** — Involves things that move, but also breath and wind

Heavenly Maps

These days we have GPS devices or ordinary, hard-to-fold paper maps to help us get where we're going. In the past, ship captains looked to the skies and steered by the stars. Ancient ancestors all over the world looked to the skies and built monuments to the sun, the moon, the stars, and their changing configurations. On certain days of the year, the sun would shine into a temple and illuminate particular carvings or statues. Similar ideas are seen all over the world. It's fascinating that ancient people could perform such feats, and it certainly gives some credence to Jung's belief in a collective unconscious. Astronomy grew out of these early observations and connections, but before that we had astrology.

According to astrologers, the day, time, and year of your birth tells something about you. The zodiac is laid out in a circle with twelve divisions, and triangles or squares are sometimes formed within that circle by various planets and have particular meanings. Most of you know your astrological sign and some of the basic characteristics associated with it. All of these signs and symbols, ordinary and unusual, make their way into our dreams as signposts to transform our waking lives.

Things to Remember and Exercises to Do

Remember:
- Vehicles may represent the way you're going or your physical body.
- Faulty brakes indicate lack of control.
- Cops or traffic signals warn you to slow down or face consequences.
- Signs give us directions.

Exercises to Do:

1. Which car best describes you? Why? Which cars best describe your friends and family? Why?
2. For countless centuries, people looked to the sky, to maps of the sun, moon, stars, constellations, and planets for guidance and direction. Astrology, an ancient esoteric art, looks at people's relationships to these heavenly maps, and grew out of a need for meaning and direction.

   Catherine Avril Morris, astrology buff and writer for online astrology sites, lists some very general and simplified characteristics in her workshop "Hey, Baby, What's Your Sign?" (Note that other astrological factors may temper these basic adjectives.) Find your own descriptors and those of friends and family. Do they fit? What would you add or delete? How do you feel these ideas could help guide you in your life or help you understand symbols in your dreams?

1. **Aries (Mar. 21–Apr. 19)** — energetic, impulsive, daring, passionate, a leader.

2. **Taurus (Apr. 20–May 20)** — practical, loyal, materialistic, stubborn, generous.

3. **Gemini (May 21–June 20)** — talkative, witty, flexible, of two minds, restless.

4. **Cancer (June 21–July 22)** — sensitive, nurturing, moody, family-oriented, a leader.

5. **Leo (July 23–Aug. 22)** — courageous, a natural leader, dramatic, loyal, generous.

6. **Virgo (Aug. 23–Sept. 22)** — practical, analytical, reserved, self-sacrificing, critical.

7. **Libra (Sept. 23–Oct. 22)** — stylish, creative, motivating, seeks justice and balance.

8. **Scorpio (Oct. 23–Nov. 21)** — intense, passionate, loyal, mysterious, sensitive.

9. **Sagittarius (Nov. 22–Dec. 21)** — dreamer, adaptable, independent, playful, honest.

10. **Capricorn (Dec. 22–Jan. 19)** — overachiever, leader, dependable, serious, organized.

11. **Aquarius (Jan. 20–Feb. 18)** — independent, loyal, free-spirited, unusual, friendly.

12. **Pisces (Feb. 19–Mar. 20)** — sensitive, insightful, nurturing, adaptable, emotional.

CHAPTER 7

What's Going On?

While people, settings, and props are critical parts of your dreams, like in films, the story doesn't begin until the director yells, "Action!" The things that *happen* provide the meat and message of the tale.

- A gigantic stone ball rumbles rapidly toward him, and he whirls and bolts back through the tunnel to escape.
- Faster than a speeding bullet, a red and blue blur streaks through the air.
- A knife slices through the shower curtain, and a woman screams and screams and . . .

Action is a big part of our internal movies as well. Even a quiet game of chess can be telling, as a symbol for some sort of challenge. Many of the actions that occur in dreams have been discussed in other parts of this book as they relate to specific people, objects, or situations. Let's look at some other common movements, actions, and emotional reactions to see what they may mean.

MOVEMENTS

Movements such as walking, running, skipping, standing up, sitting down, driving, and making hand gestures of all sorts usually give specific clues to the meaning of dreams. Note them particularly in opening scenes or when special attention is paid to the particular movement.

Walking and Other Foot Locomotion

A common dream opening is the dreamer walking along a path or other course, which typically means the way he's going, on his life path. Accompanying emotions will refine the meaning even more. The turtle dream in Chapter 2 is a good example of a walking dream. Hiking goes a bit beyond simple walking; it includes a sense of exploration and challenge.

Running draws more attention than walking and might point to running around, running from one thing to another, on the run, running away from something, or simply an admonition to hurry.

A young woman from New York asked Edgar Cayce to interpret a dream for her in which "some terrible wild man seemed to be running through the town shooting and causing great trouble, and the police were chasing him." Cayce broke in to answer, "The large man, the bugaboo, that comes to the entity in these emblematical conditions here presented, and as seen in others, is in self and self's temper, see?" [136-18]

Sounds as if her "wild man" was her own bad temper "running amok." Her reading further warned her to learn self-control.

Skipping is something children often do, especially when feeling lighthearted. To see an adult skipping might mean he's acting childish (or needs to be less serious), refer to skipping out on responsibilities, or be an admonition to skip something and let it go. Other locomotion symbols might have you jumping or leaping—into something with both feet, or warning of the need to look before you leap. The hayloft dream at the end of this chapter is a good example of a jumping dream.

Standing or Sitting?

If attention is drawn to standing up or sitting down, think of all the associated figures of speech. We can stand together, for something, at attention, or up for our rights. We can stand as in endure, take a stand, or stand up and be counted. Sitting assumes a more passive attitude: Think of sitting down on the job, sitting in for something, sitting on the fence, sitting in a waiting room or some other place. Or maybe you just need to sit down and take it easy or sit down and cool it.

Driving

We've mentioned driving in connection with what sort of vehicle appears in your dream. Besides indicating something about the physical body, driving can mean the way we're headed, or our sense of direction. And who is in the driver's seat? The person in control—or the one who's not doing such a great job of controlling the direction—is probably you. It can also mean you're driving yourself too hard or too fast. We talk about a driving force, driving someone crazy, back seat drivers, or driving around in circles. The context in all these areas carry significance.

Gail W. dreamed:

> I'm in a car with my husband. I'm driving, and the car begins to go too fast, but I cannot slow it down. I'm beginning to lose control of the car. The road turns into yellow plastic, similar to the material of a beach ball. In an attempt to slow the car down (which has continued to accelerate), I grab the side of the road. Slowly, I regain control of the car.

This is the fifth of a series of seven dreams by Gail, a graduate student who was also working full time. Most of her dreams were about anxiety in one form or another. In one dream, she was afraid of a killer and a clock played a prominent part. In another, her father had died and a perfectionist former boss had taken his place. What can you surmise about her life at that time? Stressful? Hectic? Of course. Her life was going out of control. She needed to slow down and relax (her father was the laid back sort), and time was running out to stop from "killing" herself. Her most basic needs were screaming for attention.

Hand Gestures

It's been said some people couldn't carry on a conversation if their hands were tied behind them. Gestures are an extension of verbal communication and show up in many dreams. Think of all the things you can communicate using hand movements, from the rude signals directed at a kamikaze driver to blowing a kiss to a departing child. You can wave, give a thumbs down or up, signal safe or out at the baseball game, indicate someone's crazy, wag a finger, or signal "call me." Everybody knows what the traffic cop is directing us to do, and we're all familiar with the "come forward" and "stop" signals if someone is helping us park. Various cultures and nationalities add their own unique gestures to the mix.

ACTIVITIES

Activities such as sewing, painting, cleaning, repairing, sawing, chopping, cutting, stabbing, shooting, writing, giving birth, dying, drowning, eating and drinking, urinating and defecating, beating, spilling, cooking, hunting, fishing, working, playing, and myriad others are a big part of our dreams.

The list of actions and activities can become overwhelming. The idea is to always apply the principles of association and analogy to any activity and to look for familiar figures of speech associated with them. Below are a few categories to give you an idea of possible meanings.

Negative Activities

Activities of a negative nature such as beating, shooting, stabbing, killing, and drowning often come as warnings of one sort or another. Such dreams may be talking about self-destructive behavior, or your intentional (or unintentional) behavior toward others. Look to the day before for information on the events addressed in the dream to determine if the negative vibe is directed at yourself or another person so that you can make the proper attitude adjustment. You can be shooting off your mouth or shooting yourself in the foot, beating up on yourself, blasting a coworker, stabbing someone in the back, killing yourself, or drowning in demands on your time.

Yet sometimes, dying in a dream is good. Here's why.

When we change or move to a new level of development, it's often scary to find ourselves in new and uncharted territory. We're comfortable with the old and familiar, like well-worn shoes or a comfortable, holey sweater. Many apocalyptic and end-of-the-world dreams crop up during major life transitions, complete with *War of the Worlds* scenes or erupting volcanoes and tidal waves. It *is* the end of the world for the old self, and we feel like kids plucked from our old school and old friends only to be moved to a new place we don't know. (In such a case, security needs and "belongingness needs" are threatened.) The turmoil dreamed about at such times is normal. After the apocalypse comes the dawning of a new era, a new phase in life. The swan dream in Chapter 4 is an example of a turmoil dream, with an added promise of smooth sailing ahead.

Playing and Games

Recently, a woman reported a dream that opened at a basketball game. Why a basketball game?

Her husband had been a basketball player and is a big sports fan, but she much preferred a good movie or book to watching or participating in any kind of activity that required a ball. What was significant to her about a basketball game? She knew enough about sports to realize that basketball games were all about making goals. This was a dream about scoring, strategy, opposition, contention, or skill. But the first thing that popped into her mind was goals. As it turned out, that's exactly what the dream was about—goals and using her natural skills.

Often, games and their associated toys or equipment imitate life for adults, both in reality and in dreams. They are about skill, challenge, goals and aims, interaction, teamwork, and rules. Look to the structure or purpose of the game or equipment for clues to its meaning in a dream. A batter needs to keep his eye on the ball, a charades player must think creatively and communicate effectively, and a golfer must, among other things, keep his head down.

Consider the many figures of speech associated with games and toys—making the goal, par for the course, building blocks—when reviewing your own dreams for clues.

Swimming, Diving, and Skating

Swimming, diving, and skating can certainly be competitive, especially in the Olympics, but most often they're individual activities or something to be enjoyed with friends or for relaxation. We can be swimming to something (a goal), away from something (escape or new direction), in deep water, or in over our heads. Diving in often means to get started, usually with a splash. Skating can be on a skateboard, roller skates, or ice skates, and we need good balance to glide smoothly.

Luz had the following dream about ice skating:

I was in a small college town, and most of the community had turned out for an evening of entertainment downtown. There were singers and dancers, but the focus was on the ice skating exhibition. A young Peggy Fleming and her male partner were featured. They were the epitome of balance and grace and passion as they glided smoothly and perfectly over the ice. I was captivated, and everybody's spirits were raised. There was singing and a sense of joy, partying, and celebration.

Luz had been working on a very difficult project that had her feeling frustrated and discouraged. She felt this dream pertained to something she needed to learn (the college town) to make the project go more smoothly and come together for everyone involved (the crowd of people enjoying themselves). The focus was on the effortless glide of the skaters. She needed to change her attitude, stay balanced, and enjoy what she was doing. Being upbeat, staying well balanced, and keeping a positive outlook was the answer. These characteristics can be considered part of the being needs as described by Maslow, marks of a more self-actualized person. (Maslow often reminded us that self-actualized people aren't perfect human beings; they get frustrated and discouraged, too.)

Food- and Drink-Related Activities

All sorts of activities related to selecting, preparing, serving, and eating food frequently occurs in dreams. We've spoken elsewhere about diet and food, but it often shows up in dreams, perhaps not only because of our basic physiological needs, but also because social interaction is often coupled with eating and drinking. Our modern methods of hunting and gathering food differs greatly from those of our ancestors. While they hunted buffalo or rabbits and gathered berries and bulbs, we hunt at the nearest Burger King and gather our berries at the supermarket. Food—good food—is a critical part of our survival and if we're not eating the nutrients we need, our body tells us in our dreams.

Wisdom of the Body

In 1932, Dr. Walter Cannon of Harvard published *Wisdom of the Body*, a book in which he popularized the ideas of homeostasis and the body's innate ability to maintain a constant and healthy state. Certain foods and liquids contain the particular nutrients, calories, and vitamins needed for proper functioning. Other researchers used a similar approach in maintaining that recently weaned babies, if presented with various food choices at meals, would select a well-balanced diet over time, thus exhibiting a certain "wisdom of the body" to eat properly.

Does that mean we need to eat the things we crave? Unfortunately, no.

There is a dream that I call the Fourteen Taco Dream. No food, cooking, or eating shows up in the dream, but it's about food all the same. The dreamer seems to be slogging along in slow motion. He can't run; he can barely move. And that's exactly the way a person's real body feels after ingesting a bunch of stuff the mouth had no business eating. The body can't run (function) properly. But the dreamer really *craves* those tacos. He can almost taste them before he goes to his favorite Mexican restaurant. It's more likely that Freud's pleasure principle is prompting the craving than any real need to pig out on tacos for their nutritional value.

We're not newly weaned babies. Lots of complex variables govern our cravings and our binges. Plus, overeating screws up the body's homeostasis.

JoAnn once dreamed she was digging a huge hole, dumping lots and lots of chocolate into it, and burying it with dirt. Now, JoAnn *loved* chocolate. She often craved it: fudge with pecans, chocolate cake, chocolate pie, chocolate eclairs, Snickers—all things chocolate. She sometimes overindulged. Her dream was telling her to get rid of the overindulgent habit. That was a different sort of wisdom of the body. The unconscious mind, aware of a person's functioning on all levels, was saying in essence, "Too much chocolate and empty sugar calories don't make this vehicle run efficiently. Cut it out."

For JoAnn, dreaming of eating chocolate wouldn't be a signal to hit the Godiva, it would be symbolic of something else, perhaps an over-indulgence in gossip or some other bad habit. Or it could represent a way of rewarding herself, or imply a simple craving for sweetness in interpersonal relationships. Again, the common reminder: Use common sense in your interpretations.

Selecting Food
Wendy dreamed:

I was staying at a haunted manor, and out the back door of one room was a ghost shaped like a cartoon mouse—about three feet tall and standing upright. Her face was entirely made of vegetables—lettuce made the lines, cherry tomatoes for eyes, and a squash nose. She was wearing a dress and staring at me very accusingly until I let her into the house.

Wendy knew immediately what the dream was about. She and her husband had recently joined a CSA (Community Supported Agriculture) program to obtain fresh produce from a local farmer. They'd been eating fresh vegetables like crazy, but for some reason she slacked off the program for a few days. Like Scrooge's ghosts of Christmas, her "ghost of vegetables" showed up to remind her to get back to eating her greens.

Jerry, a middle-aged man, dreamed of going into a grocery store and seeing several cases of fresh seafood, particularly shellfish and ocean fish. The seafood was displayed attractively and looked very appetizing. He said that he was a meat-and-potatoes man and didn't eat much fish, except maybe fried catfish occasionally. When urged to try a change in diet, he did and reported that he'd eaten seafood several times and enjoyed it. A few weeks later, he went in for his yearly physical. The doctor noticed an enlargement of his thyroid. A lack of iodine, an element found in ocean seafood, can cause this condition, and that turned out to be the case. His body wasn't craving fish, it was craving iodine, but his unconscious translated that need into the shrimp and ocean bass he found he particularly liked.

While eating, serving, or selecting food usually signals a dream about diet, social occasions, or even a concern with some sort of mental ingestion, it also may stand for something unrelated to food. The "cafeteria shoes" dream in Chapter 5 is a good example, as is Susan's dream below.

Food and Choices

Susan R., in middle management for a sizeable company, dreamed:

I was at a large gathering of people, perhaps a company function, and it was lunchtime. A buffet was set up, and I got a plate of food (a balanced variety) and went to sit at a table. It was a large round table with several men (eight or more) and one woman. There were a couple of empty seats. I knew these people, but at the same time I didn't. I only recognized Wally P., a manager from work, but the others seemed familiar. I said, "This looks like the most interesting table. May I join you?"

Nobody said anything. Wally only smiled weakly; the others, including the woman, said nothing. I noticed that the woman had a balanced variety of food on her plate, but the men all had only two very large pieces of cheese on their plates—like a half-inch-thick rectangle cut on a diagonal and arranged into a triangle. This was like old-fashioned rat cheese, but pale yellow and sort of dry.

Half-joking at their choice of food, I said, "Are you all on a cheese diet?" No one replied. The woman seemed slightly uncomfortable, and Wally didn't look up from his plate. Feeling decidedly unwelcome, I left to find another place.

My first question to Susan was to ask if she'd read the bestselling management book about moving the cheese. She laughed and said that while she'd heard of it, she was probably the only person in the world who hadn't read it. After we determined that this dream had no bearing on her real diet, we cast around for other meanings, particularly those that were work-related. As we talked about her goals at the company, the light began to dawn. She wanted to rise to a higher level, to "sit at the table with the big cheeses." The people in power were predominately male, rather old-fashioned, and chauvinistic. The dream seemed to be telling her not to expect a well-deserved promotion she was hoping for. As it turned out, she lost out to a less-qualified man, and decided to leave the company soon afterward.

The moral of the story? Sometimes food dreams aren't about food at all.

Elimination and Bathroom Activities

I've often heard it said that we are what we eat, think, and don't eliminate. More and more these days we're becoming concerned with the proper physical maintenance of the body. Dentists insist that we brush, floss, rinse, and use various mechanical devices to keep our teeth clean, white, and cavity free, and our gums healthy. TV ads bombard us with the same information. I discussed earlier how activities associated with teeth and mouth are often pointing to our need to watch our words. But this isn't always true. Look to the obvious first. Your teeth may *really* need attention. You may *really* need to take a bath or a shower, or wash your hands, hair, and behind your ears. Or such symbols may indicate that you need to "clean up your act" in some way. You may *really* need to watch your elimination. It's one of the basic physiological needs, according to Maslow.

Toilets and bathrooms show up often in dreams. While they may frequently signal the need for physical or internal cleansing, or attention to eliminations (bladder or bowel malfunctioning), they often relate to a necessity for figuratively eliminating certain behaviors or habits from the dreamer's life.

The Edgar Cayce readings on physical ailments repeatedly stress the importance of eliminations and their part in illness. That's why it's important to drink a fair amount of water every day. And in these times of overprocessed foods, we need to pay special attention to bowel habits and things like fiber, bulk, and going easy on junk food. That's the reason we dream about dirty bathrooms, or we find ourselves trying to get the plumbing or sewer unstopped from time to time. They may signal true need for attention in that area, or they may be metaphors relating to a need to eliminate something altogether different from your experience. There are many figures of speech relating to bathroom activities: in the toilet, flush it, potty-mouth, cleaning up (as a business deal), washing my hands of the whole thing, piss on it, and many other less delicate expressions. (I'm sure you can think of several without any prompting.) As always, context is the key.

Sex

Everybody has X-rated dreams from time to time. Often they're simply physiological reactions to the normal arousal behavior that occurs during the REM state. One of the discoveries by modern sleep research laboratories is that men, unless there is an organic reason for impotence, manifest tumescence during REM, i.e., they have erections. Women, too, have arousal reactions; they're simply less obvious and more difficult to measure.

Was Freud right then? Are dreams sexual wish fulfillment? Only partly, and only sometimes. Certainly some X-rated dreams are simply what they appear to be. But, as we've stated earlier, there is a physiological side of dreams as well as a psychological side, and the things that fill our days also fill our nights. We would expect that a portion of our dreams, as in our daily life, be concerned with sexual matters, but certainly not the majority of material. And I've found a preponderance of sexual dreams reported are fairly blatant and not disguised at all. They range from gentle kisses and caresses, to masturbation, to sexual intercourse.

Maya T. dreamed:

I am with Kevin, a classmate. I find he really likes me, and I like him as well. A lot seems to be happening. I find myself physically attracted to Kevin, and we make love. I think of my husband and hope I don't remember this dream. I decide that if I do remember it, I will either not record it at all or I will censor it. This makes me feel very controlled.

I think Maya, a graduate student in college, probably did censor this quite a bit before she submitted the dream, but she didn't disguise her attraction to Kevin. Although the details were sparse, she played out her fantasy overtly and even felt some guilt about her "adultery."

Jung, like many therapists, insisted that his patients bring a series of dreams to him before he attempted to analyze them. Doing so helped him see patterns or recurring themes. As I read through dream journals, I can easily see patterns emerging. (This serves as a good reminder to reread your own journals after a period of time.) Below are two of Beth W.'s dreams. Do you see any patterns or themes forming even in this brief sample?

A white knight on a white horse jumped over a low cement-type wall, picked me up, and carried me back over the wall to a dimly lit city. Within the city there was a carriage. I don't remember any horses or a driver, but we both got in. His white knight clothes changed to street clothes. We sat very close to each other. On the opposite side of where we sat was my husband, Matt. I moved even closer to the knight, putting my arms around him and vice versa. The two men's faces were not too clear, but I could see my husband's face better. I kept switching seats to be with each man. Each man then took me for a carriage ride separately. There was lots of hugging and kissing, and I felt nice.

Beth explained that she always dreamed and talked about white knights just like the ones in fairy tales. The white knight figure is handsome, intelligent, loving, caring, and adventurous. She described her husband Matt as into adventurous sports, thoughtful, and loving. To her, carriage rides were intimate, old-fashioned, and an exciting way to travel. It's easy to see that she is a romantic.

This was her next dream in the series:

I was at a county fair of some sort with my husband Matt. He was hungry and wanted to eat something. He also wanted me to eat some food. All that we could find for sale were hot dogs on a stick and corn on the cob. I didn't want any of those things. My husband seemed to get a little upset, and he kept saying that I must eat.

Matt kept switching and reappearing as another man who I didn't recognize, but he and Matt had similar hair. This man also wanted to buy me something to eat, but I kept seeing the hot dogs and corn on the cob on slides, and they were very greasy and gross. I think they look obnoxious. Both my husband and the other man still wanted to please me, and they were feeling hurt that I didn't want to eat.

Any thoughts? Although there's no intercourse involved, these are both sexual dreams. We know that Beth is a romantic and old-fashioned. What about Matt? Beth has already said that he's very thoughtful and loving and supportive. She's also told us that he's into adventurous sports. We might suspect that Matt might like to be more adventurous in the bedroom as well. If we look at the hot dogs and corn on the cob as fairly obvious phallic symbols à la Freud, we might see they're having a difference of opinion regarding oral sex. In this dream she was really struggling with the issue, which was "obnoxious" to her, and she saw her husband as two different men. She was not ready (and may never be) to give up her idealized man and his romantic demeanor.

When Sex Means Something Else Altogether

While some sexual dreams are just that, others with sexual themes may be symbolic of something else entirely. In fact, many dream authorities suggest that dreams that seem blatantly sexual often have an alternative meaning instead of, or at least in addition to, sexual experience. These dreams may be interpreted in the same manner as any other dream. In fact, it's entirely possible Beth's dream of hot dogs had to do with a difference in eating habits between her and her husband, and it may relate to *both* sexual and eating preferences.

Consider Fran's dream:

> *My friend Ada was strapping on a dildo to simulate an aroused male. I knew that she intended to have intercourse with me. I was horrified.*

Fran was shocked by the dream. Both she and Ada were married, and neither had expressed any physical attraction to the other. Fran was decidedly heterosexual. With a bit of questioning, the dreamer realized that this was a dream warning that Ada was about to "screw" her. As it turned out, the friend wasn't a friend at all, and shortly after the dream she betrayed Fran in a shocking way.

EMOTIONAL REACTIONS

Without getting into an area beyond both my level of expertise and the purpose of this book, it's well accepted that various emotions cause an array of chemical changes and neurological reactions in people (and some theorists say vice-versa). While gross body movements are blocked in REM sleep, other physical reactions are simulated during this time. The eyes act as if they're seeing (thus rapid eye movement), the ears act as if they're hearing, the "fight or flight" reactions caused by adrenal secretions kick in, and so forth. That's why we often awaken from a nightmare with heart pounding and forehead damp. The emotions we experience in dreams produce the same physical reactions as our waking ones do. That may be why so many people have heart attacks and die in their sleep (we're talking about people with heart disease here, not healthy ones). Researchers have noticed that many heart patients who are being monitored die just as they're coming awake in the morning.

In our dreams, we laugh and smile, we weep and sniffle, and we express all manner of aggression, anger, and fear.

Fear Responses

Dr. Walter Cannon, the same Harvard professor who wrote *Wisdom of the Body*, is also credited with bringing us the term "fight or flight." (Actually, he *dreamed* these concepts.) When our ancestors were threatened by a wild animal, the same bodily reactions kicked in to give them energy to stand and fight with their club, or turn and climb a tree, or run like crazy. Stress, threats, and disturbing dreams or nightmares produce the same fight-or-flight responses.

Chuck T., a graduate student and former police officer, dealt with his stressful university situation in a different way than most of his classmates. He dreamed:

I left some kind of meeting in New York City. It was very much like the university. I was wearing a pistol and was somewhat worried about being found out, but evidently I was more worried about being caught without one.

I left the meeting riding in a truck with a man and a woman with whom I was friends. We stopped at an old house across from what appeared to be a park. It was a dark night and visibility was poor.

Across the street I could make out several shadowy shapes of people walking. They shouted something obscene to me. (I can't recall what.) I was on the porch of the house with my pants pulled down. I think I was trying to change clothes, and the pants were hung around my shoes. I yelled back, "F— your mother!"

I knew then that they were going to try and get me. I then experienced a very strong feeling, which I've experienced before when awake and working as a policeman. It's like fear, but not fear. Fear without being afraid. I knew that I might soon be hurt, even killed. I felt that I could stave this off by being prepared, by fighting well. I began to steel myself for what would soon come. I checked the pistol and wished I had another one, more ammunition.

I asked the man with me to get his weapon from his truck. He did so and came back to the porch with me.

All of a sudden, there was the assailant. He fired shots at me from a pistol first. I returned his fire. Then he had a rifle. I was behind a brick column, and in order to aim at him I had to come out and carefully draw a bead, sitting right in front of his muzzle, an easy target.

With a rifle, he didn't even have to aim. All he had to do was point it at me.

I don't know just when I shot him. He ran across the street and into his house. I had called the police but didn't want to be caught because I was in NY carrying a pistol. So I left.

Chuck is obviously a "fight" kind of guy. This was one of the later dreams in a series of over twenty. In many of his dreams he was back as a policeman, or being with former police friends. In one he was even wondering if he should have left police work. Obviously he felt out of his element in graduate school, threatened by his lack of authority and power, and felt defensive. Still, as we see in this dream, he was determined to stay and fight it out with the threatening situation.

The "fear but not fear" he experiences is the "flight or fight" syndrome kicking in, on high alert and ready for action. This dream functions on a couple of need levels; his security needs are certainly threatened. The dream indicates that he feels out of his element in New York (the university is really in Texas, but the unfamiliar dream location adds to his unease). His pistol represents safety and protection against the unknown (the shadowy assailant). Certainly his self-esteem is being threatened in his waking life. He doesn't want to "get caught with his pants down" (vulnerable and unprepared). The central idea of this dream is about marshaling defenses and prevailing in a threatening situation.

Of course, Freud would point to all the obvious phallic symbols and declare it to be a sexual dream. Maybe it was both.

Sadness

Often we express sadness in our dreams, and it ranges from bittersweet poignancy to uncontrollable weeping. Susan M., a teacher, submitted several dreams and each one brought comments from her like, "I want to be admired and needed," and "I'm afraid of doing something wrong and having others mad at me." In one dream, which showed the birth of a child and vignettes of her and her husband interacting joyously with the baby, she acted surprised. She said later she was surprised because she never expected to have a happy home life (a reflection of her own unhappy childhood). Her dreams and responses showed a serious need for belongingness and love as well as esteem. Her self-esteem was in the toilet.

Susan's dream:

I dreamed that my husband became involved with another woman, a friend of mine. The three of us had been attending a social function. I happened to walk into a room and saw them embracing. I first felt shock, then I felt like a fool. I wept bitterly. My husband tried to

explain that she meant nothing to him (which I knew). Then I cried
because I knew that to so many people nothing has real meaning.

Because of her background, Susan had serious trust issues. She was afraid that her husband and friend would betray her, and indeed, as she mentioned before, she didn't expect to have a happy home life. She was setting herself up for failure and/or self-fulfilling prophecy with her own attitudes. It is she who was guilty of feeling nothing has real meaning. Her scars ran deep, but Susan's husband was a patient and loving man. Hopefully, with his help, she was able to overcome her insecurities.

Happiness

Most of us much prefer happy dreams. We love to wake up smiling or laughing out loud. We adore experiencing joy as we soar over cities, visit lovely places, and arrive at happy endings.

The skating dream reported earlier in this chapter is a good example of a joyous dream. Perhaps such dreams are, as Jung said, merely compensatory and designed to prop us up when we feel down to keep us in balance. But I like to think they have other meanings as well, that they come also to encourage and reward our waking efforts. Judith W. dreamed:

I was in a hayloft with several other people who appeared to be chil-
dren. The hay was a bright, golden color and was very soft. The loft,
which was one story off the ground, was open on one side, and on the
ground below I could see ropes that had been made into circles almost
to form a bullseye. The other people began jumping from the loft one
by one, trying to land in the circles. I was reluctant to try it, but I did,
and felt very pleased with myself when I landed safely and successfully.

Judith said jumping was a pleasurable, exciting experience. She awoke feeling happy, energized, and uplifted and felt that her dream was encouraging her to go for her goals, without fear.

Things to Remember and Exercises to Do

Remember:

- Movements and activities may be symbolic and give important clues to dreams.
- You are what you eat, think, and don't eliminate.
- Sometimes sex is just sex—unless it's not.
- The feelings in and from a dream are real. Upon awakening be sure to record your feelings in your journal.

Exercises to Do:

1. Read over your dream journal and notice any patterns that crop up. For example, are your dreams mostly pleasant, unpleasant, or neutral? Are you engaging in similar activities? Do they have similar basic themes?

2. Record your answers to the following questions:
   - If you could engage in any three activities tomorrow, what would you choose to do and why?
   - If you could do anything in your dream tonight, what would it be? Why?
   - What is your favorite thing to do in the whole world?
   - If you could learn to do three things, what would you choose to learn and why?
   - What three things do you hate to do most? Why? Look back over your lists. Do you see any patterns? Have you ever dreamed about doing any of these things? How did it make you feel?

CHAPTER 8

Exceptional Dreams

In many ways, *all* dreams are exceptional dreams because most of them are unique to the dreamer, but there are particularly exceptional dreams that crop up from time to time that deserve special attention. Many people have experienced dreaming about something that later came to pass, known as a precognitive dream. At talks on dreams, audiences are frequently asked how many of them have had at least one precognitive dream. Usually a majority of participants raise their hands. There have been many reports of other sorts of exceptional dreams as well, including those "big dreams" that Jung discussed, experiences of talking with deceased loved ones, what seemed to be past-life dreams, profoundly spiritual dreams, prophetic dreams (seemingly more significant or deep than a mere precognitive dream), and many instances of recurring dreams. You may feel as if we're venturing into woo-woo territory here, but these dreams are reported too frequently to simply dismiss out of hand.

Have you ever had a dream in which you tuned in to someone else's life, known as a telepathic dream?

TELEPATHIC DREAMS

Telepathy is the ability to communicate mentally or by means other than the five senses. Of the large number of such dreams reported, they almost always involve family or other closely tied individuals.

Consider the following dream of a grandmother who lived in a different state than her son and his family.

When she dreamed of her granddaughter, distressed and covered in soot, the woman was jarred awake, her heart pounding. She called her son immediately but couldn't reach him. Later that day she discovered there had been a fire in her son's house, and it had started with a candle in her granddaughter's room. Thankfully, no one was injured.

Eerie? Perhaps, but remember the saying that nothing of any consequence ever happens to us unless it's first previewed in a dream. This woman's dream is an example of a telepathic dream. In some way, she picked up on the distress of someone close to her.

Several years ago, authors Sheila Ostrander and Lynn Schroeder traveled to the USSR to research reports they were hearing. The book on their findings, *Psychic Discoveries Behind the Iron Curtain,* is a pioneering work in the study of parapsychology and science. They tell of an experiment involving rabbits, telepathy, and a Russian submarine. (If you are squeamish about experiments on laboratory animals, you'd best skip the next paragraph.)

A noted Russian researcher of paranormal subjects reported an experiment in which a mother rabbit and her newborn litter were separated. The mother was left ashore in a laboratory and electrodes were implanted in her brain. The litter was taken aboard a submarine, which submerged and traveled some distance away. One by one, and at irregular times, the baby rabbits were "sacrificed" and the time recorded. Back at the lab, the mother rabbit registered a brain change at the exact time that each was killed.

We might surmise that a similar connection exists in humans and accounts for telepathic dreams. In fact, Dr. Robert Van de Castle, who was the Director of the Sleep and Dream Research Laboratory at the University of Virginia Medical Center for many years, was actively involved in dream telepathy research at his own lab as well as others with such well-known and respected researchers as Calvin Hall, Montague Ullman, and Stanley Krippner. Their work found that, when information was mentally sent to a subject during REM sleep, some individuals were excellent receptors and incorporated the material into dreams in a recognizable way.

PRECOGNITIVE DREAMS

Precognitive dreams differ from telepathic dreams in that they involve knowing things *before* they happen, because you've dreamed about them. Have you ever had a precognitive dream that later came true? Some people have suggested that forgotten precognitive dreams may account for the feeling of *déjà vu* that most of us have experienced, the feeling that you've been to a place before, already heard those words, or know what's going to happen next. The 276 dream from Chapter 5 is an example of a precognitive dream.

It is widely reported that Abraham Lincoln had a precognitive/prophetic dream. About ten days before his death, Lincoln dreamed that he heard weeping and sobbing in the White House, which prompted him to rise and go from room to room looking for the source of the mourning, but he saw no one. Still the grieving continued, and he kept searching. In the East Room he saw a corpse, face covered and in funeral vestments, surrounded by guards. When he asked one of the soldiers who had died, he was told that the president had been assassinated. He was so bothered by the dream that he told his wife, a close friend, and some cabinet members about it. As we all know, his dream came to pass when John Wilkes Booth assassinated him a few days later. The slain president was laid in state in the East Room.

Almost a century later, a teenaged sailor passing through San Diego had a more pleasant experience. He dreamed that his future wife was born on that day. He didn't think much about the dream at the time, but occasionally he would remember it. Thirty-three years afterward he met the woman who became his wife. Her birthday turned out to be the date he dreamed. And she was born in San Diego.

Another amazing example of a precognitive dream is documented in the Edgar Cayce readings. Mr. 137, a stockbroker, asked Cayce on March 5, 1929, for an interpretation of a dream from which he says he "got the impression regarding the market that we ought to sell everything, including the box stock."

In the reading, Cayce's rather complex response to the dream discussed specifics of the market, warning of conditions that would come about, and cautioning that Mr. 137 must watch accounts very carefully. He added this bit of information:

> *During this turmoil . . . as will be seen in a downward movement of long duration . . . [not even stocks considered] VERY safe [should be given] too much latitude. . . . As indicated in the impression [from your dream that you] should dispose of all those held—even in box—would signify the great amount of change as would come. [137-115]*

A month later, the same stockbroker asked for a reading about another dream in which he was accused of murder and being administered a poisonous injection. Mr. 137 reported that he went back to sleep and interpreted his own dream as having to do with an "underhanded fight" on the Reserve Board, and about stimulation of stocks on the market.

In his reading on the dream, Cayce suggested that there were factions who disagreed about various activities regarding the stock market, and they were furthered by money powers on each side of the issue. He stated that:

Were these [factions] allowed to run without a check in EITHER direc-
tion, there must surely come a break where it would be PANIC in the
money centers—not ONLY of Wall Street's activity but a closing of the
boards in many centers, and a re-adjustment of the actual specie and
moneys in these centers. [137-117]

These readings, given and stenographically recorded in the spring
of 1929, were obviously prophetic of the events that began in Octo-
ber of that same year when the stock market crashed. Many specula-
tors were wiped out because of stocks bought through margin buying,
and banks began failing. Even economic historians don't entirely agree
about the causes of the Great Depression, but these dreams of the
stockbroker and the accompanying readings by Edgar Cayce seem to
point to serious problems ahead.

Unfortunately, Mr. 137 didn't listen to his own dreams and suffered
heavy market losses for himself and his clients. Rumblings of gloom
and doom were hard to imagine in the prosperous roaring twenties
when things were going great.

The major problem with precognitive dreams is that they're often
best interpreted in hindsight. Still, many people encounter clues in
such dreams. In Mr. 137's dream, he got an impression of what the
dream was about in both instances. In the 276 dream, content didn't
seem to relate in a meaningful way to current events. At other times
the people or events involved are dark or shadowy, indicating they
haven't "come to light" yet.

In the most recent serious recession, Dave R., whose retirement
account was heavily invested in stocks and therefore in jeopardy,
dreamed that the market would recover after his sixty-ninth birthday.
Was his dream literal and precognitive, or was it symbolic of something totally unrelated to the stock market? Should he hang tight as
his dream suggested, or should he sell out before he lost everything as
some of those in 1929 did?

After researching the issue, he decided to discuss the situation with his broker, who encouraged him to hold on, since his portfolio was well diversified. Dave decided to sit tight, but as he watched one of his more speculative stocks drop to less than half its former high, he got anxious and sold half the speculative stock in question. Even at the lower price, he made four times what he paid for it originally, so he hadn't actually lost anything in the transaction. But Dave wanted to kick himself when, shortly after his sixty-ninth birthday, the stock in question started going up again, and was soon worth three times what he sold the half for.

Does this mean you should speculate on the stock market by following your dreams? Absolutely not. As mentioned before, precognitive dreams are best interpreted in hindsight. Always, *always* use common sense in looking at any dream. Even Dave, an experienced dream worker, spoke with a trusted stockbroker and thoroughly investigated the situation before he acted.

The award for the most romantic precognitive dream goes to Sarah C., a businesswoman who dreamed this several years ago:

> *I was with Dan, who at the time worked for the same company as I did but in another city. We were lying together like spoons, and I understood that we were relating to each other in a way that was beyond sex. I felt incredibly safe and loved.*

Puzzling over the meaning of the dream, Sarah wrote it down in her dream journal. She didn't know what it meant, but she knew it had changed her feelings about Dan and was significant in some way. Because he was a dozen years older than Sarah and married, she'd never even thought of him as a romantic possibility, although she'd been divorced for five years and desperately wanted to find a life partner. She found herself more attracted to him.

About a year later Sarah heard through the company grapevine that Dan and his wife had separated. About two years after that, she heard that the company was moving him to the city where she lived. She knew immediately that they would end up together, but they didn't begin dating until about a year after his move. They married two years later.

Sarah says, "We've been married for seventeen years now. I felt unsafe and scared all my life, and I think the love and security that my relationship with Dan brought me have made great personal growth possible for me."

Sarah's is a true love story and a perfect example of our various need levels influencing our dreams.

POLITICS AND PROPHECY

Diana M. related an interesting dream of historical significance, and said that she still had the daily dream journal that she kept at that time. From the night of June 17, 1972:

> *I saw in a dream a black and white front page of a newspaper. A big headline announced: NIXON RESIGNS.*

"I was very puzzled by this," Diana said, "and I couldn't conceive of it. He was quite popular at that time, and I had great admiration for him. I had campaigned for him in both elections. I didn't know why on earth I should dream this.

"When he did resign on August 9, 1974, I was hurt in my soul. I cried and mourned. As everyone knows, he was much vilified by then, and friends couldn't believe I cared that much. I could only say, I loved him!"

It was not until years later that, while paging through old journals, she found that dream entry and realized that June 17, 1972, was the date of the Watergate break-in. She felt that her bond with Nixon was so strong that her unconscious, dreaming self realized that what had happened on that date would be his undoing.

Lyle T. had a different sort of political prophecy. In the weeks before the conventions that nominated George H. W. Bush for a second term, he was watching some of the candidates vying for the Democratic nomination. He liked Bush fine and was somewhat ambivalent about the Democratic candidates wanting a place on the ballot. That night Lyle reported this dream:

> I saw a large poster on a door. It was of Bill Clinton smiling and standing behind a podium. A beautiful rainbow was arched above his head. I knew at that moment that God had a covenant with Clinton, and he would be the next president.

When he awoke that morning, Lyle said he didn't have a doubt in his mind that Clinton would win the Democratic nomination and be elected president. That feeling never wavered, and his conviction was validated.

EXTERNAL STIMULI IN DREAMS

Sometimes it's difficult to determine if a dream is telepathic, precognitive, or simply an awareness of external stimuli or subliminal environmental cues. In one such instance, a sleeping woman saw the word "gas" in a dream. She got out of bed, and, as she walked from the bedroom to the kitchen at the other end of the house, she sniffed the air but couldn't smell any gas. When she got to the kitchen in the dark, she could see that the pilot light in the center of the stove wasn't on.

The oven pilot was out also. Here there was a hint of a gas smell, and she carefully relit the pilot lights.

She felt she'd had a warning dream. The question is: What was the source of the warning?

Some laboratory research has been done into influencing dream content by introducing odors, sounds, misted water, or temperature changes into the sleeping experience. Indications are that such external stimuli are sometimes incorporated into dreams, but often in subtle ways and not directly. One such study using the smell of roses, the smell of rotten eggs, or a neutral smell as a control at the onset of REM sleep didn't produce dreams dealing specifically with odors. However, the rose scent frequently produced pleasant dreams, while the offensive smell produced negative or unpleasant dreams. In general, studies of external stimuli have produced mixed results, with some people tending to be sensitive, but many more are not. The jury is still out.

In an anecdotal report, Cal T., who fell asleep in his recliner while watching a poker tournament on TV, dreamed of a large hairy monster who was hungry. While the monster wasn't exactly scary, neither was anybody comfortable around him because he had the potential for harming them. Cal didn't want to rile him and, in fact, felt a little sorry for this starving animal, so he began gathering food for the creature.

When Cal awoke from the vivid dream, he puzzled over it, then laughed when he realized he'd seen a commercial featuring Sasquatch several times during the show (and probably again while he dozed). He had incorporated the catch phrase "Feed Your Wild Side" into his dream. He was convinced that external stimuli influenced his dream. Did the dream have another meaning as well? Perhaps, but Cal wasn't buying it.

BIG DREAMS

What Carl Jung called "big dreams" have been discussed elsewhere, but merit further mention here because of their potency and nature. They're those exceptional dreams, often described as spiritual or trans-formative in nature, with such a profound effect that they stay with the dreamer for years. They're usually powerful, highly emotional, and the dreamer awakens with a sense of awe and wonderment.

These special dreams are very like the waking peak experiences described by Abraham Maslow, and which he attributed to some self-actualized people and most transpersonal self-actualized people. It's only logical that they would also appear in dream form.

Ford W. dreamed:

I was dressed in a wetsuit and standing on a river bank with some friends. One person and I left the group to enter the river and went into an underground area to find the source of the river. We each had a small oxygen tank and lights on our foreheads. My oxygen ran out, but I got some air by holding my head up close to the top gaps in the tunnel. I told my companion to go back with what little air he had left, but I was going on without him. He turned back.

I continued swimming on and finally reached an open area with tall, sheer sides. On one side was a beautiful, very high waterfall, the source of the river I'd been looking for. However, I could see light fad-ing at the top, and I crawled onto a shelf because I was tired, cold, and exhausted. Suddenly, a robed figure that I thought of as a guide was above me in mid air. He said he would help me get back to my friends, but he couldn't guarantee that I would make it. I decided to rest and said I would think about it.

In the morning, I looked up to the sunlight. Knowing I couldn't climb out, I wondered why my guide couldn't just lift me to the ground at the top. As soon as I had the thought, I found myself standing on the ground above and knew this was a miraculous event. My thought or intention had propelled me upward. I was awestruck, seemed to glow inside, and felt immensely blessed as I stood beside the waterfall. Those feelings lingered long after I awoke, and I was on a high for days.

Ford said he felt this dream was about the serious struggles in his life and how a powerful inner need had compelled him to find his way to the Source, God. Even though he had the dream some years ago, he still remembers the awe he felt and considers it an important spiritual dream. Just thinking about it is uplifting for him.

While Carl Jung would call this a big dream, Abraham Maslow would say that it resembles a peak experience of the sort experienced by self-actualized or transpersonal self-actualized people.

PAST-LIFE DREAMS

Have you ever had a dream about being in another time period, such as a soldier in Alexander's army, a farmer's wife in China, or a shopkeeper in France during the time heads were rolling? Were these dreams filled with emotion and shown in brilliant color and detail? Could you feel yourself in that different skin? Do you remember it still? If so, you may have experienced a past-life dream.

It's okay if you don't believe in reincarnation. Whether or not you believe your dream took you back to a real experience or a fantasy one, you can deal with your dream material in the same way you would approach any other. Every dream comes for a reason and should be interpreted as if it brings you a message. How can you apply information from this story of the past to enrich your life today?

Leslie B. had this dream:

I was an officer in charge of a ragtag bunch of Confederate soldiers on a mission behind enemy lines. We had to run a river blockade and arrive at a railroad station on a particular day, capture an important doctor and his daughter, and take them back south. As we made our way north we procured Yankee uniforms wherever and however we could, so that we could disguise ourselves and accomplish our mission. We had a few skirmishes along the way, and I remember one of our young boys with black curly hair always crawled among the dead and wounded, studying their faces to see if one of them was his brother. It was a sad sight.

We were able to take the man and girl fairly easily, but we had to move fast through a vast wooded area on our return, and we were without any food supplies and had damned little ammunition. We foraged as best we could as we traveled on foot to our destination. Still, our bellies were all stuck to our backbones, and I'd never been so hungry in my life. I could have kissed a grizzled, bandy-legged sergeant when he showed up at camp with a pair of squealing little pigs, one under each arm. I didn't ask where they came from.

Leslie reported that she (yes, Leslie is a woman) could see, feel, and smell every element in the dream. Color and emotion were very vivid. For a moment after she woke, she could still feel a sense of danger, apprehension, and gnawing, awful hunger. She felt as if she'd actually been that young officer.

Was this a past-life dream? Had she really lived that experience a hundred and fifty years before? She was open to the idea of reincarnation and felt that she had lived that life, but what else could account for such a realistic tale? Had she seen a movie or read a book with similar events and characters? She didn't recall such a scene. Was this part of some sort of genetic memory? She was from the South, and she had several ancestors who fought in the Civil War. Perhaps genetic memory could account for it. Was it, as Carl

Jung might suggest, something from the collective unconscious? Such reports (and they happen fairly often) are next to impossible to explain or prove in any scientific way.

We are still left with the question of why Leslie had this dream. What was the central idea of the experience? The gist of the story was about someone doing his duty and accomplishing a mission. But there's more. What did she feel upon awaking? She felt apprehension, danger, and a true sense of what real hunger was like. Her thoughts immediately went to mail she'd received the day before, pleas from two organizations asking for help, one to feed disaster victims, the other to provide meals for the homeless. She often donated to such causes and was on everybody's mailing list, so she'd tossed those pleas. This dream had materialized from her unconscious so that she could experience true hunger and fear for her own safety. Leslie retrieved the mailings from the wastebasket, got out her checkbook, and helped feed those hungry people with a better sense of empathy.

Edgar Cayce might say that, after the dream, she could put herself in the shoes of other people in a similar plight and remember that we must help one another. Maslow might suggest that her empathy was a being need of a self-actualized person.

Nick T., a medical researcher, recounted a very vivid dream he'd had several years before, one that he says has stayed with him for more than a decade and probably will always be with him.

I was a Native American. It was probably sometime in the 1700s or 1800s. I was in a canoe and was in the Straits of Mackinac. I was bringing someone to the West End of Bois Blanc island. The person was dead, and there was a great sadness about his passing. I brought him to shore on Bois Blanc island, and a small group of people met me there and took the body. With great weariness and sadness I left the west end of the Island and paddled to the next island, Round Island.

Once I came up on Round Island, several native men met me. They all knew what had happened. Sadness was shared by all. We stood together in silence. I was given a blanket to put over my shoulders, and a few minutes later I was directed to a small hut to rest. As I stretched out on the ground to get ready to sleep, a young beautiful woman entered the hut, as was tradition, to comfort me. I held her close but did not do any other thing because the sadness was so heavy, yet I was very grateful for her presence.

Nick also reported that there was something he knew about this land prior to the dream, and then something he discovered afterward. "Bois Blanc Island is a place my family used to take us children every summer when I was growing up. My grandfather owned quite a bit of property up there. It is next door to Mackinaw Island and four times bigger, but less well known, *and* there is an actual Indian burial ground on the west end of the island. It's called the Juntunen Site, named after the owners of the land at the time of the discovery. A University of Michigan team came down to study it in the 1960s. I remember seeing the burial site and looking at all of the graves while the U of M team was there. I was only a child. My mother said that I stood there, very still, watching them for a long time.

"What I found out about the area *after* the dream startled me. I found out that they had discovered an ancient burial ossuary interred on Round Island, in the exact location I dreamed that I went to. I had to look up this word. It means more of a box that the bones were placed in, not laid out like in a coffin. I don't know what it all means, but I have always had great reverence for this area. And I believe that I had been there in a previous lifetime as a Native American warrior. I think the tribe that is buried on Bois Blanc Island is the Ojibway."

What precipitated such a dream? When asked that question, Nick said that he was going through a very painful breakup at that time. The grief had triggered the dream or the memory of those feelings from a previous life, or, as Jung might suggest, a grief archetype from the collective unconscious. Nick also felt that some of the people in the dream were people with whom he might have shared that life, including the one who'd died in his dream and the girl, a brief previous acquaintance who comforted him again.

Those who entertain the idea of past lives and karma (the cosmic law of cause and effect) have suggested that people from the past often re-enter our lives so that old misunderstandings, betrayals, and grievances can replay with more positive outcomes, and loved ones can share our lives again.

Consider this report by Karla L. who said, "I've had a number of dreams that were set in a past lifetime and explained situations or conditions in this current one." The following is an example:

> I'm lying in bed in what I sense is a stone building with a broad open-to-the-outside corridor that runs past my open door. I feel that I'm an older woman.
>
> A man walks past my door, and I recognize him as a person I'd worked with here in my area some years ago. He turns back and enters my room. He's the same person but with another identity, and I call him by the name of his previous identity, don Teodoro. He was my doctor, and he often came in to check on me. But it surprised me this time when he came to the side of the bed, reached across me, and grabbed a pillow that he held over my face, smothering me. I was too weak to struggle and evidently died!

"When I awoke," Karla said, "I realized why I'd never completely trusted the man I'd been working with in the present lifetime, although he'd felt so familiar when we first met. A very psychic friend some months later when hearing me tell the dream said I mustn't hold it against him, for it had been an act of euthanasia! He had wanted to end my suffering."

Was Karla's experience a past life dream, genetic memory, a dream in a historical setting, or something from the collective unconscious? Can anyone be sure?

Karla believes it was a recall of a past life along with the trauma that she clung to from the original incident. She also said that, "Up to the time of the dream in my current life, I'd often struggled for breath with asthma, allergies, bronchitis, and pneumonia. After the dream recall of that experience of the earlier lifetime, I've had no more breathing problems! And it's now been many, many years of easy breathing." She seemed to have released the smothering reaction to this possible past-life event at some level of her consciousness.

ENCOUNTERS WITH DEAD PEOPLE IN DREAMS

We've dealt with the issue of the dead previously, but the dreams in this section are a bit different. They seemed to the dreamers to be *real* experiences and encounters with people who have died in this lifetime and subsequently shown up in their dreams. Most of the time, such appearances can be treated as any other character would be. They are emblematic of some aspect of you, represent a situation or a trait, or might bring to mind an earlier part of your life. At other times these encounters seem very real—and very realistic.

A couple of years after the death of her father, Fran B. saw him in her dream.

> *I met my father, who looked very healthy and happy. He seemed glad to see me, and I was thrilled to see him. I threw my arms around him, and we hugged. I laughed and said, "I thought my arms would probably go through you since you're dead."*
>
> *He laughed as well. "No," he said, "I'm very real."*

When I awoke I felt elated and was sure that I had actually been
with my dad.

Did Fran actually meet with her father in some ethereal dimension? Or was her dream simply a wishful fantasy to comfort her? Your own belief system must determine your answers, but the result of Fran's dream (or experience, as some would call it) was contentment and a renewal of her faith. She felt her dream was a real meeting.

In a different sort of dream encounter, Ellen M. recounted the following:

It was nighttime, and I was at some kind of open-air festival. The site
was a grassy valley among gently rolling hills. There were several areas
of activity where campfires were lit, and there was a general feeling
of gaiety among the many groups of people gathered. As I wandered
around taking in the sights, I met Lucy, an old friend I hadn't seen in
ages. We exchanged warm greetings, and I asked what she was doing
these days.

"I'm with Jenna and her twins a lot. She's had some difficulties
lately."

I nodded. Recalling at that moment what a beautiful voice Lucy
had, I said, "I'm going to that gathering over there. Come with me. I
know they'd love to hear you sing."

She smiled and said, "I'd better not. Not everybody can hear me,
you know."

I remembered then that Lucy had been dead for several years and
not many of the living people would be able to hear her sing. We chuck-
led, chatted for a bit, then parted.

Did Ellen have an actual encounter with Lucy? Was this a dream to
be interpreted in the usual ways instead? Was it both?

If this was a dream to be interpreted, what is the central idea? This is about a woman who, in gatherings of people, discovers when to "give voice" to something and when to remain silent. Ellen was a very opinionated person (as had been Lucy) who needed to realize that many people didn't pay any attention to her opinions, and there were times she should keep her mouth closed.

Sounded like good advice to Ellen. But who was Jenna, and what about her twins? Ellen recalled that Lucy had a daughter, but she wasn't sure of her name. Jenna seemed vaguely familiar, but Ellen knew nothing of twins. Since Lucy had lived in another city, Ellen called a mutual friend there to get more information.

"Oh, yes," the friend said. "Lucy's daughter Jenna had twin girls about six years ago, and she has been going through such an ordeal. She's just had surgery for breast cancer, and her husband has lost his job."

Indeed Jenna had had some difficulties as Lucy had said, and she had twins, born a couple of years after Lucy had died, that Ellen knew nothing about. Did this new knowledge change the interpretation of Ellen's dream? Did it verify that she'd had a real encounter with her dead friend? Perhaps. Or maybe it was both. To be sure, she vowed to curb her tongue *and* to pray for Lucy, Jenna, the twins, and the husband.

RECURRING DREAMS

Have you ever had the same dream over and over? Recurring dreams sometimes plague dreamers. Such dreams are like exclamation points, shouted messages calling attention to important information that needs to be dealt with—most often something related to emotional or high-anxiety issues. With varying frequency, these dreams pop up to capture your attention and call out a desperate inner need. Sometimes these dreams are weeks or months apart; sometimes they're years apart. Rarely do they occur almost every night as in the following example.

A shy high school girl reported this dream:

I'm walking down the aisle in my wedding dress. The church is full of people and the groom (a stranger) is waiting at the altar. I'm very excited and happy. Just as I reach the altar, a monster comes roaring in the side door, disrupts the wedding, and everyone flees for the door.

She'd been having the dream almost every night for the past two years. When asked what disrupting events had been going on for the past two years, she replied that her family had moved seventeen times during that period. Hard to believe, isn't it? This is a perfect illustration of her powerful need for love and belongingness (the wedding) and the profound effect this lack of fulfillment has on her. She desperately wants to join in and be a part of the group, but she has learned that just as she begins to make friends and form attachments to special people, another move comes to uproot her. Now she hesitates to join in at new schools and in new neighborhoods. She has become withdrawn because she knows the moving monster will eventually ruin everything. What she didn't recognize is that the monster is her fear, and it's of her own making. Hopefully, counseling helped her overcome her fear and learn to make the best of her time—however long or short—with new friends.

Faith T. began having a recurring dream when her children were small. She noticed that it always happened just before a long visit from an older family member, who was both extremely narcissistic and a troublemaker who invariably caused family problems. She recalled:

I dreamed I was a nurse in a large charity hospital. I looked out the window and saw a large tornado approaching. My immediate concern was for the patients. We held hands and made a long rope out the win-

dow, down the building, and to the ground. I led them along a specific path to safety.

This approaching tornado dream begins in a charity hospital setting, which lets her know this is a dream about charity, healing, and "patience" (patients). The approaching tornado is the destructive emotional turmoil sure to be a result of the visit from the family member. The message to Faith was that she was to be an example (lead the way) by being patient and charitable in her dealings. She said that her children still laugh and say that they can deal with any recalcitrant soul because their mother trained them so well to cope with that relative.

Erica recalled having a recurring dream as a teenager that she'd never figured out but still remembered.

I was with a group of girlfriends and werewolves were after us. The werewolves drove red pickup trucks. We tried to protect ourselves from these roving bands of creatures, but the only way we could do it was to wrap quarters in aluminum foil and throw them at the werewolves chasing us.

Freud wasn't familiar with pickup trucks, but I suspect that most modern psychoanalysts as well as dream experts in a variety of fields wouldn't have any problem with this one. Erica, like most teenaged girls, was coming to grips with her sexuality. This is a contemporary version of Little Red Riding Hood and her encounters with a wolf and the dangers of the world. How could she protect herself? With little foil-wrapped packets from vending machines that took quarters—with condoms. She was being reminded over and over of danger (red) and a need for protection.

When the dream's meaning hit her, Erica's expression clearly signaled that inner "ding" that comes with a correct interpretation—she even blushed a bit.

Another dreamer, Alexandra, reports that for the past twenty or so years she has had a very different sort of recurring dream. Whenever she has trouble in her life such as a bad relationship, financial woes, difficulty getting along with her family, or some similar circumstance, she dreams of pulling her teeth. "It starts out with one, then that feels soooo good that I begin pulling out all my teeth. I think this symbolizes the tooth being the source of pain, and the pulling of it being the resolution of the trouble. In other words, get rid of the problem."

RECURRING THEMES

Recurring themes are similar to recurring dreams except the content isn't exactly, or almost exactly, the same. For example, Melanie, a businesswoman who is also an aspiring novelist, dreams frequently of trying to get something that is just out of her reach. She is frustrated, but she keeps trying. In her waking life she has won many contests for her writing and has been accepted by an agent. She's even had interest by several editors, but for various reasons, a publishing contract has eluded her thus far. Should Melanie give up? Her dreams seem to encourage her to keep trying.

Suzanne, a physical therapist, often dreams of being pursued by a ferocious fire-breathing dragon. Sometimes the dragon flies, at other times it's in the water or various other places, but it's always after her. She's even learned to transform the dragon mentally when she encounters it, to something playful and harmless like Puff the Magic Dragon. When asked who the hot-tempered or fire-breathing person was in her life, Suzanne replied, "Oh my teenage son, definitely. He's very hot tempered, and we get into some heated arguments." She found she dealt with these times best by walking away or teasing him into a better humor.

But she later added that she'd been having the dragon dream since she was a child, long before her son came on stage. Who was the dragon back then? Suzanne identified her father as the one who scared her with his "fire-breathing" manner when she was young. It sounds as if Suzanne has been trying to escape from fire-breathing dragons—her father and her son. She's been trying to transform those scary dragons into harmless ones even in her sleep.

This idea of being aware you're having a dream and influencing dream content (lucid dreaming) is something that we'll look at in more detail in the next chapter.

Things to Remember and Exercises to Do

Remember:
- Nothing of any consequence in life happens without being previewed in a dream.
- Big dreams often come at times of great spiritual growth.
- Past-life dreams may be real or come from the collective unconscious. They represent lessons to be learned.
- Recurring dreams or themes are like messages with exclamation points! Pay attention!

Exercises to Do:

1. Precognitive or telepathic dreams usually occur for a reason, and many people have reported such experiences. Have you ever had a precognitive, telepathic, or prophetic dream? Why do you think it happened? Inquire among at least five of your friends and family if they've ever had such a dream (or even a similar waking experience). If so, ask when and why they think it happened.

2. Have you ever had a "big dream" of the sort described by Carl Jung, the kind that seems to stay in your mind for years afterward? Do you remember the profound feelings that dream created in you? Some say that if you still vividly recall a dream, it still has relevance in your life. If you've never recorded it, record it in your dream journal now along with the approximate date it occurred. Analyze it just as if you'd had it recently using the methods described in Chapter 2.

CHAPTER 9

Consciously Directing Your Dreams

Every night you rival Steven Spielberg, one of the founders of DreamWorks, with the marvelous dreamwork *you* direct while you're asleep. Although these directorial endeavors are largely unconscious, there are ways you can consciously direct and influence your dreams. Some of these are updates on centuries-old techniques; others are more recently devised methods. They include a variety of means that range from simple suggestions to lucid dreaming, and they also include guided imagery, hypnosis, and a current approach to dream incubation.

A brief example of an incubated dream is one by Celeste C., who had broken out in hives. She'd never had skin problems before, so she consulted several doctors, but none of the remedies helped. This went on for several months. She tried eliminating various things from her diet, to no avail. A strong believer in the body, mind, and spirit connection, she finally suggested to herself that if the hives were due to estrogen pills she was taking, which were dark green, she would dream of the color green. Celeste got more than she bargained for. That night she dreamed of an air conditioning filter simply clogged with the green estrogen pills. There's not much need for interpretation there. She stopped taking the pills and the hives gradually disappeared, never to return.

As in Celeste's example, most of these techniques for influencing or controlling dreams begin with suggestion, either by you or someone else. One of those methods you may have already used if you've suggested to yourself that you will remember your dreams. The others described in this chapter you may or may not choose to pursue.

HYPNOSIS AND DREAMS

Many people think of hypnosis as something almost magical. Their only experience with it may involve seeing a stage magician or one on TV who makes people act like washing machines or clucking chickens. Actually, hypnosis is simply focusing on following suggestion while being in a relaxed state. For an assortment of reasons some people are more suggestible than others (they're the ones usually picked by the stage hypnotists), and there are various stages ranging from light hypnosis to a state so deep that surgery may be performed without anesthetic. If you are reasonably intelligent, can focus your attention, and can allow yourself to relax and follow directions, you can be hypnotized.

Hypnosis can be used as a sort of "super suggestion" to help recall dreams or to focus on a specific type of dream. Studies have shown that subjects who were hypnotized and given suggestions that they would dream a solution to a problem were much more successful than those who tried another problem-solving method. The majority of the former group attributed their success to a hypnotically induced dream.

Have you ever been interrupted by the alarm clock, a garbage truck, or a crying child before you finished an important or interesting dream? Did you know that you can be hypnotized to return and finish the dream? Have you ever worked and worked with what you knew was an important dream, but the meaning continued to elude you? Usually a hypnotist can take you back to the dream, and you can interpret it easily, often with great emotion, insight, and sometimes surprise.

Nicole reported this dream:

I was swimming deep underwater, without scuba gear but with great ease, and came to a gate. A beautiful dolphin guarded it, and as I approached, he opened the gate and gave me a book, a very old and weighty volume. I felt a tremendous sense of awe at this marvelous gift.

Nicole always had loved dolphins in waking life, even noting that if she couldn't be a person, she'd want to be a dolphin. She thought of them as majestic, almost spiritual creatures that loved people, were playful and very intelligent, and always made her heart leap when she saw them. The ocean represents both the vast unconscious and the mysteries of the spirit. Gates are places of passage or entries to areas that are protected or barred from intrusion. Books, particularly like the one in her dream, are ancient sources of learning or information.

Nicole couldn't remember the name of the book she was given, although she knew it was very important. She didn't understand the entire meaning of the dream, but she knew that it held significance in her life. Being a hypnotist herself, she knew that hypnosis could help her retrieve the information she wanted, so she called on a fellow hypnotherapist and friend to "put her under."

Under hypnosis, Nicole re-entered the dream and easily came up with the central idea. This was a transformative dream telling her that she had learned the appropriate lessons (the book) in her life and it was time to move on (the open gate). She continued the dream while still hypnotized and at the end she broke forth from the sea as an eagle and soared far above the water, unfettered and free.

When she came fully awake tears were running from her eyes, but she was smiling and had a radiant expression. She later reported that, even months afterward, she had only to think of the eagle to recapture the exhilaration of soaring in the boundless sky. She said the memory was always enough to lift the foulest of moods or overcome any frustration. She felt a renewed sense of purpose and felt that "the sky was the limit."

Hypnosis can also help you deal with nightmares and troublesome recurring dreams in a similar manner. Such dreams can be fully explored with a hypnotherapist so you can pinpoint and work on the precipitating issues.

Can you have a dream while you're hypnotized? Yes, hypnosis can be used to generate a dream—or something akin to a dream—while in a trance. The resulting material may be interpreted the same way as a regular dream, either when fully alert or still under hypnosis. It's a viable therapeutic technique. While hypnosis is a fairly simple process, it's important to remember that it isn't a parlor game or something to be used to assuage curiosity. Such digging around in the unconscious is best done with the help of a trained mental health professional. It can sometimes be risky to meet "monsters of the mind" before you're ready.

GUIDED IMAGERY

Guided imagery techniques aren't usually thought of as hypnosis, but they may be a distant cousin in that they begin with relaxation and follow with suggestions by a guide or leader who gives a particular protocol to follow, usually some sort of fantasy journey. For example, the leader might say, "Picture yourself walking down a road . . . notice your surroundings."

You place yourself in whatever setting pops up spontaneously. You may be on a country lane, an asphalt road through the woods, the street where you live, or any other place your mind conjures. The guided imagery trips may be done with individuals, but they're often done with groups, particularly as an exercise to explore self-awareness or any of several motivational topics.

The cues given by the leader are minimal and deliberately ambiguous to encourage the use of your own creative, imaginative abilities to weave a story similar to a dream, but more than a daydream.

But *are* these journeys dreams? No, but if done properly (and the images aren't forced), they come from the same place (the reservoir of your own conscious and subconscious experience) and may be interpreted in the same way. When we talk about the whole area of directing your dreams, the boundaries of what *is* or what *isn't* a dream get a little fuzzy.

Guided imagery exercises help you use your imagination to explore your unconscious in prescribed methods for several reasons: to solve simple problems; clarify specific issues; remove creative or mental blocks; recognize your talents, purpose, and ambitions; engage in a sort of meditation; and gain a better understanding of symbolism.

Roberto Assagioli regularly used these kinds of exercises, and current practitioners of his psychosynthesis methods frequently use such techniques for identifying and working with various subpersonalities or other parts of the psyche. For those interested in learning more, search for websites online using some combination of the following keywords: psychosynthesis, subpersonalities, or psychosynthesis exercises.

DREAM INCUBATION

In the days before psychotherapists, suppliants went to the temples in places like Delphi or Alexandria and performed stylized rituals to incubate, or induce, dreams to help solve their problems. The next morning the priest would interpret the answer received during sleep. We can perform a modern version of this custom by devising our own rituals to incubate dreams in order to help with our own life problems. Many people claim that inventions, musical compositions, and literature have resulted from dreams.

A well-known inventor from Houston told me that he first dreamed about an invention, then mulled over the information and tinkered with the idea on paper and in his workshop. When he was ready to proceed, another dream would come to help him refine the product. (Note that he used and applied the information first, then was in an *expectant* state for the second dream.)

If this indeed works, does it mean we can look to our own inner self for guidance? Yes. You can learn to incubate a dream to help you solve problems, provide information, or give direction. As in ancient days, you can perform a ritual for incubation, although it's unlikely that you can use a temple or church to sleep in as the Greeks or Egyptians did.

Several contemporary dream workers outline a process or ritual to observe for good results, among them Dr. Gayle Delaney, co-director of the Delaney & Flowers Dream Center in San Francisco. In her book *All About Dreams*, she gives a long version of the incubation process, a short version, and a very short version. I prefer a modification of the short version. I would add that before you begin, you should think about the issue you want to address in your dreams and what you intend to do with any information you receive. Intention is a very important prerequisite. Are you going to use the information to improve your life, understand yourself, or foster your growth in some way? If so, you might want to add a short prayer or meditation if it's your habit to do so, then follow these steps to incubate your dream:

1. Clearly and succinctly write out your question in your dream journal.
2. Repeat the question over and over to yourself as you relax and fall asleep.

Follow your normal procedure for recording dreams. If you don't remember your dream, try again the next night.

An Incubation Dream Experiment

Several years ago, Janet P. was brushing her teeth one morning and noticed a large brownish spot on the left side of her neck. It was an irregular circle about two inches in diameter and looked more like dirt than a bruise. She examined it more closely in the mirror and poked at it. The spot didn't hurt, wasn't sore, and wouldn't wash off. Then she noticed two more such discolorations. One was on the inside of her left wrist, and the other was on the inside of her elbow. They looked like larger versions of her grandmother's age spots, but she was too young for such things. It was a puzzle. She became concerned. Was this some sort of disease?

As part of a group that worked with dreams, Janet had recently heard about incubating dreams for information. Knowing that her subconscious mind was aware of the cause of her skin problem, she decided this was the perfect time to experiment with dream incubation. That evening before bed, she examined the places on her skin again and decided that it was important to know the cause of the discoloration for both health and cosmetic reasons. She prayed about the situation and wrote in the journal she always kept beside her bed: *I will have a dream about the cause of these three large spots on my skin so that I can attend to the problem.* Then she changed the statement to a question spoken aloud: "What is causing the three large spots on my skin?"

Janet got into bed and, as she relaxed, repeated her question over and over. She awoke the next morning with the following "sniff" dream.

I went to a doctor's office, and he ushered me to his desk and asked me to have a seat. He was an ordinary looking man, middle-aged with dark hair and wearing a white lab coat. He was a stranger, but very pleasant. The doctor sat down at his desk across from me and picked up a file folder with some papers inside. He opened the folder, looked up at me and said, "It is sniff . . . sniff . . . sniffficant. It is sniff . . . sniff . . . sniffficant. It is sniff . . . sniff . . . sniffigant."

He repeated this several times until I grew impatient. I thought to myself that I'd be there all night waiting for him to say "significant." I decided that I'd just call my own doctor in the morning.

Janet was deflated that she hadn't gotten the information she sought, but she followed her dream's suggestion (did you notice that she was aware that she was dreaming during the doctor visit?). She called her dermatologist and made an appointment. Luckily he could see her the following morning, and the spots were still there when he examined her.

The dermatologist asked immediately, "Do you wear Shalimar perfume?"

Surprised by the question, Janet told him that she did. As it turns out, she had something called Berloque dermatitis. Shalimar and a few other perfumes and colognes contained something called oil of berga-mot, which often caused phototoxic reactions. Basically, it becomes a super-fine tanning agent when it comes in contact with the sun—and in some cases, also causes a rash. The day before she'd noticed the spots, she'd showered and dressed as usual, spraying her cologne on her wrist, elbow, and neck, and had gone out. That afternoon she'd come home, changed into her bathing suit, and taken her son to the neighborhood pool. She read and sunbathed while he had swimming lessons. The cologne-sprayed areas tanned really, really well. (The issue has since been resolved by most perfume companies using bergamot in their formulas.)

On the way home from her dermatologist's office, Janet thought again about her dream. Why hadn't she gotten the information as she slept? Disappointed that her incubation experiment was a flop, she was mentally grumbling when it dawned on her that her dream *had* provided the information. She'd simply missed it in her impatience. The dream doctor had told her over and over the problem was sniff . . . sniff . . . sniffican*t*—a perfect replication of the sound and smell aspects of her cologne atomizer as she spritz . . . spritz . . . spritzed it her customary three times.

A Caution about Incubation and Directed Dreams

Elated that her dreams *had* come through for her and realizing her own impatience and interpretation skills were to blame for her disappointment, Janet P. was determined to try incubation again and again. She figured she could incubate dreams about anything and everything! The mysteries of the ages were open to her.

Night after night she went through her incubation ritual—asking weighty questions, expecting profound answers. Morning after morning she awoke with nothing. No dreams. Nada.

After a week or so, Janet had the following dream:

I was in some sort of shop in town, talking on their phone. I made one call after another and talked and talked. The proprietor of the store came up behind me and poked me on the shoulder with his finger to get my attention. I looked up at him, and he said, "Lady, would you please limit your personal calls? This is a business phone."

The message couldn't have been clearer, and Janet got it immediately. Dreams have a purpose, to conduct "business" communication. Tying up the line and attempts to over-direct dreams interfere with that purpose. Janet backed off and decided that dream incubation was fine and really worked, but it should be used judiciously.

Incubation and Adjunctory Prayers

Sometimes life situations seem so difficult that simple prayers are inadequate, and cries for direction become desperate adjuring, beseeching, and pleading for help or information. Paula M. found herself in such dire straits. A deeply religious woman, she had been struggling for many years with her husband's hurtful, demeaning communication problems and behavior patterns with both her and others. Wanting to solve the problem, she'd been praying, meditating, and trying to consciously understand the issue, but she was about at the end of her rope.

One night as she was preparing for bed, she picked up her Bible and opened it randomly. She found a passage in Proverbs that she'd always loved: "Trust in the Lord with all thine heart and lean not unto thine own understanding. In all thy ways acknowledge Him, and He will direct Thy paths" (Proverbs 3:5–6).

Paula pondered this message deeply as she went to bed and prepared for sleep, and she prayed: "Creator of all that is good and divine, help me. I have done all I know to do, and it's not working. I need your help, and I need it *now*." The following "ticker-tape" dream is the result of her plea.

I was sound asleep, and I saw the word "Asperger's" repeated in a continuous line, moving across my visual field like an old-fashioned ticker tape message. It seemed to be urging me, and it stirred me deeply in my sleep. Then I sat straight up in bed and, in the dark room, I saw the shadows of my bedroom furniture. The word "Asperger's" continued to move across my visual field, though I knew I wasn't asleep any longer—

a first for me! I sat up for a long time, and the message continued till I lay down and went back to sleep.

Paula said that when she thought about the dream the next morning, she *knew* her prayer had been answered with this message. She went immediately to her computer and Googled "Asperger's." She was astonished by all the information she found that explained her husband's behavior, which has helped her learn to deal with this syndrome, sometimes described as similar to high-functioning autism. Adults with Asperger's syndrome are usually intelligent but have difficulty in social situations and in showing empathy, and use ordinary communication skills in a way that makes them often seem rude and uncaring. Because of what Paula learned, she changed her relationship, expectations, and communication style with her husband. Now things are much smoother. And she says that she's learned from her dream it's true that if she *asks*, she will receive.

Group Dream Incubation

In his book *Our Dreaming Mind*, Robert Van de Castle describes a different sort of dream incubation in which a group participates as a service to one of its members. He and Dr. Henry Reed, another well-known dream expert (check out Reed's website *www.creativespirit.net/ henryreed* for lots of interesting information), worked with a person who had a problem, and the other members of the group became dream helpers. The helpers weren't told any particulars about the issue of concern, but they did offer to forgo their own dreams for one night and try to incubate a dream to help with the presenting problem. The group engaged in waking interaction to become acquainted and establish rapport with each other, and meditated and prayed together.

After a night of dreaming, Van de Castle stated that the participants gathered and reported dreams, many of which seemed to have a common element including "a black car driving into the town of

White Hall, someone being hesitant to accept an Oreo cookie . . . an ice cream cone with one scoop of chocolate and one of vanilla . . . black and white keys on a piano keyboard, and Martin Luther King, Jr., preaching in front of the White House." Besides the obvious black and white theme that developed, some dreams also depicted elements of family discord. One dreamer dreamed about a slow watch, and another about a movie in slow motion.

It turned out that the presenting issue was that the target person was a Caucasian woman who had been dating an African American man, and she was sure that her family would object. Her question was how to broach the subject with her parents. No single dream addressed the whole problem, but as they discussed the issue and combined the information from all the dreams, the helpers suggested to the target that she move slowly with her parents until she was sure that the relationship was going to be a permanent one.

This dream helper method illustrates not only dream telepathy but also that incubation can be used in service to others.

LUCID DREAMS

Have you ever awakened from a dream, engaged in some activity, then later really woken up to discover that you'd been dreaming when you thought you were awake? This event is called "false awakening" and is sometimes a precursor to lucid dreaming. (Paula's feeling that she woke up and still saw the message "Asperger's" in her physical field of vision, then went back to sleep, may have been an instance of this phenomenon, i.e., she may have been asleep the entire time.)

Have you ever become aware that you were dreaming while having a dream? That's a lucid dream. In this sort of event, dreamers become aware (though happenstance or training) that they are dreaming and can sometimes influence their dream characters or situations.

In Janet's sniff dream related earlier, she was aware that she was dreaming. You've probably had at least one or two of those experiences. While not common, neither are they rare. Researchers have suggested that women are more likely than men to have lucid dreams, and people who meditate experience them more frequently than those who don't.

Going back to ancient times, there are many reports of lucid dreams scattered throughout the literature of the major religions of the world, particularly in Christianity, Tibetan Buddhism, and Islam. Aristotle, St. Augustine, St. Thomas Aquinas, Nietzsche, and even Freud spoke of lucid dreaming, as did the Russian philosopher P. D. Ouspensky, so this isn't a new phenomenon. As long as there have been dreams, there have been accounts of lucid dreaming.

Suzanne's recurring dragon dream in the previous chapter is a good example of a spontaneous lucid dream. She becomes aware during the chase that she can transform the scary, fire-breathing dragon on her tail into Puff, a friendly dragon. She intuitively found a technique that some therapists use: dealing with recurring nightmares through confrontation in lucid dreams . . . *if* the client can be taught to be a lucid dreamer. However, that isn't always easy and may not even be wise.

Bill R.'s frosting bowl dream is another example of a spontaneous lucid dream. He reported that he often has unusual dreams when away from home, and in this instance he was spending the night at his cousin's house. His cousin's wife had made a cake earlier, and he licked the frosting bowl, which shows up here:

In my dream, I'm in a travel agent's office with my two male cousins. We're planning a trip together. I'm sitting on a high stool leaning back against the wall, listening more than participating. I fall asleep and have a dream.

In the dream-within-a-dream, I'm walking in a small town at night. The stores are all closed. I'm carrying a bowl with frosting in it and licking the frosting off my fingers.

> *I realize that I'm dreaming and have fallen asleep in the travel
> agent's office. I immediately wake myself and find I'm back in the travel
> agent's office. Shortly after that I wake up in bed at my cousin's house.*

What's so interesting about this example is that Bill dreamed that
he had a lucid dream. It wasn't his waking self that became lucid, but
his dreaming self. Boggles the mind, doesn't it?

Dr. G. Scott Sparrow's 1976 work *Lucid Dreaming: Dawning of the
Clear Light* was the first book published in North America on the subject, and is largely based on his personal experiences with being conscious while dreaming and research from his master's thesis. His lucid
dreams were first spontaneous; he later induced them using various
methods, the most successful of which was meditating in the middle
of the night after the deepest, more restorative sleep time had passed.
Some of his lucid dreams produced fear and anxiety, but most were
spiritually oriented experiences, hence, the "clear light." Sparrow is
currently a university professor and transpersonal therapist. He uses
dreams in his practice with clients but says he hasn't been very successful in teaching them lucid dreaming, and he prefers to use other
methods of dream work in the majority of cases.

Stephen LaBerge, whose PhD is in psychophysiology, is one of the
foremost current proponents of lucid dreams. In his classic 1985 book
Lucid Dreaming he credits both Ann Faraday and Patricia Garfield for
their popular dream books of the seventies with bringing the notion
of lucid dreaming into public awareness. It is still a popular—and
somewhat controversial—subject, and LaBerge continues to write and
research. He conducts training in lucid dreaming, primarily through
the Lucidity Institute, which he founded.

During the seventies and eighties something called Senoi Dream
Theory became popular, and some of the best-known dream workers
latched on to the ideas presented first by Kilton Stewart, a psychologist
who, in the thirties, visited the Senoi, a native Malaysian tribe. This tribe

was purported to be a dream-based society who practiced lucid dreaming and other interesting, unique approaches to dream work. More recently, Stewart's reports have largely been debunked by a number of diligent researchers. It seems that Stewart was more raconteur than scientist or scholar.

A LAST WORD ON DIRECTING YOUR DREAMS

While we've proven that it's possible to direct your dreams to a certain extent, the question is, is it a wise thing to do, or is it perhaps even dangerous? Experienced dream workers and researchers have opinions on both sides of the issue. The fact is that there are some psychologically vulnerable people for whom such practices might be questionable or even harmful because they could push deeply into unconscious areas and encounter repressed things they aren't equipped to deal with. Some psychologists have reported frightening and disturbing experiences of their own or with research subjects when trying to direct lucid dreams.

Alarmed when I recently heard that a young man allegedly went on a killing spree, I was further concerned when I heard that he had been obsessed with lucid dreaming. Did lucid dreaming cause his senseless behavior? I doubt it, but it's an ill-advised practice for someone as loosely tethered to reality as he was reported to be. In fact, it's probably wise to entertain those lucid dreams that come spontaneously and forgo efforts at directing lucid dreaming unless you're in a supervised situation with a mental health professional.

Dreams have an agenda, and I appreciate the advice relayed by Janet's business phone dream earlier in this chapter. Janet's experience can be generalized to most of us. While all types of directed dreams, and even regular dreams, hold a fascination for us, it's important to remember to not become so preoccupied with these phenomena that we forget to participate fully in the concerns of our waking life and lose our balance.

Things to Remember and Exercises to Do

Remember:

- You can use hypnosis to help with dreams and their meaning.
- A modern version of dream incubation can help with problem solving.
- Lucid dreaming is being aware that you're dreaming while you're dreaming.

Exercises to Do:

1. If you wish to try incubating a dream, first identify some issue or concern that you want help with. Give it serious thought. Decide what you intend to do with any information you receive. Are you going to use the information to improve your life, understand yourself, or foster your growth in some way? If so, you might add a short prayer or meditation if it's your habit to do so. Follow the procedure outlined earlier.

   - Clearly and succinctly write out your question in your dream journal.
   - Repeat the question over and over to yourself as you relax and fall asleep. Follow your normal procedure for recording dreams. If you don't remember your dream, try again the next night. Were you successful? Have you deciphered the meaning? Act on the information to transform your waking life.

PART 2

YOUR PERSONAL
DREAM SYMBOL GUIDE

Introduction

While it is true that consulting dream dictionaries isn't the best way to interpret dreams, people still like the idea of guidelines. This part provides a list of various symbols along with some possible meanings other people might associate with each symbol. Your associations may be entirely different. Space is provided for you to note your personal associations with each symbol.

As you read through this guide or look up various words, notice that some common clue words or possible meanings are presented using a variety of techniques learned earlier. For example, sometimes the clues or descriptions use roleplaying techniques, free association, metaphors and figures of speech, analogies, and often a combination of these methods and others in a random pattern. I encourage you to do the same when adding your personal associations. Write down what pops up.

Underline the suggestions that seem to ring a bell with you. The blank spaces marked as "Other" are meant to be filled in by you to personalize the symbol's associations—either with different meanings you think of, or with connections you discover through working with your dreams. You are also encouraged to add pages for symbols not listed, thus expanding the guide as you work with your own distinctive dream symbols.

The various sections are arranged to mirror the order of Chapters 3 through 7 in Part 1, which deal specifically with symbols concerning dream characters, settings, props, and actions.

Remember: Don't try to fit the suggested meanings to your dreams and assume they are correct. Your personal symbology and associations are always paramount. In addition, be sure to always look at both the literal and figurative meaning of definitions and suggestions. For example, a sponge might be defined at something that absorbs. Literally, to absorb means to soak up liquid; figuratively, to absorb may mean to internalize information or surroundings.

PEOPLE

Here you'll find an alphabetical listing of people, referencing some common professions, relationships, and categories. Descriptions are given using the roleplaying technique, and in no particular order of significance. Underline the ideas that are meaningful to you.

Remember: These are only suggested possibilities. Your personal associations are always more meaningful, so be sure to fill in the blank space after each entry. Add other entries as needed.

Acrobat — I am strong and agile; I can flip and turn and twist, often in unnatural ways. I'm a performer, an entertainer. I am flexible and well coordinated. Sometimes my surroundings turn into a real circus. Other: _____

Actor/actress — I play a part, a role, and pretend to be somebody I'm not. I put on a face (persona) for an audience and can disguise my real self very well. I change the way I act depending on the circumstances or the role I'm playing. Some say I'm an exhibitionist. Sometimes I can be a drama queen. Other:_____

Animal trainer — I teach animals to behave in desired ways. I exact discipline; I'm patient and confident. Freud might say I am the ego taming the id. It's important not to show fear.
Other: _____

Artist — I am very creative and often free spirited. My keen eye brings new insight to paper, canvas, or clay, and I pour my emotions into the medium I work with. Because creating beauty from paint or clay or stone is usually messy, my hands are rarely clean.
Other: _____

Astronaut — I am rigorously trained, and I aim for boundless space. I often fly high. I'm not tethered or restricted by earth and its laws. I'm an adventurer, a new breed of pioneer. Sometimes I'm your higher self. I'm fearless, and I enjoy seeing things from a different perspective.
Other _____

Auto mechanic — I fix things that are wrong with your car (sometimes your body), or I keep it tuned up and working properly so that you can get around without breaking down. I'm good with my hands, and I can diagnose problems.
Other: _____

Baby — I am new, helpless, and full of promise. Sometimes I'm a newly born idea or a project that needs tending. (My age can give you clues as to how old that something is.) Sometimes I'm very wise, and sometimes I'm a dumb or bad idea. And sometimes, depending on how I appear, I make people smile. I can't verbalize my feelings or control my body very well yet. I belong to you, and I need tender loving care to grow.
Other: _____

Baker — I rise early and cook up things. People who have a sweet tooth enjoy my wares. I give you sustenance, and provide your daily bread.
Other: _____

Banker — I'm in charge of your money. I encourage people to save as well as pay their loans on time to avoid trouble. Most people think I'm conservative and trustworthy, but since the recent difficulties in banking have developed, some folks don't trust me as much as they used to.
Other: _____

Bank robber — I'm furtive but brazen, and I take valuables that don't belong to me. I like to get stuff the easy way, and I steal from you. I think I can get away with things. Sometimes I am you robbing yourself in various ways.
Other _____

Bartender — I deal with spirits and sometimes listen to people's woes. I usually work at night, and I see lots of lonely people. I mix up stuff. I watch people try to drown their sorrows. It rarely works.
Other: _____

Baseball player — I'm physically fit and play for a living, for fun, or for an education. I'm a team player who's out to win. I'm into keeping score, making pitches, catching what's coming at me, and keeping my eye on the ball. Kids admire me; sometimes I'm a good role model, but sometimes I'm not. To do well, I must cooperate, but being a star has its perks. I can be a Pirate or an Angel.
Other: _____

Basketball player — I'm tall and physically fit, aggressive, play for a living, for fun, or for an education. I dribble, shoot, pass, and fake. I'm into teamwork, winning, keeping score, making goals, and defending my position. Kids admire me; sometimes I'm a good role model, but sometimes I'm not. To do well, I must cooperate, but being a star has its perks. I'm called by many names, including Bulls and Jazz.
Other: _____

Beggar — I make my way by asking for handouts from others. There's a reason I don't work for a living, but my sense of shame is long gone or well hidden. People don't like to look me in the eye. A cardboard sign with a sad story or a catchy turn of phrase is a big asset in my line.
Other: _____

Bellman — I serve by carrying a heavy load and getting folks settled into a temporary situation. I help people who need my strength. I give guidance and directions.
Other: _____

Boxer — I'm a fighter, aggressive and determined to put down my opponent. I dance around and take jabs at people. I'm strong and powerful. My ears and my nose take a real beating. Sometimes I take it on the chin, or knock you out.
Other: _____

Bride — I'm in love, newly united, and looking forward to a new wholeness and new experiences. I dress in white, walk down the aisle, and go to meet my fate. I'm hopeful and optimistic, and strengthened by joining with the masculine side. (See also Groom.)
Other: _____

Bullfighter — I am fearless and proud. I pit my cunning and skill against a ferocious opponent out to gore or kill me. Sometimes *el toro* that I must fight is stubbornness, aggression, and pride. I'm a master of cape tricks. Many think I'm inhumane.
Other: _____

Bus driver — I'm in charge of a large vehicle (sometimes a body) that takes skill to control. It's stop and go with me. I take a load of people where they want to go along a prescribed route. We're all on a journey together.
Other: _____

Butcher — I'm a cut-up. I hack up things—sometimes the English language, they say. I get to the meat of matters and provide meat for your table. Some folks think I have a gruesome occupation, but I'm used to it.
Other: _____

Butler — Although I'm a servant, I'm very formal and proud. I greet people at the door and know everybody's business. I run the household and am often the one "whodunit" in mysteries, because no one would ever suspect I have another side to my facade.
Other: _____

Carpenter — I build structures, houses, and furniture; I hammer home my point, put things together, and hit the nail on the head. I measure, lay out the framework, and do finishing. I'm industrious and humble. I'm a stickler for being on the level. Jesus was a carpenter, and I'm proud to follow in his footsteps.
Other: _____

Celebrity — I'm very well known. I show up at the "in" places and parties. Often paparazzi dog me to take my picture. I may be an entertainer, a sports figure, or simply interesting. Sometimes I cash in on my name and popularity.
Other: _____

Cheerleader — I am agile and loud. I'm very supportive of my team by urging them onward and involving the crowd. I never give up or get disheartened. I'm always on your side, pepping you up.
Other: _____

Chemist — I can be a mad scientist or magician who turns basic elements into something entirely different (sometimes even gold). In your body I can turn beans into gas, alcohol to sugar, and spinach into energy. Sometimes I blend stuff; at other times I'm good at figuring out what's in a concoction, and I can get things down to basic elements.
Other: _____

Child — I can be immature, sure, but I like to be carefree and have fun. I don't want to be an adult and have to do grown-up stuff. I'm your inner child who sometimes needs attention, or I'm memories of your earlier years. I'm playful, and sometimes scared. I need to feel safe, secure, and loved. I dream about animals a lot.
Other: _____

Clown — I have a great sense of humor. I like to get attention by making people laugh when I do goofy things. I'm a show-off, a prankster, a jester. My clothes (attitudes maybe?) are outlandish, but that's part of my role. Sometimes, underneath my makeup, I'm not so happy as I appear. Jung says I'm an archetype.
Other: _____

Coach — I work with sports teams. I direct players, help hone their skills, and promote teamwork to win games. I sometimes work with individuals to help them improve various skills including speech, drama, and life skills. I give pep talks and provide encouragement, but I'm also demanding, and I expect hard work and discipline.
Other: _____

Computer programmer — I'm very bright and technical. The computer I program may be your brain. I can store your experiences and memories and transform them into the way you think, feel, and behave. It's amazing how much stuff is stored inside that you can't see and don't know about.
Other: _____

Construction worker — I do similar work to the carpenter, but I'm often a helper doing various jobs. You don't need a college degree to do my job, but you do need to be willing to help, hard working, and fit. I help erect structures, buildings, homes, and other things.
Other: _____

Convict — I'm paying for my crime, but I'll swear on a stack of Bibles that I'm innocent. Prison is a tough life, and I long to be free. I can hardly wait to get out; I don't look good in stripes.
Other: _____

Cook, chef — I cook up things (mostly food, but sometimes ideas or projects or nefarious deeds). I get all fired up, but I also can put things on the back burner. I've been known to do a slow simmer or a slow burn. I love to make high calorie sauces and desserts with butter, but I can be persuaded to make egg white omelets and salads.
Other: _____

Counselor — I'm very perceptive and wise. I listen to your concerns and often give advice or direction. Sometimes I'm your inner counselor, there to help you along your best pathway. Guidance is my game.
Other: _____

Cowboy — I ride herd and keep things rounded up, together, and going in the same direction. I'm tough and not afraid of hard work. I often sleep under the stars. Some folks think what I do is romantic. It's not.
Other: _____

Dancer — I leap and twirl and stay on my toes. I am graceful and disciplined and balanced. With a partner, I am cooperative and in sync. I can be energetic and fun, or express great joy or other emotions. I can dance around or do a tap dance to avoid providing direct answers or making a commitment.
Other: _____

Daughter — I'm the result of my mother and father, and similar to both of them in many ways. I can be dutiful and loving and usually take my responsibilities seriously.
Other: _____

Dentist — I take care of your teeth (and maybe your words). I can repair and restore, and I know the drill. I'm the guy with his hands in your mouth reminding you to floss. Sometimes people dread seeing me because I can cause pain or discomfort.
Other: _____

Detective, investigator — I look into things, mostly crimes. I can be private or with a law enforcement agency of some sort. I find out who did what by nosing around. I see that perpetrators pay in one way or another. Sometimes I'm the hero of a mystery.
Other: _____

Director — I'm in charge, and I may show up as your higher self. In bands and orchestras I keeps things harmonious, rhythmic, and together. I foster cooperation by leading and conducting myself well. In making movies and television shows, I'm the one who tells actors where to go and yells, "Action!"
Other: _____

Doctor — I am a diagnostician and a healer. I'm concerned with your body and physical health, and I encourage good health habits. I know that your mental well-being is also tied to your physical issues, so often I'm a counselor as well. Sometimes I cut things out or give you medicine. Some people doctor the books.
Other: _____

Doorman — I let the desirable in and keep others out. I am a protector. I can be the ego or the censor of your psyche. Nobody gets by me who doesn't belong, or who is disturbing.
Other: _____

Drug addict — I've lost control, and the desire for harmful things rules my behavior. I'm overwhelmed by my baser instincts (the id). I'm compulsive and weak. I don't want to deal with the world or my problems; I'd rather get high and drift than change. You can't help me unless I want to be helped.
Other: _____

Drug dealer — I take advantage of the weakness of others. I'm more interested in cash than ethics. Hey, it's not my fault the mess they're in; I'm just a businessman, and I've got bills to pay.
Other: _____

Electrician — I work with wires and electrical energy. I can juice people up, turn them on, or get them wired; I keep people going. In the body I'm usually involved with the nervous system or the kundalini. I'm sometimes associated with the Holy Spirit, and I'm a powerful guy.
Other: _____

Elevator operator — I do ups and downs, sometimes in moods or states of consciousness. I work at many levels. I don't have a lot of job opportunities; most people are into self-service these days.
Other: _____

Entertainer/comedian — I thrive on making people enjoy themselves. I'm not *self*-conscious; I'm focused on making *you* happy or uplifted. I'm a ham. Sometimes that part of me is a facade and, down deep, I'm very serious. I often hide my serious side.
Other: _____

Entrepreneur — I'm a risk taker, an extrovert, and a leader. I love coming up with new ideas for businesses or for promoting other projects (sometimes social issues) and getting them off the ground. I'm a wheeler-dealer, and I can always get my hands on some cash.
Other: _____

Ethnicities — I'm different from other people in some way. Stereotypes often define me, ones like the Irish temper, the dumb Pole, and on and on. Sad, but true. At our core, we're all alike.
Other: _____

Exes — I'm a significant person or lesson from your past. Memories of me may be bittersweet or really negative. I represent endings, old business. Our karma has ended—or has it?
Other: _____

Farmer — I grow things and tend the land. I'm productive and hard-working. I provide the food you eat, the milk you drink, or the hay for animals. Sometimes I just grow trees.
Other: _____

Father — I'm the masculine energy of the person or family, the sire of attitudes and institutions and new beginnings. I'm the father of the country, of psychoanalysis, of Heaven. I can be the authority, the protector, and the judge. I am sometimes your higher self. At other times, I can be feared. I'm strict but loving and forgiving.
Other: _____

Firefighter — I'm courageous and often rescue people in trouble or cats up a tree. I work at putting out fires that come from many sources: from your belly, your fever, your anger, or from battling factions. I wear protective gear and promote fire prevention. So keep cool and don't let things get out of control. It can happen quickly.
Other: _____

Fisherman — I seek things from below the surface, or within the waters of lakes, rivers, and seas. These may be insights from the unconscious or spiritual realms. I am patient, and know about lures, bait, and nets. Many of the apostles were fishermen. Eat more fish.
Other: _____

Fitness trainer — I help people get in shape and maintain optimum flexibility, strength, and endurance. I make you look good, too. I'm part coach, cheerleader, teacher, and conscience. I'm tough, but I'll help you reach your goal. That's what you pay me for.
Other: _____

Flight attendant — I like flying high and helping others on their journey. I'm here to serve and make your trip easier. I offer directions for your safety.
Other: _____

Football player — I'm physically fit, aggressive, and play for a living, for fun, or for an education. I'm a team player who's out to win. I'm into keeping score, making goals, and keeping the other fellows from beating me. I can be defensive or offensive. I can pass, catch, run, or block. When I'm in a jam, I can punt. Kids admire me; sometimes I'm a good role model, but often I'm not. To do well, I must cooperate, but being a star has its perks. I have many names and can be a Titan, a Ram, or a Saint.
Other: _____

Foreigner — I'm from a different place or orientation. Other people don't always understand my ways or speak my language. You may think I'm strange, but I have the same problem with you.
Other: _____

Friend — I'm a buddy, a companion, a listener. I keep your secrets. We share laughs and troubles. We also share a history. I'm there when you need me. Just let me know if you want help; don't be too proud to ask.
Other: _____

Funeral director, undertaker — I mark endings. I handle passings with dignity, compassion, and grace. My job is to handle details and arrangements, and to make things easier for you when it's time to let go. Life goes on.
Other: _____

Gambler — I take chances. I get high on risks, and I hate playing it safe. I play the hand I'm dealt. Shady guys deal from the bottom of the deck, or mark cards to give them unfair advantage. I can read people well, but I keep a poker face so others can't read me.
Other: _____

Garbage collector — I pick up stuff that's no longer useful and dump it. While not many people want my job, everybody appreciates what I do. You can think of me as the colon of the system.
Other: _____

Grocer — I provide physical sustenance for people and offer choices. The bigger my store, the more selections I can offer. Folks may choose the freshest and the best, and I'm happy when they do.
Other: _____

Groom — I am the masculine, assertive part of the couple (see also Bride) that merges and unites with the intuitive, feminine side in a new beginning and partnership. Sometimes I'm nervous.
Other: _____

Hoarder — I keep junk around that I no long need. My house, my mind, my body, and my unconscious are filled with stuff I no longer have a use for but won't let go of. I hang on to things, to guilt, to grudges, to pounds, and to bad memories. You'd think I'd learn better.
Other: _____

Horseman — I ride for business or pleasure, and sometimes I bring messages. I keep a tight rein on things. I race, or sound alarms, and have been known to go headless. Sometimes I'm a jockey and, though I'm small, I control a lot of power, and ride to win. My three cohorts and I are in the Book of Revelation.
Other: _____

Housewife — I keep the family running smoothly, provide for their needs, and see to the children's care. A woman's work is never done. I sometimes feel undervalued.
Other: _____

Hunter — I look for things and often kill them. I love the outdoors and a good challenge. I frequently camouflage myself to be more effective. I'm a good tracker, and usually find what I look for.
Other: _____

Husband or man — I am the masculine principle, and represent strength and assertiveness. Currently my roles are changing. I'm not sure how I feel about that.
Other: _____

Janitor — I clean up other people's messes. Many people don't respect me, but I'm good at mopping up. I'm often invisible to others.
Other: _____

Judge/jury — I decide people's fates. I listen to both sides and make decisions. I'm usually wise. I weigh, balance, and dispense justice.
Other: _____

Killer — I cut people down needlessly. I shoot down their ideas, their self esteem, and kill their hopes and dreams—even my own. I overwork them and foster deathly bad habits with glee. I should be locked up, but you have to catch me first.
Other: _____

King — I am royalty. I can be your higher self or any authority figure who has power over you. Some believe I'm a dying breed.
Other: _____

Lama — I am a spiritual teacher in Tibetan Buddhism. I wear distinctive clothing that is particular to my order or sect. I meditate daily and practice compassion and ethics. The Dalai Lama is the spiritual leader of my group and head of the Tibetan government (in exile).
Other: _____

Lawyer — I defend people and stand up for them when they're in trouble. I also give advice on various matters, including business and real estate transactions. Some people make jokes about me and call me a shyster. Everyone deserves to have someone on their side.
Other: _____

Librarian — I love books and learning. I catalogue and organize things, and help people find information about the world or about themselves. I provide the means for entertainment, knowledge, and inspiration. I like peace and quiet.
Other: _____

Lifeguard — I'm a people watcher and a rescuer. I help people who get in over their heads, are floundering around, or get caught in undertows. I like working around water and in the sun.
Other: _____

Maid — I clean up messes and quietly serve. I make people's life go easier. I'm fairly invisible except when I don't do my job properly.
Other: _____

Mason — I build with strong bricks or stone and mortar. Line upon line, level and true, I erect walls, churches, banks, and jails. I even have an old and secret organization named after me.
Other: _____

Messenger — I deliver messages from your unconscious or superconscious self. I can come in several forms, and I've been known to wear various outfits, from uniforms to wings. Sometimes I use a bullhorn; other times I speak with a still, small voice.
Other: _____

Minister — I offer spiritual guidance, preach sermons, and tend the flock. I can represent your higher self.
Other: _____

Mother — I am the nurturer, the earth mother. I am creative, intuitive (with eyes in the back of my head), and comforting. I kiss boo-boos and give hugs.
Other: _____

Musician — I express emotions through harmony, melody, and sound. I keep time and hear the beat. I sometimes march to a different drummer.
Other: _____

Native (appearing as an uncivilized aboriginal) — I am unspoiled with a child-like approach to life, but I've been known to eat people when they intrude into my territory. I'm pure id.
Other: _____

Neighbor — I live close to you, or am the one who lives nearest in less-populated areas. I'm the other people around you. You're supposed to love me.
Other: _____

Newsperson — I report on the latest happenings. I'm supposed to be unbiased and current; I'm up on things. Sometimes the news is sad. Folks often have a tough time. Can you help?
Other: _____

Nun — Religion and the church are my life. I pray and serve and remain true to my vows. Some people would call me a goody-two-shoes. That's their problem, bless them.
Other: _____

Nurse — I'm a caretaker and provide TLC when you're ill. I do what I can to make you comfortable and see to your needs when you're in the hospital or doctor's office.
Other: _____

Oarsman — I skim the water with my oars, sometimes in cooperation with a team, to glide over the surface. I can paddle my own canoe, and I've been up the river without a paddle. I'm powerful, and I know where I'm going.
Other: _____

Oil driller — Sometimes I have to dig deep within to find what I seek: wealth, a source of great energy, hidden treasures.
Other: _____

Ophthalmologist, optometrist — I help you see clearly, and I'm concerned about any problems with your vision or viewpoint. I test you and correct you when necessary. (See also Eyes.)
Other: _____

Pilot — I fly high among the clouds. People's lives are in my hands, and I take my responsibilities seriously. I'm high-minded and can represent the higher self.
Other: _____

Plumber — I keep the pipes clean and the water running freely. Sometimes things get clogged up or break down for one reason or another. I'm the guy metaphorically in charge of the urinary system of your body. Drink plenty of water.
Other: _____

Policeman — I deal with those who break the law and remind others not to get into trouble. I'm tough but fair. I protect you and keep you in line. Most of the time I'm a good guy, but mine is a stressful job.
Other: _____

Politician — I represent you, or should. Sometimes I talk out of both sides of my mouth. Many people don't trust me. I would like to be a true statesman, but temptations are very great to go along with pressure and get along with everyone. Sometimes my power goes to my head.
Other: _____

Postman — I bring messages. Pay attention to what I leave for you.
Other: _____

President — I'm the person in charge, the ultimate authority in business or government. The buck stops here. I am powerful and hopefully wise, decisive, and compassionate. Yes-men can be an issue.
Other: _____

Priest — I'm a spiritual leader, a higher-self figure, who engages in church rituals and forgives wrongdoing.
Other: _____

Prince, princess — We are heirs to royalty. We're storybook heroes and heroines, a perfect ideal or fantasy partner. We're sometimes pampered and spoiled.
Other: _____

Principal — I'm the authority figure of schools and learning. You have to answer to me if you get into trouble. I truly love children, but sometimes I make them nervous.
Other: _____

Private detective — I observe, investigate, and dig through your secrets. You can't hide from me. (See also Detective.)
Other: _____

Prosecutor — My aim is to prove you guilty and make you pay for your crimes. I'm tough and assertive, dogged and dedicated. Usually I'm also poorer and less experienced than high-powered defense attorneys.
Other: _____

Psychologist, psychiatrist — I listen, analyze your behavior, and help you understand why you do what you do. I probe the unconscious and examine your motivations. I'm non-judgmental and say "hmmm" a lot.
Other: _____

Queen — I am the ruler of the realm, the queen bee, the authority—or possibly I'm married to him. Some call me haughty; I'm often just lonely.
Other: _____

Rabbi — Sometimes I'm the wise higher self. I'm the temple authority and a leader who serves. I study; I teach; I counsel.
Other: _____

Relative — We're connected by act of birth or fate. I'm associated with family matters and reunions. I'm related to various issues. I'm also kin to Einstein's theory of relativity.
Other: _____

Religious figures — Our appearance in your dreams usually signals that the subject is about your spiritual life. (Make a list here of the religious figures important to you and what they mean. Is Jesus loving? Is Buddha serene? Is John the Baptist passionate?)
Other: _____

Runner — I can run away from something (escape), toward something (goal), or for my health. I make great strides, and I like it when things are running smoothly.
Other: _____

Salesperson — I can be helpful, convincing, or sell you a bill of goods. If I'm sharp, I can convince people to buy anything. What I sell and my approach gives you more clues as to my meaning. Beware of fast talkers who sell used cars.
Other: _____

Secretary — I'm a helper, often undervalued, who makes my boss's life go more easily. I keep things organized and running smoothly. I'm a buffer and sometimes a personal shopper. I take dictation.
Other: _____

Server/waiter — I serve. I deal with food and make suggestions. Often I just wait. I appreciate tips, and I've learned that when I'm helpful and pleasant my tips are bigger.
Other: _____

Sheriff — Sometimes I'm stereotyped, but I deal with the law in the outer areas. I'm tough. I'm usually elected.
Other: _____

Ship captain — I'm the ultimate authority of your ship, and I steer the vessel in its proper path. I'm often a spiritual symbol. I am the master or the Master. We're all in this together.
Other: _____

Shopper — I am the seeker. I'm looking for something to buy. I examine choices carefully and try to make good decisions. I like a good bargain.
Other: _____

Singer — I'm all about melody, harmony, and the emotions I can portray with my voice. I am gifted in a special way to bring joy or sing praises. Sometimes I hit sour notes.
Other: _____

Skater — I am grace and balance and smooth gliding. I can have sharp edges, or just roll along. Sometimes I "skate" when I don't have to pay for my wrongdoings.
Other: _____

Skier — I'm fast and I'm strong, and it's all downhill, baby.
Other: _____

Soldiers, military — Whether with the army, navy, air force, or marines, I do my duty; I serve and protect. I'm a fighter, a warrior. I'm disciplined. I look out for my buddies.
Other: _____

Son — I'm the heir, the creation of my parents. Sometimes I'm a son-of-a-gun; sometimes I'm Christ.
Other: _____

Spy — I'm a watcher. I stick my nose into everybody's business. I know where all the bodies are buried. If I'm good at what I do, nobody ever suspects me.
Other: _____

Stranger — You may not have met me or acknowledged me yet, or I may be just passing through. Are you afraid of me? Why don't you just stop and talk to me? I'm part of you.
Other: _____

Student — I'm here to learn lessons. I must gain information about myself, the world, everything. Sometimes those lessons are hard.
Other: _____

Swimmer — I am strong. I cut through the water with various strokes and styles. (See also Runner.)
Other: _____

Tailor, seamstress — I make and alter clothing (sometimes meaning attitudes, or what is shown to the world). I make things fit, and update old styles to make new ones. I bind things together.
Other: _____

Taxi driver — I take you where you want to go—for a price. I usually know my way around. There are lots of stereotypes about me. What's yours?
Other: _____

Teacher — I help you learn. Sometimes I'm a tough taskmaster, but I have students' best interests at heart. I'm an authority. I'm both revered and resented by some. I hope my students remember me fondly.
Other: _____

Thief — I'm sneaky, and I take what I want without conscience and in secret. Maybe I'll get caught, but then again, maybe I won't. The nine-to-five life isn't for me.
Other: _____

Traffic director — I keep things moving by telling people which way to go. I like to avoid confusion and snarls. I'm in the middle of things, blowing my whistle and pointing.
Other: _____

Truck driver — I handle big rigs, often over long distances. I have to be in control, or I'm in trouble. I haul and supply. I keep schedules and deliver.
Other: _____

Usher — I assist in finding the right place and leading people there. I bring in the mother of the bride, the new year, or a change. I provide light in dark places.
Other: _____

Vintner — I make wine from grapes (or sometimes water) using various processes. I'm in charge of the vineyards and hope for good fruit.
Other: _____

Watchman — I protect property at night. I provide security and keep my eyes open when things are quiet and people are sleeping. I make rounds.
Other: _____

Welder — I make sparks when I join things together securely and permanently. I make strong bonds.
Other: _____

Wife or woman — I'm the feminine principle. I'm receptive. Things are changing for me, and sometimes the old roles don't fit.
Other: _____

Writer — I'm a creative idea person. I weave pictures and stories in my head and put them on paper. I produce work that is entertaining, informative, or inspirational. I have a way with words and expression.
Other: _____

Zookeeper — I see that the wild and exotic animals are cared for and not allowed to run amok. I keep things under control.
Other: _____

BODY PARTS

Here you'll find an alphabetical listing of body parts or systems. Descriptions are given using a variety of techniques, and in no particular order of significance. Underline the ideas that are meaningful to you.

The body and its parts are common dream symbols. Their appearance may signal a literal need for attention to that body part or, more commonly, it may be figurative. Other symbols may be representative of the body and its parts. Automobiles, houses, and buildings can portray the body; plumbing systems may call attention to the kidneys or urinary tract; a pear, the uterus; a pump, the heart.

Remember: These are only suggested possibilities. Your personal associations are always best, so be sure to fill in the blank spaces. Add other entries as needed.

Adrenal glands — Associated with energy, anger, fire, the fight-or-flight system. (See also Solar Plexus.)
Other: _____

Ankles — Associated with balance and support. Strong ankles are important in dance, walking, and sports activities; weak ankles can mean unsupported or lacking faith; fettered ankles can mean captive, enslaved.
Other: _____

Arm — Associated with comfort, service, work, entanglement, grasping, hugging, loving arms, sheltering arms, arms like an octopus, strong-arm tactics, long arm of the law, an arm and a leg, good right arm.
Other: _____

Back — Associated with the past (what's behind you), warning of back ailments, strength (strong back), monkey on his back, get off my back.
Other: _____

Beard — Associated with disguise, that which keeps coming back, growth, a nuisance (for some), a mark of distinction, masculinity.
Other: _____

Belly — Associated with bellyache (complain), belly like a whale, belly up to the bar, belly laugh, fire in the belly. Having a bellyful can mean the end of endurance.
Other: _____

Blood — Associated with the life force, danger, may indicate physical problems or injury; related by blood, blood is thicker than water, cold-blooded (unfeeling); bad blood between them can mean old feuds or hatred; bloodshed signals a serious contention between two or more forces; blood brothers, symbolic of Jesus' sacrifice, Passover mark.
Other: _____

Bones, skeleton — Associated with underlying structure or framework; that which holds you erect; sometimes associated with Halloween, pirates and poison (skull and crossbones), or death; having a skeleton in your closet can mean embarrassing or damaging secrets from the past.
Other: _____

Brain — Associated with thinking, ideas, intelligence; the physical control center, body's computer; having half a brain or not a brain in your head can mean not having enough sense or intelligence.
Other: _____

Breasts — Associated with feminine attributes, motherhood, sustenance, comfort, development of female aspects, nurturing concepts of love, compassion, tenderness, gentleness, spirituality.
Other: _____

Buttocks — Associated with past (what is behind), rear; several derisive slang expressions (ass, butthole), showing your butt or ass; the bottom, weight problems if large; too big for your britches can mean arrogance.
Other: _____

Chest — Associated with pride (chest swelled), breathing, respiratory concerns, beating one's chest/breast, getting something off your chest. (See also Heart, Thymus.)
Other: _____

Chin — Associated with strong chin (strength, courage, determination), keep your chin up, lead with your chin, take it on the chin, weak chin; stroking the chin while thinking can mean considering alternatives.
Other: _____

Complexion — Indication of health, shade, protection, clue to personality, outward appearance, changes the complexion of things. (See also Skin.)
Other: _____

Ear — Associated with hearing, understanding, listening (lend me your ears), he who has ears to hear, ear to the ground, big ears (eavesdropper), bending your ear, pointed ears (devilish).
Other: _____

Eyelashes — Associated with protection of the eye from foreign matter, an aid to clear vision. Fluttering or batting eyelashes can mean flirting; long eyelashes can be an attractive trait. (See also Eyes.)
Other: _____

Eyes — Associated with sight, I/ego, perception, insight; imperfection in eyes or sight may indicate that one isn't looking at something correctly; shifty eyes or eyes too close together can mean untrustworthy; roving eyes, eyes to see, an eye for an eye, eye-opener, eyes are windows to the soul, the night has a thousand eyes.
Other: _____

Face — Associated with the persona, that which is presented to the world, ego identity; makeup on face may mean hiding or enhancement of certain characteristics; recognition, confrontation, slap in the face, I can't face it, face-to-face, face value.
Other: _____

Feet and toes — Associated with foundation, understanding (feet are how or where you stand on issues), sensitivity; big toe can represent balance, path/direction you are taking, that which connects you to the earth and/or keeps you grounded; being barefoot may be freedom from restriction or being overly sensitive; tenderfoot, foot in mouth, two left feet (clumsy), one foot at a time, foot in the door, follow in footsteps, feet on the ground. In reflexology, parts of the body have a corresponding area on the bottom of the feet, e.g., the brain and the pituitary gland are related to the big toe.
Other: _____

Fingernails — Extensions of finger qualities, activities, work, status symbol, nervousness or anxiety when nails are chewed, clawing, an indication of health, sharp nails; hanging on by the fingernails; dirty nails can mean unclean or hard work, false fingernails may indicate false or unrealistic activities or involvement.
Other: _____

Fingers/thumb — Associated with feeling, talent, agility, service, activity, work; the index finger may denote identity (fingerprint) or pointing the way/pointing the finger; ring finger may indicate marriage, marital situations, or symbolize love; middle finger may show contempt; a lifted pinky may be pretense (sipping tea). Palmistry and acupuncture both assign specific meanings to finger and hand points. (See also Hands.)
Other: _____

Forehead — Indication of fever or emotions, intelligence, psychic center (the third eye), indicator of life direction (the mark of the beast or of the lamb, the scarlet letter of adultery, the mark of the thief, etc.).
Other: _____

Gonads (male or female genitalia) — Associated with reproduction, sexuality, creative energy, concern with male/female characteristics. A dream of possessing both male and female genitals is often a positive dream indicating a masculine/feminine balance.
Other: _____

Hair — Associated with thoughts, thinking (that which comes out of the head), strength (Samson), vanity; matted or disheveled hair may indicate mental problems; an overabundance of body hair may refer to animal nature; gray hair can mean wisdom or age.
Other: _____

Hands — Associated with help, friendship, greeting (offer a hand, lend a hand, join hands), right-hand man, praise (give a hand as in applause), handy, surrender (hold up the hands); ask permission, take an oath, or volunteer (raise the hand).
Other: _____

Head — Associated with sense (use your head), hard-headed, thick-headed, conceit (have a big or swelled head), pin-head. (See also Brain.)
Other: _____

Heart — Associated with the core, love, stamina; generous and warm (have a big heart), cold-hearted, heart on your sleeve, heartbroken, heartless. (See also Thymus.)
Other: _____

Heel — Associated with a jerk or a cad; weakness (Achilles heel), obey (as bring to heel), dominate (under his heel).
Other: _____

Intestines — Associated with guts (nerve or courage), intestinal fortitude; gut wrenching; may indicate digestive problems.
Other: _____

Kidneys, urinary tract — Associated with cleansing the body of impurities at all levels, releasing emotional tension; filtering and getting rid of things.
Other: _____

Knees — Related to on bended knee (as a plea, asking for marriage, prayer, show of respect), weak-kneed, a knee-knocker (frightening experience).
Other: _____

Legs — Associated with underpinnings or principles, support, foundation, a leg to stand on, on its last leg (about to die or give up), get a leg up (helpful advantage), pulling your leg (joking), shake a leg (hurry).
Other: _____

Lungs — Associated with breathing, the breath of life; needing to catch your breath can mean needing to rest or slow down in any activity. Emotional reactions such as fear or passion affect the lungs and respiration by panting, heaving, sighing.
Other: _____

Mouth and lips — Pertains to the part that takes in (food, for example) and sends out (words or spewing venom); speak out or speak up; big mouth, smart mouth, all mouth, loose lips, keep a stiff upper lip, get a fat lip. The lips and mouth are also erogenous zones and may be concerned with romance or sex.
Other: _____

Navel — Related to the body's center, connection to mother and birth; to contemplate your navel means to be totally self-absorbed.
Other: _____

Neck — Associated with stick your neck out (take a chance), making out. (See also Throat.)
Other: _____

Nose — Associated with prying, be nosy, nose in the air, "knows"; paid through the nose, lead around by the nose, win by a nose (very close call).
Other: _____

Pineal gland — An endocrine gland in the head (the sixth) that represents the Christ center. It produces the hormone melatonin, which regulates the sleep/wakefulness cycle.
Other: _____

Pituitary gland — The master gland, associated with the seventh or God center. Its hormones regulate homeostasis, growth, and the function of other glands.
Other: _____

Saliva or spit — Digestive aid, mouth dried up (fear), spit on you (disdain), not worth spit (valueless).
Other: _____

Shoulders — Associated with strength, broad shoulders (attractive or a good listener), assuming burden (shoulder the load).
Other:: _____

Skeleton or bones — Associated with framework, support, what's inside, death, good bones (attractive); bone up on (study); a hint, temporary distraction or something to chew on (throw a bone).
Other: _____

Skin — Associated with sensitivity, protection, the outer self; gets under my skin (bothersome), skintight, skin of my teeth (barely), skinflint (cheap), no skin off my nose (doesn't matter); can mean the self or self's situation (you should be in my skin, save your skin).
Other: _____

Solar plexus — A nerve network behind the stomach; associated with the fourth chakra or energy vortex in some medication systems and represents energy, fire, courage, and power. A punch to the solar plexus hits a vulnerable part of the body.
Other: _____

Spine or backbone — Associated with fortitude, strength, spineless (lacks courage), support, path of the kundalini.
Other: _____

Stomach — Associated with endurance (I can't stomach that), butterflies or bees in my stomach (upset or nervous). Often pertains to diet or digestion.
Other: _____

Teeth — Associated with words (teeth falling out = talking too much or need for dental care); sink your teeth into (getting involved), pulling teeth (difficult or removing discomfort), scarce as hen's teeth, tooth for a tooth (revenge). (See also Mouth.)
Other: _____

Throat — Associated with voice, communication, swallowing, will (see also Thyroid); a lump in the throat (moved by emotion), shoved down your throat can mean forced upon you, cut your own throat or someone else's, jumped down my throat can mean chastised. (See also Neck.)
Other: _____

Thymus — The fourth endocrine center or chakra, associated with the color green, and located near the heart; love. (See also Heart.)
Other: _____

Thyroid — The fifth endocrine center or chakra, associated with the color blue; will, the Holy Spirit. (See also Neck and Throat.)
Other: _____

Tongue — Associated with speech; hold your tongue, the tip of my tongue, foreign tongues; silver-tongued orator can mean a glib, talented speaker; tongue-lashing (chastising). (See also Mouth.)
Other: _____

Veins or arteries — Associated with circulation, carries life force, provides nourishment and cleans the blood; in that vein (on that subject, along that line), sacrifice (open a vein or artery), lifeline. (See also Blood.)
Other: _____

White blood cells — Associated with the body's immune system; rally to defend against foreign bodies or intruders. May be symbolized by white knights or other defenders or a cleaning crew dressed in white.
Other: _____

FLORA

Here you'll find an alphabetical listing of some plants found in the dream world. Plants or their characterization usually represent some aspect or trait in you or concerning a situation. Look for figurative meanings. Descriptors are given using a variety of analytical techniques and in no particular order of significance. Underline the ideas that are meaningful to you.

Remember: These are only suggested possibilities. Your personal associations are always best, so be sure to fill in the blank spaces. Add other entries as needed.

Aloe vera — The plant sap is healing (especially burns), soothing; used in beautifying skin and in a number of products; sometimes used to treat stomach, digestive problems. Grown in containers, except in very warm regions.
Other: _____

Banyan tree — National tree of India; associated with eternal life because of expansive growth pattern; important in both Hindu and Buddhist religions; represents enlightenment, knowledge, and insight. (See also Trees.)
Other: _____

Cactus — Prickly, survives dry spells; may represent a prickly person who repels with barbs and needles. At home in dry, rocky terrain but can grow most anywhere.
Other: _____

Carnation — Simple ruffled flower that comes in many colors, is common in flower markets, and is inexpensive. Reminds some of high school proms or of funerals; a brand of canned milk.
Other: _____

Cedar tree — Fragrant wood that repels insects, weathers well; strength, protection; often mentioned in Bible, especially the once vast and majestic Cedars of Lebanon. Wood often used to line closets, make cedar chests for storage, and wood used for decks and outdoor furniture. (See also Trees.)
Other: _____

Chestnut tree — Spreading tree of Longfellow's poem "The Village Blacksmith"; some Native American tribes considered chestnut trees as symbols of fertility and abundance because of the large number of nuts dropped in the fall. (See also Trees.)
Other: _____

Chrysanthemums (mums) — Autumn bloomer, often seen potted and given as gifts, traditional football corsage for teens.
Other: _____

Clover — Soft cushion, good luck (four-leaf); good forage for livestock, hence living in clover (easy life of prosperity).
Other: _____

Cypress tree — Italian cypress (tall, slender) often planted as memorials; bald cypress lives in water, has "knees," long-lived, tough, and enduring. (See also Trees.)
Other: _____

Daffodil — Sunny flower with a trumpet that often grows in large groups and multiplies freely. Signals spring, happiness. A song tells of clouds of daffodils in spring.
Other: _____

Dogwood tree and blossoms — A small flowering tree frequently found in the shelter of larger trees. It blooms around Easter and has become a Christian myth related to Christ's crucifixion because of the shape and symbolism of the four-petal blossom. Often represents eternal life, sacrifice, and rebirth.
Other: _____

Fern — A very old type of plant, reproduces by spores; grows in hidden, shady places; may be associated with new life, endurance, antiquity.
Other: _____

Fig tree — Often mentioned in Bible, small but productive, fertile, noted for the abundant, sweet fruit it bears. Some medicinal purposes.
Other: _____

Fir tree — Strength, immortality; reminiscent of Christmas trees, decorations, and holiday spirit and activities. (See also Trees.)
Other: _____

Flowering tree — Springtime, new beginnings, weddings (apple and orange blossoms); promise of fruit or results to come. (See also Trees.)
Other: _____

Flowers — In general: allure, beauty, fragrance, maturity (from bud to full flower); tokens of love or admiration, celebration, talents, spiritual gifts.
Other: _____

Forest, woods — Often venerated for majesty and mystery; sanctuary, the unconscious or hidden, the positive or negative unknown or secrecy; being lost or overwhelmed; can't see forest for the trees (too much attention to detail and missing the big picture). (See also Trees.)
Other: _____

Fruit trees — Productive, sweet results, yielding, bearing, nourishing; forbidden fruit (temptations), fruits of the spirit, the fruit doesn't fall far from the tree. (See also Trees.)
Other: _____

Garlic — Often noted for its smell and abilities to protect against or ward off evil spirits; valued for its flavor and some medicinal purposes.
Other: _____

Grass — Covering (lawn), growth, marijuana, fodder, grass doesn't grow under his feet (acts quickly).
Other: _____

Hedge — Bushes that hide or separate, a fence or boundary, to dodge or avoid (as answers); hedge your bets (avoid risk), hedge fund (investment strategy to spread the risk).
Other: _____

Holly — Prickly, self-protective, keeps people from getting too close; Christmas greens used for decoration, and reminiscent of the holiday season.
Other: _____

Lilies — Easter and immortality, death (calla lilies), motherhood (Greek mythology), innocence; lily of the valley associated with perfumes and scents (often old-fashioned).
Other: _____

Lotus — Spiritual growth, the divine within, enlightenment, unfolding into great beauty, at home in the water (spiritual realm); sacred in some cultures.
Other: _____

Magnolia tree — Stately, the South, alluring (fragrance). (See also Trees.)
Other: _____

Maple tree — Fall color, inner sweetness (sugar maple), valued as a wood for furniture or flooring. (See also Trees.)
Other: _____

Mistletoe — Romance (kissing under it), Christmas decoration, parasite; ancient mystical symbol; highly esteemed by Druids as a remedy for poison; healing properties, used in some modern medicines.
Other: _____

Morning glory — Often represents a morning person or an early bird because of its habit of blooming early and closing later; greeting the day; a clinging vine.
Other: _____

Oak tree — The mightiest of trees, strong, courageous, sturdy, deep-rooted; valued for its hard wood used in building houses, furniture, cabinets, and floors. Once considered an oracle tree. (See also Trees.)
Other: _____

Orchid — Flower often noted for its rare and exotic beauty; highly prized and luxurious; aloof and aloft, it doesn't grow in dirt but in high places.
Other: _____

Palm tree — Joy and happiness, sacred symbol of life and promise, often religious symbol (Palm Sunday); signals water nearby (oases); date palms are valued for their fruit and its sweetness. (See also Trees.)
Other: _____

Pine tree — Longevity, majesty, taps deep within (long tap root); pine (long for), pine box (death); valued for kindling wood because of its rich resin. (See also Trees.)
Other: _____

Poison ivy — Irritations (often hidden), may symbolize a warning to avoid people or situations, an irritant or allergy that causes a rash. .
Other: _____

Poppies — Veterans, remembrance, bloodshed, soporific drugs (opium poppies).
Other: _____

Potted plants — Life and growth out of their natural habitats; restricted; that which introduces life into a house (state of consciousness) or buildings (various activities).
Other: _____

Rosemary — A fragrant plant used as an herb and seasoning; ordinarily signifies remembrance.
Other: _____

Roses — Love, remembrance, romance, a rose by any other name, English rose, "I Never Promised You a Rose Garden." The color is usually significant: Red roses can mean love and romance, yellow roses are often associated with Texas, and white roses can indicate purity or spirituality.
Other _____

Shrubs — Planted for their decorative value on roadsides, in parks, and around buildings and houses to provide color, interest, balance, or symmetry.
Other: _____

Trees — Rooted, grounded, stable, rising toward the heavens, provide shade and shelter; Tree of Life, family tree, Tree of Knowledge; up a tree, out on a limb, treed. (See also individual varieties.)
Other: _____

Tulips — Spring, Holland, "two-lips," romance.
Other: _____

Vegetable plants — Home grown; healthy; can indicate productivity; attention to food and diet. The particular variety is important to note, e.g., squash may imply a need to squash a rumor or a behavior.
Other: _____

Venus flytrap — Enticement to destruction, a seductive but harmful person or situation.
Other: _____

Vines — Climbs, chokes, or covers; entanglements; grape or berry vines can indicate fruitfulness, productivity, fulfillment of promise.
Other: _____

Violets — Sweet romance, innocence, simple and unassuming.
Other: _____

Weeds — Unproductive, useless, choking out the positive things, marijuana.
Other: _____

Wheat, other grain fields — Usually associated with freedom and abundance (amber waves of grain); time for reaping benefits or something is coming into fruition; nurturing.
Other: _____

Wildflowers — Natural beauty, signal seasonal change, promise; they're also effortless and simple.
Other: _____

Willow tree — Magic, healing (leaves and bark), inner visions and dreams; may commemorate death, represent mourning and tears (weeping willow). (See also Trees.)
Other: _____

FAUNA

Here you'll find an alphabetical listing of many of the animals found in the dream world. Animals often represent some trait or aspect of the dreamer or an issue. Descriptions are given using a variety of analytical techniques, and in no particular order of significance. Underline the ideas that are meaningful to you.

Remember: These are only suggested possibilities. Your personal associations are always best, so be sure to fill in the blank spaces. Add other entries as needed.

Alligators, crocodiles — May refer to something with a tough hide or exterior that is ugly but inherently valuable; a dangerous thing that glides just beneath the surface of murky waters, perhaps devouring fears or something with a deadly bite (a big, powerful mouth with sharp teeth can indicate powerful and harmful words), trying to drag you under or do you in.
Other: _____

Ants — Industrious, they work together to cooperate as a community in food gathering and other pursuits; small irritations, pests at picnics or in the pantry; can sting in defense; ants in your pants, antsy; fire ants sting viciously and ruin lawns and pastures.
Other: _____

Bats — Creatures that live on the dark side and hang on by their toe-nails; may represent hidden fears or shadowy parts of the unconscious. They're helpful in that they eat insects, especially mosquitoes, but they also can carry disease (rabies). Someone who is bats or batty or has bats in the belfry is crazy.
Other: _____

Beaver — Dams up things (perhaps emotions), interrupts natural flow, gnawing teeth, busy as a beaver, eager beaver; often destructive to land by blocking streams of water and causing it to overflow and flood surrounding areas.
Other: _____

Bees — Active, industrious, defensive, ecologically helpful (pollina-tion), produce honey (sweetness); work cooperatively for the good of the colony; busy as a bee, bee in her bonnet, queen bee, drone, like a worker bee; Africanized bees are aggressive and inflict painful and sometimes fatal stings when disturbed.
Other: _____

Birds — Messengers, harbingers of spring, cheery; early bird gets the worm, bird in the hand. Various birds represent different things: peace or spirituality (dove), happiness (bluebird), imitation (mockingbird), new birth or ideas (stork), fearfulness (chicken). (See other specific birds.)
Other: _____

Bull — Usually aggressive, territorial, brave, represents the masculine principle; bred for fighting in some countries; bull-headed (stubborn), bull in a china shop (indelicate), take the bull by the horns (take con-trol), full of bull, don't take any bull from anyone; Taurus, the bull, is a sign of the zodiac.
Other: _____

Butterfly — Symbol of transformation, rebirth, coming into spiritual awareness, colorful and delicate; a social butterfly may be a superficial or gregarious person who loves parties and other social occasions and flits around having a good time; butterfly kisses (brushes with eyelashes).
Other: _____

Buzzard, vulture — Scavenger, often an omen of death and dying; someone who preys on others who are in a weakened position; buzzard on a fencepost (pessimist waiting for something bad to happen), buzzard breath.
Other: _____

Calf — Immaturity, helplessness, youth, innocence; making calf eyes (looking longingly at someone you're attracted to); the fatted calf; a golden idol in time of Moses.
Other: _____

Canary — Singing, caged to provide entertainment or amusement for another, vulnerable, flitting around, Tweety Bird; sing like a canary (blab everything).
Other: _____

Cats — Independent creatures, stalkers, quiet; they may be self-sufficient, demanding of attention or interaction with others on their own terms; cuddly, soft, and playful (especially kittens); play cat and mouse games, cat-eyed, catty, cats have nine lives and land on their feet.
Other: _____

Cow — Docile, slow, contented, continually eating; large matronly female, provides nourishment; sacred in some cultures.
Other: _____

Deer — Quick, delicate, gentle, a dear; some people hunt them for sport or food.
Other: _____

Dogs — Pets, man's best friend, guard dogs, keen hearing, good trackers, dog days, dogged (relentless); like a dog with a bone, my dogs (feet) are killing me. Various breeds have different and distinctive characteristics.
Other: _____

Dolphin or porpoise — Playful, intelligent, they often represent spiritual ideas or positive aspects of the unconscious, sometimes they signify purpose (porpoise), freedom, leaping for joy; they're easily trained and enjoy interacting with people, and have been known to come to the aid of someone in trouble in the water.
Other: _____

Donkey — A pack animal that bears heavy burdens; tough, plodding, stubborn; act like a jackass.
Other: _____

Duck — Water-loving swimmer; to avoid (duck or duck out), like a duck to water (naturally compatible with some element), rubber ducky. Baby ducks are cute, soft, and fluffy, and follow their mothers. If it walks like a duck . . .
Other: _____

Elephant — Huge, good memory, strong and powerful, big ears, tough hide, conspicuous, has a long life; can rampage and be destructive when frightened or raging. Associated with wisdom and spirituality in India, symbolic of the Hindu god Ganesha.
Other: _____

224 Into Your Dreams

Fish — Things below the surface (unconscious), of the spirit (early Christian symbol). Look to various types for other clues, e.g., slippery as an eel, flat as a flounder, hungry as a shark. To be fishy (something's not quite right).
Other: _____

Fox — Sly, crafty, quick as a fox, foxy (sexy or attractive), outfox (outwit).
Other: _____

Frog — Symbol of ugliness, a creature awaiting transformation into a prince; change, a long-tongued amphibian; a jumper (leapfrog); you have to kiss a lot of frogs before you find a prince (means keep trying); a frog in your throat can indicate difficulty speaking or speaking up.
Other: _____

Giraffe — Very tall, stick your neck out, something that is high or far reaching, someone who has her head in the clouds or is high-minded.
Other: _____

Gnats — Small irritations that are difficult to deal with, peskiness.
Other: _____

Goose — Silly, naïve, has a distinctive way of walking or waddling; the goose that laid the golden egg, my goose is cooked (I've been found out; I'm in trouble and have ruined my chances).
Other: _____

Gorilla — Primitive parts of people, they can represent great strength and size; huge, live in groups in the wild; King Kong; thug or gangster, big and dumb.
Other: _____

Horse — Messages, racing, carry riders, work animal from plow horses to thoroughbreds, some spirited, others steady and reliable; wild horses can represent instinctual urges; acting horsey, horsing around, a real workhorse; look to the type of horse for distinctive traits.
Other: _____

Hound — Good trackers, hunters, bay at the moon, hounding (insistent, relentless pursuit); hellhounds are mythological dog-like demons covered in fire.
Other: _____

Hummingbird — Small but fast, flits around, territorial and assertive despite size, timeless joy, accomplishing what seems impossible, loves nectar of life.
Other: _____

Insects, bugs — Bothersome, many flies bite or sting, various wasps sting painfully, some destroy gardens or crops while others help (ladybug). Beautiful dragonflies eat mosquitoes; grasshoppers and locusts can wipe out whole fields, yet children love to play with them; something may be bugging you.
Other: _____

Lamb — Often associated with sacrifice and with Jesus; gentle, pure, meek; like a lamb to slaughter (going innocently and helplessly, not knowing the danger); soft, cuddly, and childlike; associated with Passover. (See also Sheep.)
Other: _____

Lion — King of beasts, king of the jungle, associated with the third endocrine center (the adrenal glands), power, energy, a symbol of transformation, lion-hearted (courageous), the lion's share (biggest part); associated with Leo in the zodiac.
Other: _____

Monkey — Playful and mischievous, noisy, an imitator, scampering around investigating, hiding, or stealing food, sometimes entertaining; made a monkey out of me (made to look foolish), a monkey on your back (a serious problem you can't get rid of, drug addiction),
Other: _____

Mouse — Quiet, secretive, hidden, gets into things, nibbling or nagging, a pest, meek or timid; country mouse, mousey; feeling small and inadequate.
Other: _____

Octopus — Grasping, restricting, strong attachment to something, something you have difficulty shaking, all arms or hands, the number eight.
Other: _____

Ostrich — Fast runner, flightless, plumed, one who avoids unpleasantness or confrontation (head in the sand), copping out.
Other: _____

Otter — Cute, playful, a voracious appetite for fish, can be a pest in that they can quickly decimate a pond stocked with fish.
Other: _____

Owl — Messenger, wise old owl, nocturnal, a bird of prey, associated with Athena and Greece; an owlish person is studious and bright.
Other: _____

Ox — Strong work animal; pulls wagons, plows; often in pairs, yoked together; dumb as an ox, big as an ox. "Whose ox was gored?" means "Who was harmed by this plan or situation?"
Other: _____

Parrot — Talker (sometimes incessantly), imitator, a gossip who repeats everything, someone who has no original thoughts and only reiterates those of others, long-lived, colorful, associated with pirates.
Other: _____

Peacock — Pride, preening, beautiful, openness, loud and noisy, colorful. Associated with NBC. Eye pattern on tail feathers is associated with all-seeing knowledge in Greek mythology, and a spiritual symbol in some cultures.
Other: _____

Pig — Greedy, messy, stubborn (pigheaded), low-classed, a slob; getting a pig in a poke (taking a chance on something with no information about it), go whole hog (all out, to the maximum), make a pig of myself (overeat), hogging (not sharing). Often associated with gluttony, eating slop (poor diet); a pig may be an undesirable person or a policeman.
Other: _____

Poodle — Pampered, intelligent, high-strung, pet, fancy grooming, often a show dog.
Other: _____

Rabbit — Frequently associated with sexuality (breed like rabbits), fertility; large ears may call your attention to hearing or listening; meek and fearful, quick to bolt; might be an admonition to eat more fresh vegetables; a small thing that irritates or nibbles at you; to rabbit (to escape); to pull a rabbit out of a hat (to do something no one was expecting, especially to solve a problem at the last minute).
Other: _____

Rat — Nasty, carries disease (dis-ease), gnawing, destructive, laboratory rat (experiments); rat out (tell on, report), I smell a rat.
Other: _____

Robin — Sign of spring and of promise, regeneration and rebirth.
Other: _____

Seal — Cute, trained to perform tricks on command, difficulty moving on land but fast in water, flippers, Navy SEALS. May also indicate things like seal of approval, to seal an envelope or opening.
Other _____

Shark — Maneater, scavenger, must keep moving constantly, loan shark (preys on those who need cash), jumping the shark (an expression from TV meaning the climax of a series and the beginning of its downward spiral or slide), *Jaws*.
Other: _____

Sheep — Often represents those who are easily led or those who gather in groups; a Christian symbol; a wolf in sheep's clothing is someone who pretends to be meek and gentle but underneath the facade is a predator; being fleeced (bilked out of money or other property). (See also Lamb.)
Other: _____

Skunk — Something that smells bad (suspicious); powerfully defensive, all black and white; frequent road kill in rural areas; repulsive, creating a real stink, or driving you away. To be skunked means to be beaten badly in a competition; "he's a skunk" can mean he's low-down, reprehensible.
Other: _____

Snake — Temptations, sexual connotations; a raised serpent is also a spiritual symbol of power and energy (kundalini), healing when intertwined in the caduceus. Venomous in some cases. Lower than a snake, snake in the grass. The variety of snake is important to consider: boa can mean squeezing the life out of, swallowing whole; cobra can mean hooded, mysterious, venomous, sacred in some cultures.
Other: _____

Spiders — Spin webs to snare, to deceive, to entangle; secretive, frightening for those who are phobic about spiders, enticing; "step into my parlor, said the spider to the fly."
Other: _____

Squirrel — Extremely fast, energetic, and playful. They plan ahead and store things away. May be associated with hoarding or saving. Squirrelly (crazy or odd).
Other: _____

St. Bernard — Rescuer, associated with mountains and the brandy keg; huge, slobbers; protective of family members; loyal, heavy coat.
Other: _____

Swan — Symbol of transformation, spirit; graceful, magical, enchanted, peaceful and tranquil; often seen in pairs and can represent love and commitment; the ugly duckling who became a beautiful swan.
Other: _____

Tiger — Powerful, distinctive, aggressive, ferocious, dangerous, nocturnal predator; a tiger can't change his stripes, Chinese zodiac Year of the Tiger is associated with the earth and its elements. A white tiger is a mystical creature sometimes symbolizing the west.
Other: _____

Turtle — Someone who retreats into a shell at signs of trouble, won't stick his neck out in threatening situations, long-lived, has a hard protective shell, slow-moving and purposeful. A turtle on its back is vulnerable and helpless.
Other: _____

Whale — Largest of the sea mammals, magnificent rulers of the ocean, symbolic of a depth of spirit, unconscious realms; a whale of a tale, being swallowed up (Jonah and the whale), gigantic.
Other: _____

Wolf — Predator, runs in packs, sacred to some Native Americans, raw sexuality; a wolf can be a womanizer, wolf down your food, a wolf at the door (threatening danger or poverty), a wolf in sheep's clothing (one who pretends to be meek and harmless but is feral and vicious beneath the disguise).
Other: _____

Zebra — Striped like a prisoner, distinctive message, clarity (the ability to see things in black and white), integration of opposites, herd mentality.
Other: _____

OTHER CREATURES

Here you'll find an alphabetical listing of many various types of creatures or beings that don't fit into the human, plant, or animal categories. In dreams we see everything from aliens to monsters or mythical entities, and from angels to zombies. Some are benevolent, even holy or mystical; others scare the pants off us.

Descriptions are given using a variety of analytical techniques, and in no particular order of significance. Underline the ideas that are meaningful to you.

Remember: These are only suggested possibilities. Your personal associations are always best, so be sure to fill in the blank spaces. Add other entries as needed.

Aliens — Out of this world, foreign to you, something that doesn't belong.
Other: _____

Angels — Messengers, often from God or higher self, guides, heavenly, goodness, halo, a real angel (beautiful or sweet and kind).
Other: _____

Corpses, mummies — Dead issues, things long dead and buried, leavings, preserved, past, unchangeable, mother (mummy). Some people have serious phobias about corpses and panic when confronted with one.
Other: _____

Dead people — Something or someone from the past; depending on profession or relationship to the dreamer, can be treated as living people symbols.
Other: _____

Devil — The personification of evil and temptation; a force inside you (or outside) that would lead you astray (the devil made me do it); often portrayed clothed in red, with a forked tail and pointed ears, and holding a pitchfork; he lives with his minions (various demons and such) in the fiery pits of Hell; a projection of your own negative desires.
Other: _____

Dragons — Mythological creatures who breathe fire and eat people; often battled and slain by knights or other heroic characters, fearful monsters that sometimes fly, the Chinese Year of the Dragon is a significant time; Puff, the Magic Dragon, or Ollie, a puppet, are harmless, playful creatures loved by children.
Other: _____

Fairy — Supernatural creature, often related to nature; modern concepts like Tinker Bell character are very small, delicate, ethereal, and have wings like that of a butterfly or insect; possesses magical powers, capable of cunning and trickery, mischievous; a fairy tale is a fabricated story, not believable. The magical, enchanted part of the self.
Other: _____

Genie — From Arabic folklore and Islamic teachings; popularized as a magical creature that lives in a lamp and must do the bidding of the one that summons him (sometimes by rubbing a lamp). The magical, hidden part of the self; a granter of wishes.
Other: _____

Ghost — The spirit of a dead person who sometimes appears to individuals and may haunt (hang around) old habitats; fears from past, that which haunts you; a ghost of a chance is a faint possibility.
Other: _____

Gods, goddesses in mythology — Masters of particular realms, e.g., Poseidon of the seas, Mercury of communications, Athena of wisdom. Those most familiar are the Greek gods and their Roman counterparts, e.g., Zeus, the supreme Greek deity, and Jupiter, the Roman counterpart of Zeus.
Other: _____

Griffin — A creature with the foreparts of a winged eagle, the hindparts of a lion, representing the combined traits of each; vigilant strength; powerful guardians.
Other: _____

Jesus — Loving, a guide sometimes likened to a good shepherd, often seen as a symbol of the higher self, of spiritual values and compassion; also represents sacrifice, a miracle worker, a savior.
Other: _____

Mary, mother of Jesus — Motherhood, saintly, pure, compassionate; she is especially revered among Catholics.
Other: _____

Medusa — Snake-haired creature (see also Snakes), feminine rage, petrifying stare, a paradox (both enticing and horrifying), losing your head (decapitated by Perseus).
Other: _____

Menacing stranger — Threatening issues, fears, unacknowledged problems, anxiety, may be shadow-self archetype identified by Jung.
Other: _____

Monsters — Usually fears, anxieties, threatening issues from unconscious; sometimes an archetype; may also represent a monstrous situation or person in real life that causes fear and anxiety; an abusive person.
Other: _____

Religious figures — Usually represents spiritual matters, symbolic of traits of particular individual, e.g., Mohammed can mean a prophet, messenger; Buddha can mean awake, enlightened; Krishna can mean the fully realized and perfected self. (See also Jesus.)
Other _____

Saint — Martyr, miracle worker, goodness, holiness, often a higher self symbol; those achieving sainthood through the Catholic church; an exceptionally good and helpful person (she's a real saint); a football team in New Orleans.
Other: _____

Santa Claus — A magical, fat bearded fellow associated with Christmas, the spirit of giving, gifts, and toys left for children; a generous (and sometimes secret) benefactor.
Other: _____

Vampire — Someone who feeds off others, a bloodsucker, one who is draining (energy, life force, ideas); a mythological being who is bat-like and lives hidden in the dark and shadows by day; blood lust.
Other: _____

Werewolf — Hidden base nature, savage, changeable dark side (sometimes sexual).
Other: _____

Wizard — Magical, mysterious, metaphysical, wisdom, a real wizard (intelligent). Merlin is a well-known example, as is Harry Potter.
Other: _____

Zombies — Usually represents some issue that resurfaces; feeling like a zombie (out of it, going through the motions and not really here); the living dead, unconscious, controlled by another; a potent rum cocktail.
Other: _____

SETTINGS

Here you'll find an alphabetical listing of many of the indoor and outdoor settings—even weather—seen in dreams. These places often represent some trait or aspect of the dreamer, an issue, or a behavior. They may also set the stage or the mood and let you know what your dream is about. Descriptions are given using a variety of analytical techniques, and in no particular order of significance. Underline the ideas that are meaningful to you.

Remember: These are only suggested possibilities. Your personal associations are always best so be sure to fill in the blank spaces. Add other entries as needed.

Alley — May represent something hidden, something from the past (out back); a narrow passageway between two areas, often used for garbage storage and collecting. A place that's dark and foreboding. "That's right down (or up) my alley" suggests that something is suitable.
Other: _____

Ballroom — Often associated with special occasions and celebration, gaiety, formality; having a ball (having a good time); cooperative relationships (dancing).
Other: _____

Bathroom — Most often concerns cleansing, a place to escape for privacy, eliminating things from your life; personal grooming, applying makeup; a place for relaxing and soaking in a bubble bath. Often in demand in a large household.
Other: _____

Beach — A place to go for summer vacation, relaxation, warmth; life's a beach, play, swimming, riding the waves, the edge between land and sea, contentment, constant ebb and flow of life; a spot to contemplate, dig for things, and build sandcastles.
Other: _____

Bedroom — The place you go for rest, sleep, privacy, sex; your personal space; may represent hidden activities or a reflection of your inner self.
Other: _____

Cafeteria — Being offered or making choices in life, a need to look at diet selections; may be associated with overindulgence or difficult decisions.
Other: _____

Church, synagogue, other religious building — A spiritual symbol; a place of worship, learning, fellowship of kindred spirits, celebration.
Other: _____

City — Relates to activity, hustle and bustle, complexity, overcrowding, community, various aspects of yourself; city slicker, city limits, city lights.
Other: _____

Cleaners — Stain and dirt removal, freshen, iron out problems, pressing matters, get taken to the cleaners, cleaned out, clean up (make a lot of money), clean up attitudes.
Other: _____

Court, courthouse — Associated with the place you go on trial; judgment of your transgressions (attitudes or behaviors), attention to past conduct, legalities. Matters pertaining to deeds, records, licenses. (See also Judge.)
Other: _____

Dead end — May indicate that you're not going anywhere (referring to a current life situation, relationship, or thinking), and you need to rethink your state of affairs and change directions or goals.
Other: _____

Department store — Multifaceted, something on many levels, choices among many things, compartmentalized. Looking at a complex issue.
Other: _____

Desert — Lifeless wasteland, apparently infertile, hot and dry, deserted, without water (spiritless); thirst (literal need for more water).
Other: _____

Dining room — The place for family congregation, partaking of food (physical, mental, or spiritual nourishment), celebrations, belonging.
Other: _____

Family room, den — Comfort, entertainment, family gathering place for activities and sharing.
Other: _____

Fields, meadow — Harvest, reaping, openness, growth of all kinds, productivity, grazing.
Other: _____

Fork in the road — A decision about which way to go, which path to follow; a choice or division. Context is important here.
Other: _____

Grocery store — Stocking up, meal planning, choices and decisions about food at all levels, bring home the groceries (provide).
Other: _____

Gym, spa — A place to concentrate on exercise, fitness, strength; Jim; work out the kinks, pump iron, pampering the body. May refer to working out a problem, or exercising restraint or good judgment.
Other: _____

Hall — Passageway, direction, connection to various rooms; a transition from one place or situation to another.
Other: _____

Hospital — Healing, mending the body, mind, spirit; emergency attention, recuperation and regeneration. (See also Doctor, Nurse.)
Other: _____

Hotels, motels, inns — Temporary situation, state of mind; rest stop; luxurious hotel or flophouse, seedy hotel, five-star hotel; inn can mean "in."
Other: _____

House — State of mind, personality and facets of person, where you live, state of consciousness (note repair, decor, size); attic can mean higher consciousness, storage space, memories; basement can mean storage, memories, sexuality, hidden, or subconscious. (See also individual rooms.)
Other: _____

Kitchen — Food preparation, cleaning, concern with dietary habits, nurturing, being fed on any level, often center of activity.
Other: _____

Lake — Clear, tranquil, reflective of self or spirit, deep, recreation, wide spot in river.
Other: _____

Living room — Public part of self, what others see, daily activity.
Other: _____

Mine — Something very deep below the surface, buried there and waiting to be dug out (of the unconscious). May represent latent gifts, treasures, and talents, or refer to what's "mine."
Other: _____

Mountains — Great heights in understanding or awareness or consciousness; also represents problems to be overcome, climbing or ascending in life; making a mountain from a molehill, it's all downhill, "I've been to the mountain . . ."
Other: _____

Museum — Represents a repository of things from the past (like the subconscious or the collective unconscious), memories, or past experiences; where you keep valuables from the past; reminders of old lessons and events.
Other: _____

Ocean — The vast depths of the unconscious or the soul, the emotions, the spirit, something huge, mysterious. Very deep and contains vast numbers of things.
Other: _____

Office buildings — Usually associated with work or business issues, or people involved with office; commerce.
Other: _____

Park — Recreation, growth, an oasis in the city, family activities, picnics, walking or jogging, easy (a walk in the park).
Other: _____

Prison, jail — Confinement, restriction, punishment for wrongdoing, being trapped in a situation with no way to escape; prisoner of love, prison walls, jail-bird.
Other: _____

Repair shop — Mends that which is broken (shoes, hearts, promises, spirit).
Other: _____

Restaurants, other eateries — Service, special occasions, dietary issues, night out, lunch with friends, a quick bite, business lunch or dinner, nurturing or nourishment at any level.
Other: _____

River — Moving body of water, life journey or direction; destiny; going with the flow, flow of energy or time, sell down the river (betray), send up the river (jail), river of no return, lazy river, "Old Man River." Other: _____

Schools — Learning or lessons, knowledge, growth, understanding, opportunity, testing; college and university associated with higher learning, more profound lessons to be learned; the need to know and understand. Other: _____

Theater — Observing life or situations from a distance, entertainment, drama; playing at life, relationships; pretense, "all the world's a stage." Other: _____

Vacation home — Rest and relaxation, respite from daily concerns. Other: _____

Weather — Sets mood; storms can mean gloom, disagreements, emotional turmoil; rain can mean cleansing, nourishing; tornadoes or hurricanes can mean extreme mental and emotional conditions and chaos; snow and ice can mean frozen emotions, relationships, outlooks, rigidity; sunny can indicate pleasant conditions, attitudes. Other: _____

Yard — Front yard can mean the current situation, that which is presented to the world (persona); back yard can mean fenced in, hidden, private, safe for children. Other: _____

CLOTHES

Here you'll find an alphabetical listing of many of the costumes and items of clothing seen in dreams. Clothes frequently identify a character's role (like a police officer) or, most often, represent some attitude or aspect of the dreamer shown to the world, the persona, how we appear to others, or what we hide behind. Descriptions are given using a variety of analytical techniques, and in no particular order of significance. Underline the ideas that are meaningful to you.

Remember: These are only suggested possibilities. Your personal associations are always best so be sure to fill in the blank spaces. Add other entries as needed.

Bathing suit — Relaxation, recreation, prepared for diving in or getting into the swim of things, exhibition or competition (pageants), attention focused on body.
Other: _____

Black clothes — Mourning, sadness, hidden; engaged in magic, secrecy, or dark arts; conservative, formal, blending into background; little black dress, black tie, widow's weeds. Wearing black is said to protect your personal energy.
Other: _____

Boots — Usually relating to work or bad weather wear; protective elements; very high-heeled boots may refer to fashion or sensuality. Context and type of boot is important.
Other: _____

Casual clothes — Casual attitudes, relaxed, engaged in everyday activities.
Other: _____

Coat — Warmth needed (literal or figurative), suggests winter, that which warms us or insulates us, snug and comforting, protection from elements and outside forces (perhaps emotions or attitudes of others), armor; raincoat can signify protection from weather; coat of many colors, take your coat off and stay a while.
Other: _____

Colored clothes — Bright attitudes, attention-grabbing, cheerful. The specific color gives more clues, e.g., red is vibrant, energetic, and speakers and politicians often wear it.
Other: _____

Costumes — Roles we play, the way we act or appear, facades we present, pretense. The particular costume gives further clues: Note historical period and attitudes at that time, e.g., a Puritan, a pioneer, knight, royalty, caveman. May signal past life or simply things from the past. Superhero costumes can represent heroic attitudes and demeanor.
Other: _____

Coveralls — Protection, attitudes concerning work, someone who works at a particular thing, repairing or maintaining. The activity of wearer gives further clues.
Other: _____

Formal clothes — On best behavior or presenting best self, stiffness, special occasion, celebration, politeness.
Other: _____

Gloves — Protection for the hands from outside elements or work. Pull off the gloves (get serious in fighting, bare-knuckle with no cushion), put on the gloves (to fight or be in opposition), a thrown gauntlet or being slapped with a glove is a challenge to duel or fight, a gloved hand leaves no fingerprints, hand in glove. (See also Hands, Fingers.)
Other: _____

Hats — Protection for the head, ideas, thoughts, what's on your mind. May represent an occupation (e.g., chef, police officer, jester, chimney sweep). Throw your hat in the ring, take off your hat (show respect or intention to linger), pass the hat. (See also Head, Hair.)
Other: _____

Jewelry — Material wealth or success, spiritual gifts or attributes; charm bracelets can mean charm or memories, wedding or engagement rings can represent commitment; adornment, beauty, accessory. Whether real or costume may be important.
Other: _____

Kimono — A traditional Japanese costume of a loose, wide-sleeved robe, usually of patterned or delicately adorned silk.
Other: _____

Naked — I feel exposed, uncomfortable, or embarrassed. This is the real me; I'm letting it all hang out. What you see is what you get. I'm stripped, and I can't hide.
Other: _____

Necktie — Business or formal attire, attitudes, or concerns; choking or restricting, a necktie party (hanging). A tie serves no purpose except as an adornment. (See also Neck, Throat.)
Other: _____

Pajamas — Loose, comfortable garments made for lounging or sleeping. May represent an issue involved with rest or relaxation. Wearing pajamas in public might signal attitudes that are too relaxed or the opposite—maybe you need to kick back and relax your public attitudes or behavior.
Other: _____

Purse — Holds material possessions and resources; identity; what you carry with you (literally or figuratively). Losing a purse may represent that which is valuable at any level being lost or stolen, a threat to your identity and personality. If a purse is crammed full and disorganized, it may be a reflection of your life.
Other: _____

Robe — Covering for sleepwear or beachwear, and associated with rest or relaxation, cover-up, modesty, privacy, warmth. Royal robes or clerical robes can represent higher ideals.
Other: _____

Shoes — Understanding, foundation, direction in life, protection, perspective; be in my shoes, walk a mile in his shoes, big shoes to fill.
Other: _____

Suit — Often related to business or occupation; a professional appearance and attitude; decision makers or upper echelons in business are sometimes referred to casually as "suits."
Other: _____

Top hat — Old-fashioned or traditional hat worn with tails on formal occasions; stove-pipe associated with Abraham Lincoln; magician's hat; "pulling a rabbit out of his hat" can mean to do something no one was expecting, especially to solve a problem at the last minute; hidden tricks. (See also Hats.)
Other: _____

Underwear — What's beneath the surface, foundation; unprotected, not fully clothed; an underdeveloped idea or attitude, unprepared (caught in your underwear).
Other: _____

Uniforms — Identifies particular occupations, personae; uniform can make everyone the same or alike. Context and particular kinds of uniforms give important clues. (See People section for some specific types of occupations.)
Other: _____

Wallet — Valuables, material possessions and resources. (See also Purses.)
Other: _____

Watch — To observe; concerned with and focusing on time, the time is coming, it's later than you think, it's all in the timing.
Other: _____

White clothes — Purity, innocence, healing (as in brides, doctors, nurses, christening and communion dresses), spiritual attitudes and ideas.
Other: _____

OBJECTS

Here you'll find an alphabetical listing of some common objects seen in dreams, ranging from toys to weapons. Descriptions are given using a variety of analytical techniques, and in no particular order of significance. Underline the ideas that are meaningful to you.

Remember: These are only suggested possibilities. Your personal associations are always best, so be sure to fill in the blank spaces. Add other entries as needed.

Balls — Usually round and associated with catching or getting it; keep your eye on the ball, connect with the ball; having balls is to have boldness, courage.
Other: _____

Bats — Hitting, connecting, swinging, can be used as a weapon, phallic symbol, go to bat for something (support, defend), right off the bat (immediately).
Other: _____

Bed — Put to bed (finish), the place where you rest, sleep, have sex; represents intimacy, where you have dreams, comfort; strange bedfellows are unlikely companions, bed of roses can mean a life of ease.
Other: _____

Books — Associated with lessons and learning; entertain and inform; libraries are filled with them, some are electronic; some are designed especially for young children, others have large print or are on tape for those who have vision problems.
Other: _____

Carpentry tools — Hammer home ideas, saw or cut to fit; associated with building, putting things together, constructive methods. Useful things to have around the house.
Other: _____

Clay — Used to mold and sculpt, form into a desired shape; malleable; feet of clay indicate vulnerability, an area of weakness in a strong or admired person.
Other: _____

Cleaning products — Needed to clean up things on all levels including ideas, thoughts, behaviors; washing out mouth with soap means cleaning a dirty mouth of profane language.
Other: _____

Clock — Concern with time or timing. (See also Watch.)
Other: _____

Comb — May indicate a need to untangle thoughts or ideas, smooth out thinking, get your head in order; to comb through something means to search. (See also Hair.)
Other: _____

Computer — Information storage, communication, brain or levels of consciousness; that doesn't compute (doesn't make sense).
Other: _____

Copy machine — Imitate or copy information or behavior, duplication; may imply inherited traits (carbon copy).
Other: _____

Cup — Used for drinking in or absorbing life, receiving spiritual water, giving comfort with a cup of water; accepting fate (let this cup [of sorrow, of duty, of this mission] pass from me). Quest for the Holy Grail, or the cup used by Jesus at the Last Supper.
Other: _____

Curtains, drapes — Usually relating to a need for privacy (urging to have more or be more open, accountable); may concern the opening (beginning) of a situation (like a play) or the closing curtain (the end). Could indicate something hidden or concealed. It's curtains for him (the end, death).
Other: _____

Desk — A work station in office, school, or home. Relates to work, learning, keeping accounts; assigned place (at my desk).
Other: _____

Dishes — Serving others or self with either real food or metaphoric food (for thought or by being helpful), too much on my plate (over-extended with responsibilities), a real dish (attractive person), dishing it out.
Other: _____

Eyeglasses — A need to see things more clearly, get better perspective, magnification. Losing glasses can mean losing perspective or sight of goal. (See also Eyes.)
Other: _____

Fence — Something that encloses and keeps things in or out, a boundary line; don't fence me in (don't restrict me); "good fences make good neighbors" (knowing boundaries eliminates problems).
Other: _____

File cabinet — Organization and storage of material, thoughts, ideas, memories; file it away to remember it for later.
Other: _____

Fossils — Ancient relics or remnants of life captured in stone. Lasting impressions of the past; he's an old fossil (outdated).
Other: _____

Frying pan — Cooking up something, a warning to avoid fried foods, from the frying pan into the fire (from bad to worse).
Other: _____

Furniture — Look at the purpose and function for each piece for clues to meaning. An easy chair can mean relaxation, comfort; dining chair suggests eating; a chest indicates storage.
Other: _____

Garden tools — Associated with cultivating, growth, planting, maintaining, beautifying; weeding out in life as well as in the garden.
Other: _____

Gate — An opening in an enclosure for passage; the way through.
Other: _____

Gold, treasure, valuables — That which you value, real treasure or material wealth, spiritual gifts, talents, knowledge, advantages, insight; fool's gold, golden anniversary; finding gold or treasure can mean discovery of new ideas, assets, spiritual gifts.
Other: _____

Guns — Used to defend or attack, phallic symbol; bullets can be wounding words or heated exchange; jump the gun (premature action), stick to your guns (hold onto opinions), go gunning for (looking for a fight or to make trouble for someone), go in with guns blazing (put all your energy and effort into a project), go down with guns blazing (fight to bitter end).
Other: _____

Instruments — May represent a vocation, like a surgeon's instruments. Musical instruments may have to do with harmony or with mood; each instrument has its own personality and associations: piano = keys, drums = beat or tempo, bugle or trumpet = announcement; "played" like a violin, teeth like a keyboard, mellow as a saxophone.
Other: _____

Kitchen tools — Use for stirring the pot, stirring up something, making preparations, concerned with food-related issues. Look at tool for clues, e.g., rolling pin suggests flattening.
Other: _____

Knives — Pointed, phallic symbol; cutting remarks, cutting down to size, stabbing in the back, that which wounds, going under the knife (having surgery), knife happy, something (a habit or other behavior) that needs to be cut out.
Other: _____

Lamp — Something that lights the darkness of the unknown; improves ability to see (understand), shows the way; light suggests illumination, insight.
Other: _____

Letters — Messages from other parts of the self, communication, information.
Other: _____

Luggage — May suggest a trip or travel; excess baggage we haul around from the past, or filled with outmoded ideas or ways of doing things.
Other: _____

Measuring tools — Used to guide, direct, draw the line, be exacting, pertains to size or amount, not overdoing it. The particular tool will give more clues to meaning.
Other: _____

Money — Security, wealth that is either material or metaphorical, payment, possessions, success, power; the love of money is the root of all evil, in the money, not for love or money. (See also Gold.)
Other: _____

Nails — Pierce or join, something you drive; hitting the nail on the head, nailed (caught), another nail in my coffin, nailed to the cross.
Other: _____

Radio — Receiving information or understanding, insights from unseen source, tuning in, keeping up, musical harmony, noise that fills the quiet or passes the time. (See also Television.)
Other: _____

Sponge — I absorb things like water, spilled milk, ideas, my sur-roundings, reading material. Sometimes I clean up. I've been known to mooch off you for lunch or ask to borrow twenty dollars until pay-day. If I'm the real deal, I naturally came from the sea.
Other: _____

Stove — I'm hot. I cook up things. Some people put things on my back burner, others have a bun in my oven (are pregnant). I can transform things—sometimes it's trial by fire.
Other: _____

Tableware — I help you feed and nourish yourself in all sorts of ways. I cut stuff into manageable pieces. I fork things up and fork things over. Sometimes I spoonfeed.
Other: _____

Telephone — Communication, being connected; messages from the higher self, the unconscious, or a distant source; keeping in touch.
Other: _____

Television — All about entertainment, communication, information, new insights; sometimes called the idiot box. (See also Radio.)
Other: _____

Toys and games — Entertainment, playfulness, happiness, childish pursuits, immaturity, playing games, toying with someone's affections or emotions.
Other: _____

Umbrella — Associated with protection from the elements, usually rain, but may also shade from the sun (a parasol); everything under one umbrella, let a smile be your umbrella.
Other: _____

Washing machine — That which cleanses clothes (often attitudes, emotions, or facades) or other household linens. I have many cycles and can spin you around.
Other: _____

Weapons — Things used to attack or harm: words, arguments, lies, rumors, even negative thoughts. Having ammunition means possessing hurtful information to wound your opponent. (See also Guns, Knives.)
Other: _____

TRANSPORTATION

Here you'll find an alphabetical listing of some common modes of transportation seen in dreams—and some uncommon ones as well. Often these represent you, your body, the direction you're traveling, your aspirations or ideals, and a number of other things. Descriptions are given using a variety of analytical techniques, and in no particular order of significance. Underline the ideas that are meaningful to you.

Remember: These are only suggested possibilities. Your personal associations are always best, so be sure to fill in the blank spaces. Add other entries as needed.

Airplane — Soaring to exceptional heights, high ideals and purposes, higher realms, high-minded, may signal a literal trip or need for one, faster way to travel; landing may be coming down to earth, being grounded; crashing may signal a dive or loss of ideals and purposes or an abrupt ending to an activity or project (the plans just crashed and burned), a market or other crash. (See also Pilot, Flying.)
Other: _____

Ambulance — Emergency vehicle used for health crises or accidents; pay attention to something that's "sick," immediate attention needed for something, anything; warning siren about health or other non-health issue; may remind you to let something pass.
Other: _____

Automobile — Direction you're going, your vehicle; often symbolic of the body and the parts emphasized may correspond to the physical self or activities, e.g., headlights are eyes or vision, engine is heart or energy level, gas tank is fuel (food) ingested, flat tires are being tired or unable to go, brakes are the need to stop or slow down; may be associated with willpower or stubbornness; car crashing or hitting a wall can mean slow down, rest, you're overdoing it.
Other: _____

Bicycle — Exercise needed, importance of staying balanced at all levels, being outdoors, being or keeping yourself maneuverable in tight spaces or situations. A child's bike or trike may indicate immaturity or be about learning about balance and maneuverability.
Other: _____

Bus — Large vehicle with a particular destination, may allude to a body and size, path or direction you're going; may be a situation involving other people with the same purpose or headed in the same direction. Type of bus will give further clues, e.g., school bus suggests lessons or learning, tour bus suggests observing things. Missing the bus (not understanding or being mistaken, losing out on an opportunity), bus stop (waiting), another bus will come along (another opportunity will arrive).
Other: _____

Canoe — Originally a primitive boat often associated with Native Americans, light, maneuverable for river or lake travel (see also River and Lake) and for portage; basic and easy way to go; pointed craft, paddler faces the direction he's headed (looks where he's going), often a solitary journey (sometimes as a pair); paddle your own canoe (act independently, decide your own fate, tend to your own business).
Other: _____

Convertible — Openness, youth, being unrestricted, changeable, a status symbol, chick magnet; also vulnerability and lack of protection.
Other: _____

Fire truck — Sirens blaring, I go quickly to emergencies, primarily to fires of all kinds: real fires in homes, buildings, cars, grass, and woods; figurative fires like anger, business flare-ups, fires in your belly. Unless I'm driving slowly and quietly or am parked with children climbing over me, I'm a warning signal.
Other: _____

Flying without a plane — Exhilarating, uplifting, joyous experience, rising above earthly cares and physical laws; a higher perspective; may be a compensatory experience after a difficult period to lift your spirits and keep you balanced; flying high; a reminder that your abilities are unlimited.
Other: _____

Hearse — Death, the end of a situation or period, carrying things from the past around that are dead and need to be buried.
Other: _____

Helicopter — Rising above situations, maneuverability, rescue, noisy, clear view of surroundings; specific purpose of chopper gives other clues (traffic, transport, etc.).
Other: _____

Horse — Often represents messages, power (an engine's horsepower); type and color of horse give additional clues: white horse of hero or knight, racehorse indicates speed and spirit, winged horse can be a magical or spiritual message, four horsemen of the Apocalypse; horsing around, acting horsey (aloof or rude).
Other: _____

Horse and carriage or buggy — Old-fashioned method of getting anywhere, outdated, used for sight-seeing tourists, pleasant and peaceful, romantic outing, love and marriage (like a horse and carriage).
Other: _____

Limo — Luxury, a real stretch, going in style, wealth or fame, pretentious, driven.
Other: _____

Motorcycle — Powerful, loud, vulnerable to outside elements, tough, wild and crazy, dangerous, freedom and openness, a trade-off (safety versus feelings of power and being unrestricted).
Other: _____

Pickup — Used for hauling things around, a workhorse, often a masculine/macho symbol sometimes heavily accessorized, to pick up (as in hooking up with a stranger of the opposite sex).
Other: _____

Rattletrap, junker — Unsafe, body or attitudes need repair, things are falling apart or in a mess. The situation you're in or direction you're going doesn't look so good. It's time to trade up. Is your car safe?
Other: _____

Rowboat — Using pull, pulling to get somewhere, not facing your destiny and destination; many rowers suggest cooperation to reach a goal, pulling together.
Other: _____

SUV — Popular utility vehicle, good for hauling or transporting family, children, pets, and equipment; tough, practical.
Other: _____

Sailboat — Glides with the wind, may be associated with a spiritual journey; go with the flow, relax, set sail (aim, begin); smooth sailing; other meanings dependent on type of boat, era of popularity, and weather, e.g., a pirate ship or the *Mayflower*.
Other: _____

Scooter — One who scoots or hurries, child's toy, motorized wheelchair or other small vehicle designed for ease of getting around; can be fun or an aid used for convenience.
Other: _____

Semi — Tough, powerful, in for the long haul, work-related. The cargo gives other clues: Load of oranges may suggest a need for more citrus in the diet, load of beds suggests that more rest is needed, a moving van may represent movement in reality or in consciousness.
Other: _____

Ship — Life's journey, a spiritual journey; waiting for your ship to come in (waiting for success or good fortune), ship arriving (success or good fortune achieved); your emotional self or an emotional journey. (See also Sailboat.)
Other: _____

Spaceship — Boundless, into the heavens; an astonishing or alien message or idea or one from another realm; the unknown, may be a message from a higher power.
Other: _____

Sports car — Fast, powerful, showy, sleek, a masculine or phallic symbol; sometimes indicates a change in lifestyle, may indicate wealth or ostentation.
Other: _____

Submarine — Deep (in terms of thought or the unconscious), below the surface, hidden or submerged; exploring your emotional or unconscious waters safely; enclosed, confining, and restrictive, especially if you're claustrophobic.
Other: _____

Tank — Tough shell, armored against attack; built like a tank; aggressive, protective, used both offensively and defensively against enemies.
Other: _____

Taxi — Someone else is in control; being delivered, carried along, temporary state of transition; what drives you, being taken for a ride (cheated or deceived).
Other: _____

Train — Train of thought, many things connected, your life's journey, destiny, goal, being derailed (off the track), loss of direction, depressed, temporarily sabotaged (by self, others, or circumstances) from reaching goal; one-track mind.
Other: _____

Van — Associated with work, carrying things including many people. (See also SUV and Bus.)
Other: _____

SIGNPOSTS AND MAPS

Here you'll find an alphabetical listing of things that give us directions and guidance in our life journey, from common traffic or road signs, to maps of all sorts, to GPS units, to signs seen in the heavens. They may be messages from the unconscious or the superconscious to you. Descriptions are given using a variety of analytical techniques, and in no particular order of significance. Underline the ideas that are meaningful to you.

Remember: These are only suggested possibilities. Your personal associations are always best so be sure to fill in the blank spaces. Add other entries as needed.

Billboards — Big messages, advertisements, commercialization seen as a blight on landscape and natural elements, something that grabs the attention, larger than life.
Other: _____

Compass — I help you find your way, get your bearings. I keep you from getting lost in the woods because I always point north. I'm magnetic, and a good guide.
Other: _____

Constellations — Any of the eighty-eight named groups of celestial bodies (primarily stars) that form a pattern in the sky. Their names are primarily of Greco-Roman origin. More familiar are those named in the zodiac. Represent patterns or the attributes of the named group, e.g., Orion, the hunter. (See also Heavenly Maps, Stars, Zodiac.)
Other: _____

East — Awakening, rebirth, new beginnings (sun rises in the east). Often associated with Asia and the Orient. May indicate a new situation or experience.
Other: _____

Elements (four basic) — It was once thought that all matter was comprised of four basic elements: air, earth, fire, and water. Astrological signs are divided so that each belongs to one of the categories.
Other: _____

GPS instrument — Modern guidance system based on global positioning. Represents guidance, direction at all levels to help you on your life journey and get you to your goal.
Other: _____

Heavenly maps — The basis for astronomy (science) and astrology (esoteric art); in olden times ships were steered by the stars; guidance from afar; star-gazers, dreamers; the far reaches of imagination, destiny, heaven, infinity. (See also Constellations, Stars, Zodiac.)
Other: _____

Hot or cold — If moving close to a goal or destination, you're said to be getting warmer and hot when you've reached it, cooler and cold when far away from it. Typically, hot water is the left faucet and indicated by red; cold water is on the right and indicated by blue. Emotional climate.
Other: _____

Maps — Any of many types of instruments that give directions and point the way may represent guidance and advice for your life journey, from fold-up paper maps to computer-generated ones. They give the bigger picture as well as your particular journey in relation to the whole. Old maps represent the past, old paths, or ancient wisdom.
Other: _____

Moon — Emotional influence (control of tides), the light in the darkness, cycles, feminine influences, romance, inspiration, the man in the moon, mooning (baring the bottom, or yearning for someone or something); full moon is supposedly associated with madness, birthrate of babies, increase in criminal activity.
Other: _____

North — The basis for direction on a compass or map; may represent wisdom and the higher self. The North Pole is home to Santa Claus and Old Man Winter; cold, frozen; in *The Wizard of Oz*, the good witch was from the north.
Other: _____

Planets — Heavenly bodies, particularly those closest to Earth that also revolve around the sun. Associated with astrology and influence on us, something distant that is still within our sphere of experience.
Other: _____

Right and left — May indicate the right way to go; right is associated with the east, the future, political conservatism, and the conscious mind. The left is more often associated with the west, political liberalism, the past, open-mindedness, and the unconscious self. The left may indicate the wrong way to go rather than the right (correct) way.
Other: _____

Signal lights — Color of lights give definite direction. Red and flashing red mean stop, amber or yellow mean caution, green means go. These signals are often symbolic of the direction you're going, the path you're following, and the action needed (a warning or a go-ahead).
Other: _____

South — Slower pace, relaxed as in southern life, rebellion (Civil War), the lower centers, sensuality, emotionally warm; may indicate the past.
Other: _____

Stars — Aspirations, hopes and dreams (reach for the stars), higher realms, infinite space, to shine, a starring role, get a star (reward), become a star (excel in a particular realm), a five-pointed star can represent the human body, a six-pointed star is a Jewish symbol.
Other: _____

Sun — Gives life and light, illumination, energy; the center of our universe, the spiritual force, power and clarity.
Other: _____

Symbolic shapes and figures — Ancient archetypal symbols across cultures that are said to resonate with the unconscious and the spirit. The circle: wholeness (Jung's mandala figures), completeness, oneness, the circle of life, circle the wagons; square: symmetrical, equal, balanced, on the square, fair and square, he's a square (a dork, old-fashioned); the triangle or pyramid: any triune, the physical, mental, and spiritual, the Holy Trinity, ancient wisdom, spiritual initiation, enduring, balance, a pyramid scheme.
Other: _____

Traffic and road signs — Messages that give specific instructions in dream travels relating to your life and behavior: turn right, stop, straight ahead, no U-turn (no going back), yield (give in to another on an issue), slow, school zone.
Other: _____

Treasure map — Indicates inner resources, gifts, and talents that may be buried or latent. Your treasure is within; find it.
Other: _____

Up and down — Ups and downs of life; elevators, stairs, and escalators can take you to higher levels of awareness or down deeper into the unconscious self. Up (upbeat), down (sad or depressed). Up may be the right way and down the wrong way, or up may be uppity and down may be down-to-earth.
Other: _____

West — Sunset, the end, death and dying, resting; the end of a cycle, a relationship, a testing period; the western world, the old west; moving west may indicate moving into new frontiers, new challenges and opportunities.
Other: _____

Zodiac — The twelve astrological houses designated by particular constellations with each having meaning to an individual and based on birthdate. (See the list in the Exercise at the end of Chapter 6.)
Other: _____

WHAT'S GOING ON? (ACTIONS AND ACTIVITIES)

Here you'll find an alphabetical listing of some actions and activities seen in dreams. A full list would be extremely long. Descriptions are given using a variety of analytical techniques, and in no particular order of significance. Underline the ideas that are meaningful to you.

Remember: These are only suggested possibilities. Your personal associations are always best so be sure to fill in the blank spaces. Add other entries as needed.

Arguing — People with different points of view or experience claiming to be right, often vehemently; inability to agree or come to a common understanding, debating both sides of an issue; being defensive or offensive.
Other: _____

Attacking — Threatening verbally or physically, often with a weapon; going on the offensive; a battle to vanquish an enemy; attacking a problem (begin to make a vigorous effort to solve an issue); attacking someone's reputation or veracity.
Other: _____

Beating — Using fists or a weapon to repeatedly strike someone or something; winning against an opponent in a game or competition (besting me at chess, the Yankees drubbing the Red Sox); striking an object to shake loose dirt (like a rug) or make noise (like a drum); taking a beating in the stock market (losing money).
Other: _____

Begging — Asking for a handout on a street corner; pleading for mercy, for forgiveness, for one's pardon for an offense; earnestly beseeching a favor or for help. In some cultures alms for the poor or for holy men is common.
Other: _____

Building a fire — Literally piling wood and kindling to burn; lighting a fire under someone is an effort to motivate or get him started; igniting passion.
Other: _____

Chasing — Running after (on foot or in a vehicle) another person to catch or do harm to him; trying to catch up; chasing rainbows (spending energy on futile or unrealistic goals); chasing his tail (not making progress), one drink following (chasing) another, as whiskey with a beer chaser. Chasing a person of the opposite sex may mean romantic pursuit.
Other: _____

Chopping — Cleaving with an ax or a hatchet; cutting into small pieces or making shorter; chopping him off at the knees (squelching or humiliating, bringing down to size); chopping off a head is to execute or disable, render harmless.
Other: _____

Cleaning— Scrubbing, removing dirt and impurities; cleaning house may mean a literal need to sanitize and neaten surroundings, or getting rid of all the disruptive or ineffective people; cleaning up at the poker table or on a business deal means you made money and were successful.
Other: _____

Cooking — May indicate attention needed to preparation of healthful food; cooking up something may mean making plans, plotting (sometimes to no good end); what's cooking (going on)?
Other: _____

Coughing — May be a warning of a literal throat problem (cold, allergies) or metaphorical need to cough something up (the cash, the truth, words stuck in your throat); trying to get attention or cover a faux pas.
Other: _____

Crying — Indicates sadness, grieving; releasing of emotions may be cleansing; sometimes the tears are of joy, happiness; crying over spilled milk means ruing an incident that can't be changed; crying out for help, a need for comfort from another.
Other _____

Cursing — May be literally casting a spell, a dark arts kind of curse or a vitriolic recitation of invectives concerning family members and your heritage. Or are you the one doing the cursing? In either case, anger and negative energy bolts are being flung with no good reason. What caused the anger? Aim for a solution to ease the tension.
Other: _____

Dancing — Rhythmic movement alone or with a partner, an emotional expression through the body. May indicate grace and beauty, the ability to keep in step; dancing with a partner requires coordination and cooperation; an expression of joy, celebration.
Other: _____

Defecating — Cleansing the body of waste and impurities, getting rid of what is no longer useful. If done in public, this may be reminding you to keep certain things in their proper place; don't thumb your nose at convention. May be a need to release toxins at all levels, physical, mental, and spiritual, not to hold on to things or hold things in—what Freud would call being anal retentive.
Other: _____

Diving — Plunging into something (deep water?) head-first, starting things with an immediate fervor; diving in at the dinner table means start eating; a dive is a sleazy place; taking a dive (pretending to lose, throwing a fight illegally).
Other: _____

Drinking — May be a literal reminder to drink more water or fluids; if drinking alcohol, it might be a reminder to do so responsibly or a warning of impaired judgment. Drinking in (absorbing and appreciating the things around you).
Other: _____

Driving — Controlling, in charge of your path or direction. Who is the driver? It may relate to being driven in an obsessive manner. Problems driving indicate a lack of control, a need to slow down, to know your limits.
Other: _____

Drowning — In over your head, out of control, sinking in responsibilities, being inundated with work, stress, pressure. May signal a need to call for help, represent being overwhelmed with emotional or mental issues.
Other: _____

Dying — Dying is an end of something, a relationship, a responsibility, the old self. "I'm dying here" is an expression of frustration, of being pushed to your limits or being at the end of your rope. Comedians are dying when they aren't getting any laughs. Dying isn't always a bad thing; it can be the end of a phase of your life and indicate the time to move on to the next level or lesson.
Other: _____

Eating and drinking — Ingesting physically, mentally, and spiritually from surroundings. May indicate a need to note concerns in one of those areas. Are you drinking too many sodas? Taking in too many negative comments on TV? Too much lack of concern for those in need?
Other: _____

Fight or flight — An emotional reaction to fear or any extreme stress: The adrenal glands pump adrenaline into the bloodstream according to a primitive system that equips us with extra energy to run like blazes, or turn and battle the enemy or the bear. If this energy isn't used, it takes a toll on the body. Physical exercise is a good remedy.
Other: _____

Fishing — Seeking spiritual insights or nourishment, need for relaxation, trying to catch or capture understanding; fishing for compliments, fishing for answers or information.
Other: _____

Giving birth — Being productive, giving birth to new ideas, new ideals, any new beginning. Can represent an awakening or being fruitful, bringing to life a concept, a project, or even a business deal.
Other: _____

Hand gestures — Expressive symbols as substitutes for the spoken word. Hands and fingers may be used to signal okay, hello, call me; a thumbs up or thumbs down denotes opinion of good or bad, go or no-go; an extended middle finger is an insult, as is a raised fist.
Other: _____

Hiding — Signals that you're being secretive or feeling threatened and don't want to face an issue. Keeping things from others, the hidden parts of the self (archetypes or sub-personalities). Looking for a place of safety and security.
Other: _____

Hiking — Trek or journey through the countryside to enjoy the natural beauty of territory; hiking is more arduous and purposeful than walking; take a hike (leave), hiking up the price or the rent (raising, increasing), hiking up his pants (pulling up).
Other: _____

Hobbling — Walking with difficulty because of injury or lameness; may indicate a problem with feet or legs, or with the way you're headed. Hobbling a horse is restricting movement with a rope or strap around the legs to keep it from running away overnight, or when a pen is not available.
Other: _____

Jumping or leaping — Hurdling an obstacle in the path; going to a lower place below or the unknown, similar to diving without water; jumping in with both feet (becoming totally involved or committed), jump the gun (start too quickly or before you're ready), she jumped all over you (lambasted or chewed out).
Other: _____

Killing — Trying to do away with, as with undesirable parts of the self or a situation. Some behavior or bad habit that may be harmful to you; to make a killing (be successful or make money as in the stock market or with some deal or sale), you're killing me here (you're putting me in a bad position).
Other: _____

Kissing — Usually pertains to affection, love, romance; a greeting between friends or family. Kiss of death (something potentially ruinous), Judas kiss (betrayal), kiss off (end a situation or relationship), kissing babies (making political points), kiss my ass (dismissive insult), kissing up to (fawning over, flattering to boost someone's ego and curry favor).
Other: _____

Laughing — Indicates joy, happiness, amusement, usually a positive symbol of levity, uplifting energy; laughing at someone derisively is to ridicule and embarrass, making or being made to feel foolish and diminished. Laughter is sometimes a facade to hide discomfort (laughing on the outside) or a reminder not to take yourself too seriously.
Other: _____

Listening — A metaphor for meditation; being open to hear, understand, and commiserate with others; valuing others by hearing what they're saying, paying attention, using listening skills.
Other: _____

Lying — Often refers to areas of deceit with self as well as others; fear or avoidance of the painful truth; denial of the truth, an ego-defense mechanism, not wanting to see or feeling threatened by the truth. Hiding behind a lie. (See also Hiding.)
Other: _____

Mailing — Sending a message to yourself or another, offering new ideas, insight, information.
Other: _____

Moving — Making changes or progressions within; moving to a new level of consciousness or understanding; growth, emotional or spiritual maturation; a change in your situation or life path; may signal a literal move. The destination provides more specific clues to meaning. Something moving is emotionally touching.
Other: _____

Painting — Painting a house or a room relates to positive changes in attitudes or appearance; colors provide important information as to meaning. Painting a picture is more apt to be about a growth in creativity and inner expression. As exciting as watching paint dry (really dull and boring); to paint yourself into a corner is to put yourself in a difficult position by not planning ahead.
Other: _____

Playing games — Having fun, relaxing. The kind of game gives more clues to meaning. May be about goals, competition, or teamwork. If someone is playing games with you, they may be messing with your head, or being coy or insincere.
Other: _____

Playing golf — Hitting the target, making your goal, measuring yourself against a standard. May be a reminder to relax and get some exercise.
Other: _____

Playing music — Being in harmony or in tune with the creative flow of the universe. Playing an instrument is the ability to express your

creativity in a harmonious manner; being part of a band or orchestra is a cooperative aspect of that creative power.
Other: _____

Playing poker — Taking chances in the daily activities or in the game of life, gambling on outcomes instead of using your own talents and intellect. A poker face is the ability to hide your thoughts, be expressionless.
Other: _____

Reading — Studying, gaining new insights or reading for leisure and pleasure; reading between the lines is intuitive understanding of nuances or something not specifically stated; reading someone means picking up clues to understand another person.
Other: _____

Rowing or paddling — Exerting yourself to move toward your destination under your own power, by your concerted effort, working with the flow of life. (See also Canoe and Rowboat.)
Other: _____

Running — Important to know if you're running toward, running away, or running for exercise and pleasure. Running toward means moving forward to a goal, making strides; running away means escaping a fearful or unpleasant situation; running for exercise means a concern for endurance and physical care. A runner may deliver a message, be run down, or running around.
Other: _____

Running amok — Disruptive, crazy behavior. Someone or something out of control and needing attention.
Other: _____

Sewing — Putting things together creatively, making new clothing, attitudes; following the proper pattern, binding together.
Other: _____

Sexual activities — May relate to the creative merging of two energies, self-gratification, reproduction; the blending of the male and female attributes; an act and expression of love and fulfillment, or simple pleasure and physical release. The physical expression of becoming one with something beyond yourself.
Other: _____

Shooting — Firing a gun at a target that may be paper, animal, or human. The motivation behind the shooting and the specific target is important to understand the meaning. A soldier may be attacking or defending; a robber may be committing a crime. Shooting your mouth off can mean talking too much, boasting, telling secrets; shooting yourself in the foot can mean you're the cause of your own misfortune.
Other: _____

Shopping — Making selections, choices from many options; looking around and making wise decisions. The type of store and merchandise will give further clues to meaning. For example, a grocery store will be associated with food, a dress shop with facades and attitudes or adornment.
Other: _____

Singing — Using the voice to express emotions, joy, praise; being in harmony. Uplifts the spirit. Sing out (speak up), sing (confess, tell all one knows).
Other: _____

Sitting down — Resting, recharging the batteries; not standing up for one's beliefs or principles; sitting down on the job (not being fully engaged).
Other: _____

Skating — Requires balance and agility, ability to glide gracefully; smoothly managing any situation, agility, poise, skilled, in control of the situation. Skating on thin ice (taking foolish chances, flirting with disaster); skating (getting away with criminal activity without serving time). The kind of skating is indicative of the associated issues: ice skates, roller skates, skateboards.
Other: _____

Skiing — Requires power, agility, and balance. Strong legs are especially important. Going downhill quickly; a race against the clock.
Other: _____

Skipping — Often a child's way of getting around, carefree and happy. Might signal an adult to adopt a more carefree attitude. Skipping can also mean omitting, leaving out; skipping town can mean leaving to avoid responsibilities or paying bills.
Other: _____

Sleeping — A time for rest. May signal you to pay attention to your sleep needs. Delving into the unconscious and dreams. May indicate a lack of awareness and a need to wake up and pay attention. Sleeping on the job can mean not being fully engaged in work.
Other: _____

Slow motion — To feel as if you're moving in molasses or in slow motion may mean that you literally need to slow down, or it may indicate that your body isn't running efficiently because of diet, lack of rest, or weight problems.
Other: _____

Smiling — Pleasant, joyous demeanor, indicates happiness, satisfaction. (See also Laughing.)
Other: _____

Smothering — The feeling that you can't get your breath; may be connected to lung disorders, illness, or someone may be smothering or stifling your growth by being overprotective. Alternately, you may be the overprotective one.
Other: _____

Spilling — Not being careful, or unable to manage the things you must carry; may indicate a lack of balance or attention to tasks literally or metaphorically. Spilling the beans can mean telling secrets.
Other: _____

Standing up — Standing up for what you believe or to be counted. Rising to the occasion; defending your ideals and beliefs.
Other: _____

Stealing — Taking what doesn't belong to you, often stealing from yourself by not being honest with yourself or making your best effort. If someone is stealing from you, do you need to stand up for yourself and defend your position and possessions?
Other: _____

Sweating — What is the cause of the sweating? Fear? Fever? Overexertion? Often anxiety makes you sweat, or fear of being exposed causes the same reaction. Sometimes this is a call to be courageous (don't let them see you sweat). Pressure (by police or authorities) to be truthful or make admissions is called sweating.
Other: _____

Swimming — Going with the flow, with the spirit, following your spiritual or emotional path. Feeling weightless and supported by the water is like being buoyed by unseen forces. Being in the swim of things can mean being engaged in important and current activities. The ease or difficulty of swimming as well as the environment will give additional clues as to meaning.
Other: _____

Taking a test — Going through a testing period to determine if you have learned your lessons (tested by the self). Feeling nervous about the test or unable to find the testing place indicates anxiety about some issue in your life, a common theme.
Other: _____

Talking — Concerns communication and messages, an exchange of information or ideas. Who is talking? What is being said? Are you talking too much? (See also Listening.)
Other: _____

Throwing — Tossing out ideas, making a pitch, taking aim, or hitting a target; throwing a tantrum, throwing a fight (purposely losing). Who is the pitcher and who is the catcher?
Other: _____

Traveling — Going on life's journey or taking a vacation both require travel. May indicate a real trip, or a figurative one as you move toward growth and understanding.
Other: _____

Urinating — Cleansing the body of impurities at all levels; releasing emotional tension; filtering and flushing unneeded things. (See also Defecating.)
Other: _____

Walking — Proceeding along your path, your direction in life. May address your current situation, activities, state of mind, or issues at hand. A need to walk the walk; walking out on someone or something (leaving); walked all over someone (dominated, took advantage).
Other: _____

Washing hands — Need for cleansing; may literally or figuratively be reminding you to keep your hands clean. Washing your hands of the matter can mean abdicating further responsibility and involvement.
Other: _____

Watching a movie or TV — Calling attention to these activities. Are you spending too much time here? Do you need to relax and get your mind off more weighty matters? Being able to see a situation objectively.
Other: _____

Working — May relate to current job or occupation and your feelings about the situation, the people involved. Dreams are about current events, and a good part of your day is spent working. Who are the characters in your dream? What are your feelings? What are your work related issues? This may also relate to working out a problem or working on a relationship.

Other: _____

Writing — Relates to communication and messages as well as self-expression and creativity. May indicate a need for communication with the inner self or a reminder to write a friend.

Other: _____

Further Reading

Assagioli, R. (1975). *Psychosynthesis*. New York: The Viking Press.

Cayce, H. L. (1968). *Dreams: the language of the unconscious*. Virginia Beach: A. R. E. Press.

Delaney, G. (1998). *All about dreams*. San Francisco: HarperSanFrancisco.

Faraday, A. (1974). *The dream game*. New York: Harper & Row.

Freud, S. (1965). *The interpretation of dreams*. New York: Avon Books.

Garfield, P. L. (2001). *The universal dream key*. New York: Cliff Street Books.

Jung, C. G. (1974). *Dreams*. From *Collected works of C. G. Jung, Vol. 4, 8, 12, 16*. NJ: Princeton University Press.

Jung, C. G. (1989). *Memories, dreams, reflections*. New York: Random House.

LaBerge, S. (1986). *Lucid dreaming*. New York: Ballantine Books.

Maslow, A. H. (1987). *Motivation and personality, Third edition*. New York: HarperCollins.

Maslow, A. H. (1975). *The farther reaches of human nature*. New York: The Viking Press.

Sechrist, E. (1968). *Dreams your magic mirror*. New York: Cowles Education Corporation.

Thurston, M. A. (1978). *How to interpret your dreams*. Virginia Beach: A. R. E. Press.

Van de Castle, R. L. (1995). *Our dreaming mind*. New York: Ballantine Books.

Index

Dogwood tree and blossoms, 214. *See also* Trees

Dolphin or porpoise, 163, 223

Donkey, 223

Doorman, 187

Dragons, 158–59, 173, 232

Dream dictionaries, 21

Dreamgate.com, 98

Dreams: The Language of the Unconscious (Cayce), 13

Dreams: Tonight's Answers for Tomorrow's Questions (Thurston), 13, 24

Dreams: Your Magic Mirror (Sechrist), 37

Drinking, 268. *See also* Eating and drinking

Driving, 120–21, 268

Drowning, 268

Drug addict, 187

Drug dealer, 188

Duck, 67–68, 223

Dying, 122, 269. *See also* Dead people

Ear, 205

Earth, 114, 115

East, 261

Eating and drinking, 87–89, 124–28, 269

Electrician, 188

Elements (four basic), 114–15, 261

Elephant, 223

Elevator operator, 188

Elimination and bathroom activities, 128–29. *See also* Defecating; Urinating

Emotional reactions, 132–36

Endocrine glands, 56–57, 98

Entertainer, comedian, 188

Entrepreneur, 188

Esteem needs, 8, 9, 25, 26, 30, 50

Ethnicities, 188

Exes, 189

External stimuli, 145–46

Eyeglasses, 249

Eyelashes, 206

Eyes, 55, 206

Face, 206

Fairy, 232

False awakening, 172

Family room, den, 238

Faraday, Ann, 29, 46, 47–48, 94, 174

Farmer, 189

The Farther Reaches of Human Nature (Maslow), 9, 16–17

Father, 189

Fauna, 59, 65–75, 220–30

Fear responses, 133–35

Feet and toes, 54–55, 206

Fence, 249

Fern, 215

Fields, meadow, 238

Fight or flight, 269

Fig tree, 215. *See also* Trees

File cabinet, 250

Fingernails, 207

Fingers, thumb, 53, 207. *See also* Hands

Fire, 114, 115, 266

Firefighter, 189

Fire truck, 107, 256

Fir tree, 215. *See also* Trees

Fish, 224

Fisherman, 189

Fishing, 269

Fitness trainer, 190

Flight attendant, 190

Flora, 59, 60–65, 212–20

Flowering tree, 215. *See also* Trees

Flowers, 60–63, 215

Flying without a plane, 111, 256

Food- and drink-related activities. *See* Eating and drinking

Football player, 190

Forehead, 207

Foreigner, 190

Forest, woods, 215. *See also* Trees

Fork in the road, 238

Formal clothes, 243

Forty, 99

Fossils, 250

Four, 99

Fox, 224

Freud, Sigmund, 4, 5, 7, 13, 36, 71, 95, 98, 125, 129, 131, 135, 157, 173

Friend, 190

Frog, 224

Fruit trees, 215. *See also* Trees

Frying pan, 250

Funeral director, undertaker, 191

Furniture, 250

About the Author

Janece O. Hudson, EdD, is a certified hypnotherapist and a former licensed psychologist who received her BS and MEd degrees from Stephen F. Austin University, and her doctorate in counseling from the University of Houston. During her doctoral training, she studied "Psychophysiology of Sleep Disorders" and conducted research on laboratory dreams at the Baylor University School of Medicine's sleep lab; did independent study and research with a clinical psychologist who specialized in dreams; presented a variety of studies and papers on dreams as well as publishing academic articles; and wrote her dissertation on dreams. Before leaving the profession to become a full time writer, Dr. Hudson taught college psychology for twelve years. She is currently a popular speaker in the fields of dreams, hypnosis, motivation, creative imagery, parapsychology, and creative writing. She is a member of the International Association for the Study of Dreams and lives in Austin, TX.

BEYOND HERE

Sure, this world is fascinating, but *what's beyond is even more intriguing...*

Want a place to share stories and experiences about all things strange and unusual? From UFOs and apparitions to dream interpretation, the Tarot, astrology, and more, the **BEYOND HERE** blog is the newest hot spot for paranormal activity!